DUSE
ON TOUR

GUIDO NOCCIOLI'S
DIARIES, 1906-07

translated and edited
with an introduction and notes by
GIOVANNI PONTIERO

The University of Massachusetts Press
Amherst, 1982

First published in the USA in 1982
by The University of Massachusetts Press
Box 429 Amherst, Ma. 01004

ISBN 0-87023-369-6

Printed in Great Britain

FOR MY PARENTS

CONTENTS

Illustrations

PREFACE

The good diarist has three talents: a sustained enthusiasm for the task; an inner gift for perceptive observation of people and events; and an unfailing sense of relevance and economy. As a young actor and fairly inexperienced man of the theatre, Guido Noccioli shows himself in the following pages, previously unpublished in their entirety in any language, to have kept a good, though brief, diary of his professional association for a full year with one of this century's greatest actresses, Eleonora Duse.

These diaries are the only ones known to provide a day-to-day account of Duse in rehearsal and performance. This unique document was written just before and during her second tour of South America, 1906–07, when she was at the peak of her career.

The introductory essay dealing with the life and career of Eleonora Duse up to the relevant period will help to prepare the reader for the remarkable yet strangely tortured personality described by Noccioli. For only by taking into account the early years of privation and solitude can one fully appreciate Duse's resilience of character in middle age; only by pondering on the crucial experience that hastened her development as a woman and artist can one hope to appraise her true stature.

The essay is also intended to clarify the powerful formative influences of three men – Arrigo Boito, Gabriele D'Annunzio and Henrik Ibsen – who guided and inspired the actress in her unsparing search for higher objectives in art and a 'theatre of poetry'.

Through Noccioli's steady but sympathetic eyes, we see a Duse at the height of her career yet close to physical exhaustion and emotional collapse, a woman of unpredictable, almost neurotic, temperament. Edgy and solicitous in turn, authoritarian but at times uncertain and indecisive, infuriatingly unbending yet ever quick to express remorse and confess

PREFACE

herself mistaken, Duse emerges, all the same, as dignified and honest in her dealings with others. Seriously ill as she was, she remains for Guido Noccioli a real presence, but one shifting in and out of focus: courageous and determined on some occasions, solitary and vulnerable on others.

No less revealing is Noccioli's record of Duse the actor–manager. Her efforts on behalf of new dramatists, Italian and foreign, have been sadly neglected by biographers, who have taken their cue from D'Annunzio's description of her as *la grande amatrice*. However slow and painful her progress from being a provincial child-actress, who was thrust into adult roles far beyond her years, to being a performer, who was hailed everywhere for her subtle and intense power on stage in roles beyond the experience of her audiences, the diaries clearly show Duse at work. Her self-discipline is intransigent, and her passion for deeper and broader values in dramatic art spares no one. Perfection was her goal for herself as well as for the least important member of her company. She is obsessed not with 'her art' but with 'the work' to be done.

At the conclusion of these diaries, the Duse we leave is an actress who has, in a real sense, completed her mission. Retirement came unexpectedly in 1909, and her all-too-brief comeback in 1921 until her death in Pittsburgh in 1924 is not only another story but a shadowy reincarnation of the actress described some eighteen years earlier in these pages by Noccioli.

The research for this book was carried out with generous financial assistance from the University of Manchester, the British Academy and the Small Grants Research Fund in the Humanities.

I am indebted to the following libraries, institutions and editorials: The Library of Congress, Washington; The Library of the Performing Arts at the Lincoln Center, New York; The Biblioteca Teatrale Livia Simoni; the Biblioteca Comunale; The Biblioteca Nazionale Braidense; The Centro di Documentazione Teatrale del Piccolo Teatro; and the Editorial Staff of the *Corriere della Sera* in Milan; the Fondazione Giorgio Cini in Venice; the Teatro della Pergola in Florence; the Management of Cappelli Editore, Bologna; the Biblioteca Teatrale del Burcardo; the Istituto Centrale per il Catalogo e la Documentazione and The British School in Rome; the Research Departments of *O Estado de São Paulo, O Jornal* in Rio de Janeiro, *La Nación* in Buenos Aires; and the Instituto de Investigaciones Estéticas at the Autonomous University of Mexico.

I also wish to express my heartfelt thanks to the following colleagues and friends who have given me much valuable help and advice, and their unfailing support while collecting material for the book: Sr Teo Tomás Moralejo, Signor Renato Partenope, Professor T. G. Griffith, Dra. Paola Seganti, Sig. Guido Lorenzetti, Mr Roger Evans, Dr Arnold P. Hinchliffe, Sister Mary Mark and Dr Gerardo Guerrieri.

Finally, much gratitude is due to Miss Mary McDonald who typed the manuscript in its various stages with admirable speed and efficiency; and to Mr Martin S. Stanford who played a major role in planning this book and corrected both the typescript and proofs with exemplary care.

THE LIFE AND CAREER OF ELEONORA DUSE

And she speaks fictitiousness, wherein
some too common lot is made to moan,
and she makes it with her soul akin,
till it sounds like something all its own:
like the crying of a stone –

Rainer Maria Rilke, 'Portrait of Eleonora Duse' (August 1907)

More than half a century after her death, Eleonora Duse continues to be remembered as one of the most expressive and magnetic actresses in the history of modern theatre. The daughter of strolling players, she was born on 3 October 1858 in the Hotel Cannon d'Oro at Vigevano in the Italian Veneto. By her early twenties, Duse was already established throughout Italy as the most remarkable actress of her generation, and when she died at the age of sixty-five on Easter Monday 1924 in Pittsburgh during her fourth tour of the United States, the whole world mourned the loss of this unique personality who had become a legend in her own lifetime. Yet her progress from hardship and obscurity in the Italian provinces to success and acclaim in the most important European theatres of the day was neither sudden nor easy.

Duse's paternal grandfather, Luigi Duse, had been an actor–manager whose performances were admired by Alfred de Musset and George Sand. With mixed success Luigi Duse had attempted to adapt the techniques of the waning *commedia dell'arte* to nineteenth-century taste by virtually discarding the masks and eliminating most of the traditional improvisation. But thwarted by circumstances and changing fortunes, the old man was poor and forgotten when he died in 1854, four years before the birth of his famous granddaughter. This was generally a critical period for theatre companies throughout Italy. Throughout the 1840s and 1850s wars and political upheavals made their financial situation precarious. Increasingly, actor–managers found it more and more difficult to arrange profitable tours: travel permits were strictly controlled and governmental and ecclesiastical censorship curtailed company activities and scrupulously vetted the plays in their repertory. During the last years of Austrian domination in Italy, the restrictions became so serious that provincial theatre companies found themselves struggling for survival. And scant audiences reflected the prevailing atmosphere of tension and unrest.

This bleak situation did not discourage at least four of Luigi's sons from becoming actors, although none of them was to equal their father's success or popularity. Vincenzo Alessandro Duse, Eleonora's father, appears to have been more interested in painting than acting without ever really fulfilling his ambitions in either profession. His wife, Angelica Capelletto, was of farming stock and took up acting only out of necessity after her marriage. Persistent ill health dogged Angelica's modest career on the stage, and the rigours of touring the provinces in the most depressing conditions hastened her death, leaving Eleonora, who was still in her teens, withdrawn and inconsolable.

Duse's formation as an actress

By the age of seven, Duse was already a seasoned trouper travelling with her parents from theatre to theatre throughout the provinces of Northern Italy – Lombardy, Piedmont and her native Veneto – and she soon found herself being carefully rehearsed in children's roles, including a small part in Shakespeare's *Coriolanus*, recorded at Trento as early as 1863. A thoughtful and responsive child, Duse revealed an aptitude for absorbing things quickly as she watched the adult members of the company perform. The family's itinerant existence ruled out the possibility of any formal education.

The young Duse soon became familiar with the vicissitudes of life in the theatre. When her grandfather died, there were at least eighteen members of the Duse family connected, in various ways, with the stage, and the Duses did not escape the domestic tensions that were all too common in small repertory companies dominated by family ties and obligations. However provincial or modest the theatre company might be, a strict hierarchy of status among the actors was strictly observed; and as the youngest and least important member of the Compagnia Drammatica Italiana, under the management of her uncle Enrico Duse and Giuseppe Laganuz, Duse was exposed even as a child to petty intrigues and fierce rivalries.

When her mother became seriously ill, Eleonora was persuaded to take over her roles. Barely in her teens, she found herself playing parts wholly beyond her powers or understanding – Silvio Pellico's *Francesca da Rimini* and Giuseppe Marenco's *Pia dei Tolomei* as well as the fashionable heroines of Scribe and Schiller. The young actress was gradually promoted from *ingenue* roles to those of *prima amorosa*[1] and by 1874 she was appearing on a joint contract with her father in the Benincasa Company.[2] Her next engagement with Luigi Pezzana raised her to the status of *seconda donna*, but professionally she made little impact in a repertoire of mediocre plays that were badly produced and acted in the declamatory style of the day. Further engagements with second-rate companies provided few opportunities for self-improvement, and Duse must have felt increasingly more frustrated and discouraged by her inability to make any real impression on audiences, managers, or her fellow actors.

The turning point in her career came when the actress signed her first important contract as *amorosa* with the management of the reputable Ciotti-Belli-Blanes Company. Francesco Ciotti was an actor of some distinction who favoured a natural and sober style of acting as opposed to the emphatic gestures and mannered diction of the so-called 'heroic' school. In this more congenial atmosphere, Duse was able to reveal something of her true potential when she was asked to replace the company's leading lady at short notice as the heroine Maia in Emil Augier's *Fourchambault*. The originality of Duse's performance attracted the attention of another well-known actor–manager, Giovanni Emanuel, who was to comment some years later: 'Here was a young woman who could grip your heart night after night in the theatre and crumple it like a handkerchief.' This heartrending humanity to which Emanuel refers was indeed to become the hallmark of Duse's

[3]

acting and the sheer intensity of her performances, even at this early stage of her career, singled Duse out from other members of the cast. Emanuel's professional interest in the talented new-comer prompted him to arrange an interview with Giacinta Pezzana, one of Italy's most gifted actresses. An audition soon followed, and Duse was engaged to play supporting roles opposite the experienced Pezzana, whose methods were in the traditional mould but greatly enhanced by admirable diction and excellent stagecraft. Despite obvious differences of age and temperament, Duse improved her technique while working with Pezzana. She made her debut with the company at the Teatro dei Fiorentini in Naples during the Spring of 1879 as Electra in Alfieri's *Oreste*.

The actress was now exposed to a wider range of new and demanding roles, which often had to be prepared without sufficient time for study or rehearsal. The repertoire included all the major dramatists of the late nineteenth century – Alfieri, Sardou, Scribe, Beaumarchais, Schiller and Zola. In *Teresa Raquin*, which was adapted from Zola's novel, Duse scored her first personal triumph by playing the title role alongside Pezzana's historical interpretation as Signora Raquin. Pezzana predicted a great future for the company's juvenile lead. Audience reactions were also favourable and a small group of loyal admirers in Naples pledged their support led by the novelist Matilde Serao who was to become Duse's lifelong friend and confidante, and by a handful of influential drama critics led by Boutet and Verdinois.

The last decades of the nineteenth century saw some promising new developments in the Italian theatre. There were nearly a hundred theatre companies around the late 1870s presenting plays either in Italian or dialect, and better standards of production were becoming evident under the able management of pioneers like Luigi Bellotti-Bon. This actor–manager had toured with the celebrated Adelaide Ristori when the Reale Compagnia di Sardegna visited Paris in May 1855 during the Great International Exhibition. He dreamed of creating a national theatre in Italy along the lines of the Comédie-Française, where plays by national authors might be fostered. And with this goal in mind, Bellotti-Bon produced the works of young Italian dramatists like Achille Torelli and Gherardi del Testa and built up a strong company of experienced artists capable of sound ensemble acting: these included artists of the calibre of Cesare Rossi, Amalia Fumagalli, Giacinta Pezzana and Francesco Ciotti, among others.

As early as 1873, Bellotti-Bon began to expand his activities by creating three separate theatre companies, but the initial enthusiasm for this courageous enterprise soon waned. Internal factions and hostilities created unforeseen problems, and when eventually faced with financial ruin, Bellotti-Bon committed suicide. Yet his efforts on behalf of improved standards and a more adventurous policy for the Italian theatre were not in vain. Other managements were inspired by his vision and initiative, and former members of his company, such as Cesare Rossi, tried to continue his work. When Duse and her father were engaged by Rossi at the Teatro Carignano in Turin for the 1880–81 season with a joint salary of 7,500 lire, Rossi had already assembled a strong cast that included the brilliant young actor, Claudio Leigheb and his wife, Teresa, Tebaldo Checchi (whom Duse married in 1881), the handsome young Flavio Andò and Giacinta Pezzana, who was then at the height of her career.

When Pezzana unexpectedly announced her decision to abandon the stage for personal reasons, Rossi, with some uneasiness, promoted Duse to the rank of *prim'attrice assoluta* and entrusted her with Pezzana's roles. She made her debut as the company's new leading lady in Achille Torelli's comedy *Scrollina* at a special gala performance on 19 August 1881. At the age of twenty-two, Duse had achieved the goal of every aspiring young actress, but initially her new status brought little personal satisfaction or reassurance. Audiences at the Teatro Carignano seemed reluctant to accept Duse as an adequate substitute for Pezzana and the Rossi Company soon found itself playing to half-empty houses. Even their standard repertoire came in for severe criticism as the public grew tired of old and inferior Italian dramas – or new and sophisticated French plays, which were often badly translated and poorly produced without regard for authenticity. Duse's own frustrations and doubts about her future in the theatre must have weighed heavily upon her at this period as she struggled to overcome public apathy and to silence her own misgivings about the parts she was asked to sustain night after night.

The Bernhardt legend

This monotony was providentially interrupted in 1881 when the press suddenly announced the imminent arrival of the celebrated Sarah Bernhardt with members of her own company. The great French actress was at the peak of her career and a star attraction in all the major capitals of the world. Her appearance in any theatre guaranteed a full house and profitable business for the theatre management. Her Italian tour on this occasion was carefully publicized, and Europe's most elegant stage personality arrived in grand style with her familiar retinue of attendants and menagerie of exotic animals.

Rossi, who was already facing serious financial difficulties, reacted immediately to the news of Bernhardt's visit and offered her the Teatro Carignano for her performances in Turin. The shabby dressing room normally occupied by Duse was hastily transformed into a sumptuous boudoir worthy of the city's distinguished visitor, and Bernhardt's international reputation ensured a capacity audience for every performance. No one in that audience could have been more curious or enthralled than Duse herself as she studied every detail of Bernhardt's stagecraft – the pictorial beauty of the French company's sets and costumes and the studied refinement Bernhardt brought to every detail of gesture and facial expression. Turin saw Bernhardt in four of her most famous roles: *La Dame aux camélias, Adrienne Lecouvreur, Le Sphinx* and *Frou-frou*.[3] Several critics were lukewarm in their reviews but for Duse, who was watching Bernhardt for the first time, these performances made an indelible impression and helped her to clarify her own ambitions as an actress at the crossroads of success or failure. While recognizing that neither her temperament nor training was likely to mould her in the image of another Bernhardt, the example of the French actress's achievements gave the young actress the self-confidence she had lacked hitherto. When Bernhardt departed and the Rossi Company resumed performances, Duse had some firm ideas of her own about the parts she now felt ready to play. And, to everyone's surprise, Rossi capitulated.

Duse examined Bernhardt's repertoire anew and insisted upon attempting roles like *La Princesse de Bagdad* by Dumas the Younger – roles associated in France with Bernhardt's unique stage presence and visual glamour. Critics and audiences alike in Turin were soon aware of a new power and attack in the acting of Rossi's leading lady. Duse's assumption of new roles from the fashionable French repertoire of the period did not result, as some feared, in a pale imitation of Bernhardt. Much less pictorial and extrovert as a performer, Duse was obliged to work out her own interpretation of the heroines of Dumas and Sardou.

Reviewing Duse's intense performances, critics found her conception of these roles much closer to that of the late Aimée

Desclée, a French actress who was noted for the emotional power of her interpretations. Like Desclée, Duse penetrated the intimate essence of Cesarine's complex personality in *La Femme de Claude*, but whereas the French actress was said to have emphasized the violence of the heroine's morbid sensuality, Duse adopted a more restrained line by hinting at some inner tragic force. Another role associated with Desclée in France, that of Lydia in *Une Visite de noces*, was introduced into Duse's repertoire at Turin and her marginal notes to the text provide ample evidence of the Italian actress's careful preparation and extraordinary insight into Lydia's character.

News of her triumphs and growing popularity with audiences in Turin soon spread to other major theatres throughout Italy, and invitations to tour gave Duse an opportunity of perfecting her conception of the new works in her repertoire. But success in Turin did not guarantee immediate acceptance elsewhere. The loyal fans of an earlier generation of actresses, such as Adelaide Ristori, Giacinta Pezzana, Adelaide Tessero and Virginia Marini, were slow to warm to the intense acting of Duse, whose individuality was even condemned by some of her critics as bordering on eccentricity. But Duse was fast learning to counter prejudice and indifference with courage and resolve.

Increasingly aware of the limitations imposed by traditional concepts of acting in Italy, she was already searching for a new approach to every aspect of technique that would bring her acting closer to nature and truth. To Antonio Fiacchi (alias Piccolet), the drama critic of *Piccolo Faust*, she confided: 'It is far from easy to win over the public when one pursues certain ideals.' Those ideals became Duse's first priority as she gradually developed from being a competent performer into a great actress. A scrupulous reading of the original texts, followed by painstaking analysis of detail and extended rehearsals, became Duse's standard procedure in working up every play for performance.

Rossi had every reason to be proud of the controversial young actress who had vindicated his confidence, and she was never to forget Rossi's kindness. When she terminated her contract after the company's ill-fated South American tour of 1885–86,[4] Duse's decision was not provoked by any rift (a fact borne out by subsequent correspondence between the actress and her former manager) but simply because she needed to feel independent. 'My dream is to achieve virtually everything I believe to be to the benefit of my art . . . and to this ideal I am totally committed,' she once wrote to a friend.

[7]

Once released by Rossi, she was free to act upon those words and form her own company – the Compagnia della Città di Roma. Despite its title, Duse's company had no permanent base either in Rome or elsewhere. She engaged Flavio Andò as her leading man and company director and toured with a repertoire that consisted almost entirely of French and Italian plays: those of Dumas, Sardou, Meilhac and Halévy alongside those of Goldoni, Paolo Ferrari, Achille Torelli and Felice Cavallotti.

Flavio Andò was the perfect foil for Duse's style of acting. There was an immediate rapport between the two actors that remained undisturbed by Duse's tendency to alter or improvise detail from one performance to another – ever a sore point with less accommodating partners. Contemporary reviews of her acting at this period suggest that Duse's conceptions of her French roles were not simply different from those of other actresses but often succeeded in appearing altogether revolutionary. She came to be regarded by leading Italian critics as an actress of unpredictable originality who achieved 'extraordinary effects with the utmost simplicity'.

Once in control of her own company, she demanded of every actor on her payroll the same spirit of sacrifice and dedication towards greater perfection. Constant study and exhaustive preparation she counselled as the only guarantee of a fully integrated performance. From audiences too she expected civilized behaviour and undivided attention, even though any real understanding or appreciation of what she was trying to achieve might be beyond their powers. Having moved beyond the provinces and provincial standards, she laid down strict standards for all to follow or, at least, to respect. She insisted upon absolute privacy and discipline backstage; and visitors, no matter how distinguished or influential, were refused admittance to her dressing room during a performance.

As Duse went on assimilating new roles into her repertoire, her uncanny ability to transform her physical appearance without the assistance of make-up or artificial aids became one of the most intriguing aspects of her artistry. Subtle adjustments of facial expression and gesture enabled her to move convincingly from grandeur to pathos, from lyrical tragedy to sparkling comedy. First-hand observations of her acting by experienced actors intent upon analysing her technique concur: by the age of thirty Duse had already established perfect harmony between the inner essence and the externalized emotions of any woman she might be portraying on stage. Her intelligent coordination of vocal colouring and the appropriate gesture or movement helped her undergo a complete transformation of personality as she moved with deceptive ease from the roles of Magda and Cesarine to those of Marguerite and Mirandolina.

Free to follow her own instincts and indulge her own preferences, Duse read widely in the hope of finding fresh inspiration in the works of foreign poets and dramatists. She studied the English romantic poets, the French Symbolists, Maeterlinck, the Greek classics, Shakespeare, Dante, Hauptmann, Sudermann and Ibsen. She pondered over her interpretation of familiar roles in the light of new discoveries and became ever more conscious of the need to go on improving and deepening her knowledge of every aspect of the theatre. No established actress was more apprehensive of resting on her laurels. As she matured, Duse's friendships reflected her affinity with artists and intellectuals who were capable of nourishing her ideals and, at the same time, sufficiently experienced to guide her taste and judgment.

With the assistance of Lugné-Poe, the director of the experimental Théâtre de l'Oeuvre in Paris and subsequently one of Duse's most able impresarios, the actress turned to the study of Ibsen and other Nordic dramatists with renewed interest. She felt an irresistible attraction to Ibsen's world, not merely because of the poetry and mystery in his writing but, above all, because of the way in which the Norwegian dramatist explored the human soul while endowing his powerful woman characters with a spirit of rebellion and fierce individuality. In her relentless pursuit of greater truth and spirituality, Duse was anxious to draw a clear distinction between histrionics and serious acting. Her incessant tours abroad throughout the 1890s made her increasingly aware of important new developments in the capitals of France, Germany, England and Russia, where experimental theatres were already being launched and revolutionary theories about acting techniques being formulated by pioneers like Antoine and Stanislavsky, the founders of the Freie Bühne[5] in Berlin and the Independent Theatre[6] in London. Duse craved new material and fresh ideas about interpretation and production. She had steadily progressed from the crude violence of Zola to the romanticism of Dumas the Younger, from the *verismo* of Verga and Giacosa to the lyrical symbolism of Maeterlinck and D'Annunzio. Ibsen's tragic idealism marked the last phase in this remarkable career, which was prematurely halted when Duse announced her retirement in 1909.

'To stand still in art is to fall back'[7] she would often comment to fellow actors, and finally discouraged by the outcome of her strenuous efforts to combat sheer theatricality with 'poetry and ideals', she felt constrained to withdraw in silence.

The private conflicts

Duse's biographers suggest that she inherited her father's disenchantment with the theatrical profession and her mother's weak constitution. Undoubtedly, the stress and rigours of her early years seriously affected her health, and Duse was dogged all her life by weak lungs, frequent bouts of depression and nervous exhaustion. 'We actors are a cursed race', she would often exclaim, and one French critic who followed her career with keen interest throughout Europe described her as 'toujours nerveuse, inquiète . . . malade . . . hystérique'.[8]

Even after she had established her reputation and become financially independent, Duse continued to feel restless and insecure. All the evidence adds up to a complex and difficult personality, and yet the inherent contradictions in her nature as a woman exercised a hypnotic effect when exploited in her acting. The emotional relationships at various stages in her life reflect significant changes of attitude as Duse grew in stature and experience. D. H. Lawrence, in a letter dated 16 April 1916 to Catherine Carswell, wrote: 'I often think of the Duse with her lovers, how they were keen and devouring excitements to her, but only destructive incidents, really, even D'Annunzio.'[9] This idle statement is quite misleading. The relatively few men who played an intimate role in the actress's life possessed very different traits of character and coincided with specific phases in Duse's emotional development.

In retrospect, Duse saw these relationships as inevitable and self-revealing, however damaging the consequences. Her infatuation as a young and somewhat naive actress for the suave Martino Cafiero, a prominent figure in Neapolitan literary circles, came to grief when she discovered that she was pregnant and Cafiero had no intention of marrying her. A few years later in 1881, she gained respectability and security by marrying Tebaldo Checchi, a fellow actor in Cesare Rossi's company. Checchi ignored the warnings of those who tried to dissuade him from becoming involved with this moody and unpredictable young woman whom they considered something of a freak and without any real future as an actress.

The marriage was strengthened by the birth of a daughter, Enrichetta, who was born in 1882, but it soon became apparent to the couple that they were incompatible as man and wife. Duse's indiscreet affair on board ship with Flavio Andò when Rossi took his company on its first South American tour in 1885 humiliated and embittered Checchi, and when the company returned to Italy, he remained behind in Buenos Airés. There he made a new career for himself, first as correspondent for a Roman newspaper *La Fanfulla* and subsequently in the Argentine Consular Service.

In a letter addressed to Marchese Francesco d'Arcai, dated Rio de Janeiro, 27 August 1885, Checchi communicated the news of the separation. There is more sorrow than anger in Checchi's account of the events that led to the collapse of their marriage as he recognizes his shortcomings as a husband. He wrote:

> I do not believe that Eleonora is a wicked person – only spoiled by certain false acquaintances and led astray by the constant furore of success and the bad example of celebrated actresses like Rachel, Desclée, and Bernhardt . . . I forgive her for everything she has done to me, but I shall never be able to forget that by indulging some mad impulse she has banished me from the land of my birth. I may never see my own father again for he is already an old man. Eleonora's folly has also separated me from my own daughter and forced me into trying to build a new life for myself at the age of forty-one . . . Insofar as I am concerned, Eleonora Duse no longer exists.[10]

Duse's own thoughts about the scandal that abruptly ended her marriage to Checchi have never been recorded, but oblique references here and there in her correspondence betray a lingering sense of remorse. By mutual agreement she assumed full responsibility for their daughter's upbringing, and Duse made the best of a difficult situation by carefully supervising Enrichetta's education and making quite certain that she never lost touch with her father.

Subsequent relationships of any importance in Duse's life were to be much less conventional but also much more rewarding, although certain fictionalized accounts of her liaison, first with Boito and then with D'Annunzio, would have us believe otherwise.

The affair with Flavio Andò was short-lived. He continued to partner Duse for some time after they had ceased to be lovers. The shallow nature of this brief interlude was confirmed by Duse herself in later years when she commented philosophically: 'Il était bête, mais il était beau.' To Andò's credit, he was never to disclose anything in public about their relationship.

Duse and Boito

The actress's attachment to the Italian poet and composer Arrigo Boito was something deeper and more enduring. They met for the first time in the spring of 1884. Duse was fêted with a *serata d'onore* at the Teatro Carcano in Milan on 14 May, and the play chosen to mark the occasion was the ever-popular *Dame aux camêlias*. The following evening a dinner party was organized by her admirers at the Ristorante Cova and Duse found herself seated next to Boito. The intimate relationship, however, that was to last for almost thirty years dates from their second meeting in 1887 after an exchange of correspondence. Associated with progressive and reformist groups in Italian music, Boito was one of the most talented and versatile intellectuals of his generation who enjoyed the confidence and esteem of celebrities like Victor Hugo, Verdi, Berlioz and Rossini. Boito's wide cultural interests and rare sensibility made him an ideal mentor and collaborator for Duse. She was a youthful twenty-five and Boito a mature and experienced man in his early forties when they met. This difference in their ages helped Boito to convert the actress to his own lofty ideals, and he impressed upon Duse the importance of striving for absolute perfection in one's art. In Duse he could scarcely have found a more receptive pupil. When he reminded her that for the creative artist: 'Instinct in itself is not enough; it is necessary to study, to cultivate the spirit, to elevate oneself', he was only confirming what she had intuitively felt for some considerable time. Acting upon his advice, Duse began to devote more and more time to improving her mind by studying foreign languages and a much wider range of serious literature.

Addressing her affectionately as Lenor, Boito's correspondence encouraged and assisted her through frequent bouts of illness and despondency. As their friendship deepened, Boito's protective role became more apparent. In a letter dated 23 February 1888 he reassured her: 'I have promised myself that nothing will be allowed to disturb your serenity and peace of mind.'

In November of that same year, after months of intensive collaboration, mainly conducted by a constant flow of correspondence, Duse scored a personal triumph in a costly new production of Shakespeare's *Antony and Cleopatra*, specially translated and adapted by Boito. Further collaboration was no doubt intended but a combination of personal circumstances and professional commitments decreed otherwise. Boito had other commitments and emotional ties, and Duse was soon to become publicly involved with D'Annunzio. From the outset, Boito had exercised prudence and restraint in his relationship with the more impulsive Duse. The numerous letters they exchanged provide reliable evidence of the deep emotional bonds between them at the height of their romance. And those bonds survived on a more platonic note when they renewed their friendship after a short period of coolness provoked by the D'Annunzio furore. The spiritual role Boito came to assume in Duse's mind is reflected in her habit of subsequently referring to him as 'Il santo'. When the news of his final illness and death in 1918 reached her in Florence, where she herself was recovering from serious illness, the actress buried her grief in impenetrable silence.

Duse and D'Annunzio

Most of Duse's biographers have tended to give rather more space to the actress's tempestuous love affair with the 'enfant terrible' of Italian literary circles at the turn of the century, Gabriele D'Annunzio.

Ironically enough, it was Boito himself who sent Duse a copy of D'Annunzio's controversial novel inspired by Nietzsche: *Il trionfo della morte* (*The Triumph of Death*), published in 1894. Attracted initially by the title, she read the book in great haste and penned her reactions to Boito within days. She wrote: 'I should prefer to die . . . rather than fall in love with such a soul. The great test of courage, the great virtue of *bearing one's exist-ence* . . . the tremendous and anguished sacrifice of *facing up to life* . . . is totally destroyed in this book. D'Annunzio is someone whom I detest and adore.'[11] Prophetic words indeed in the light of future events.

It was while resting in Venice between tours that Duse finally met D'Annunzio in September 1894. Duse was then thirty-five years old and at the height of her career, and the poet from

[13]

Portrait of Gabriele D'Annunzio at the height of his literary fame.
Duse's love and admiration for the poet knew no bounds and
together they dreamed of building a theatre on the shores of Lake
Albano modelled on Wagner's Bayreuth. In this suggestive setting,
the great poet and actress would collaborate in reviving a classical
repertoire and a 'theatre of poetry' but this ambitious project failed
to materialize. (Photograph from the Nunes Vais Collection by
courtesy of the Istituto Centrale per il Catalogo e la
Documentazione.)

Abruzzi, at the age of thirty-one, could already consider himself a literary success. At the time of their meeting D'Annunzio's reputation was based on his poetry and several novels. As yet he had written no plays, although the idea of writing for the theatre appealed to his vanity. In his belief that 'woman and love must serve creation', Duse was to become both muse and companion as he set about working out his ideas for his first two plays. Duse's superb acting in *Il sogno di un mattino di primavera* aroused rather more interest than any intrinsic merits in the work itself. Duse acted the role of Isabella in Italian as part of her programme at the Théâtre de la Renaissance in Paris on 15 June 1897. The French critics rightly defined the play as a 'poème dialogue . . . plus qu'un drame véritable', and the doyen of French critics, Francisque Sarcey, dismissed the work as 'un poème enfantin et prétentieux . . . d'un insupportable ennui'.[12]

As early as 1896 D'Annunzio had finished writing his second play, *La città morta*, which required only forty days to complete. In her enthusiasm, Duse fully expected to create the leading female role of Anna, but D'Annunzio, who was intent upon success for his plays in Paris as the great centre of European theatre, entrusted the role to Sarah Bernhardt in a French translation by Georges Hérelle.[13] This insensitive behaviour caused Duse great disappointment and sadness, yet she insisted upon remaining loyal to D'Annunzio in the sincere belief that his genius would redeem the Italian theatre throughout Europe.

Biographers and critics alike have tended to treat this turbulent chapter in the actress's life with undue emphasis and prejudice. D'Annunzio's vanity and unfailing sense of expediency scarcely endeared him even to his contemporaries. For her part, Duse's love and misguided sense of loyalty prevented her from ever arriving at any truly objective assessment of D'Annunzio, either as a man or as a writer. The letters they exchanged in the heat of passion strike an uncomfortable note of theatricality. Grandiloquence came naturally to D'Annunzio, who was wont to address Duse as 'the great . . . and sublime Beloved One!' – ecstatic outbursts that proved to be contagious. Duse's own letters at this time reveal an effusive adulation. A letter written as early as September 1894 is full of exalted phrases: '*I see the sun* and give thanks to all the providential forces of this earth for having ordained our meeting'. D'Annunzio is hailed as 'the beneficent power' and elsewhere in an undated letter she rhapsodizes: '*I have seen the light* simply by listening to your soul – and an overwhelming affection fills my heart.' These were heady sentiments indeed, and not without danger when addressed to someone as susceptible to flattery as D'Annunzio. Eventually these ecstasies were to give way to gentle reproaches that betray something of the deep distress caused by the poet's callousness and disloyalty. On 20 December 1895, she wrote to him: 'You must not lie to me . . . as far as I am concerned you have no duty or obligation to fulfil.'

However unreliable he may have been as a lover, Duse's faith in D'Annunzio's worth as a playwright was to remain unshaken. She firmly believed in his aesthetic principles and his quest for a 'theatre of sheer poetry'. She rented La Porziuncola, a villa near Florence, in order to be near the poet's residence, La Capponcina, at Settignano. Together they made plans to build their own theatre on the shores of Lake Albano where they would revive classical drama. The actress and playwright were confident that this ambitious enterprise would capture the imagination of the Italian public and restore 'an ideal conception of drama in its purest form'. Alas, Italian actors, audiences and critics showed scant interest in the project. Because average theatre-goers in Italy lacked the culture and literary background such a repertoire would demand, the plea of D'Annunzio and Duse for a return to classicism found little support.

To her friend Matilde Serao a resolute Duse confided: 'Here at last is my dramatic poet! From now on, I shall work for my own Italian theatre where only the highest and noblest art shall flourish.' An equally enthusiastic D'Annunzio commented to friends: 'I have found my ideal heroine at last. She will give life to my unborn creations!' And undaunted by any negative reactions to his conception of the 'new drama', D'Annunzio feverishly produced some fifteen plays between 1897 and 1914, which he aptly defined as 'tragedies, mysteries, and dreams'.

Many of D'Annunzio's plays that were ultimately to gain acceptance both in Italy and abroad were received with abuse and ridicule when first produced on stage.

The first performance in Italy of *Il sogno di un mattino di primavera* at the Teatro Rossini in Venice on 3 November 1897 was given a cooler reception than that accorded by the Paris critics. Even Duse was described as appearing 'much altered . . . less convincing and more affected in her acting', and when she staged the work at the Teatro Valle in Rome the following January, the theatre was in an uproar. Audiences who knew something of the commotion provoked by D'Annunzio's prurient novels were expecting some-

[16]

thing more lively and daring from Italy's high priest of erotica. But *Il sogno di un mattino di primavera* had virtually no action as a play; matters of location and time were vaguely defined, and the work seemed to hover uncertainly between reality and fantasy. For audiences accustomed to *verismo* and plays of contemporary interest dealing with flesh and blood characters caught up in human conflict, D'Annunzio's poetic exaltations and symbolic rhapsodies were altogether too dull and meaningless. For her part, Duse had prepared her role with the utmost care and portrayed *La Demente* – a woman driven mad by sorrow when her lover is murdered before her very eyes – with extraordinary power. The great actress had mastered every detail of phrasing and inflection in D'Annunzio's text, but something more than her committed performance was needed to bring the play to life.

Accounts by persons who attended the opening night in Rome on 11 January 1898 suggest that had it not been for the presence of Queen Margherita of Savoy in the audience some very ugly scenes might have ensued. When the curtain rose after the interval for a performance of Goldoni's spirited comedy *La locandiera* with Duse in one of her most successful roles as the scheming Mirandolina, the audience cheered at length with cries of 'Evviva Goldoni! Evviva Eleonora Duse!' in order to show their utter contempt for D'Annunzio's offering.

Ten days later on 21 January 1898, Sarah Bernhardt staged in Paris a French translation of the author's first play *La città morta* (completed by the author in 1896). Curiosity attracted a fashionable audience to the Théâtre de la Renaissance which included many distinguished literary figures such as Mirbeau, Rostand, and Lemaître. Although Bernhardt scored a personal triumph in the role of Anna, the work itself received mixed notices.

The drama critic of *L'Intransigeant* considered *La Ville morte* 'a masterly piece of theatre' and the review in *La République Française* described the play as 'a marvel of tragic beauty'. Other French critics, however, were less enthusiastic. Some dismissed the work as 'un expériment italien' of dubious value, while one caustic reviewer adjusted the play's French title to *La Ville à mourir*.

La città morta had been conceived during a cruise around the Greek islands in the summer of 1895, and D'Annunzio had the Greek tragedies in mind when he worked out the details of this five-act tragedy about sensuality, incest and murder amidst the ruins of Mycenae. The plot centres on a youth (Leonardo) who idolizes his sister (Anna). Gripped by an obsessive desire to mix her blood with his own, he struggles in vain against overwhelming temptation and brutally murders her in his insanity.

The Italian critics, as might be expected, were even more acidulous in their reactions. Ferdinando Martini, in a letter to the Marchesa Matilde Gioli Bartolomei, dated 6 March 1898, wrote: 'Have you read *La città morta*? . . . If that is a drama, then I am the Pope. I read in some newspaper or other that the public, in order to understand the play, should be *in possession of the key*. If I were D'Annunzio, I should withhold it from them. With *that* drama and *those* characters, any key brought into the theatre might well prove fatal.'[14]

Both D'Annunzio and Duse were soon to become hardened to similar jibes and hostile demonstrations throughout Italy.

Concealing her own bitter feelings about the loss of *La città morta*, Duse anxiously awaited the outcome of the play's opening in Paris, and with characteristic nobility of spirit she telegraphed her congratulations to Bernhardt: 'I rejoice in your triumph and as an Italian I cannot but express my deep gratitude.'

Duse herself was soon to score a similar triumph when she created the role of Silvia Settala in D'Annunzio's next play, *La Gioconda*, which opened on 15 April 1899 at the Teatro Bellini in Palermo. A sumptuous production and strong casting ensured some measure of success. Critics were full of praise for the fine performances of Duse and Emma Gramatica (Sirenetta) while finding La Galliani in the title role and Ermete Zacconi as Lucio Settala somewhat less suited to their parts. As in *La città morta*, this third play hinges on the theme of fatal love. D'Annunzio reiterates his belief in the supremacy of genius and superhuman ideals for which all other mortals must be sacrificed and the poetic qualities of D'Annunzio's language are fully exploited in *La Gioconda*. Although press reviews were almost unanimous in stressing the musical harmonies of the dialogue, they continued to question D'Annunzio's concept of dramatic form. Technically, *La Gioconda* was undoubtedly superior to *La città morta*, but for most of the critics, D'Annunzio's plays were only beautiful poems rather than dramatic compositions. Critics in Italy and subsequently in France, where the play was staged at the Théâtre de l'Oeuvre on 21 January 1905, continued to insist that 'fine phrases, exquisite images and elevated thoughts' do not in themselves add up to theatre. As in his earlier plays, D'Annunzio's tended to ignore the importance of action by submerging his characters in a labyrinth of myths and symbols.

[18]

left Duse in the role of the blind Anna in D'Annunzio's *La città morta*. After experiencing considerable difficulty in assembling a suitable cast for the play and several inevitable postponements, Duse finally performed this role in the spring of 1901. And despite the unfavourable reviews, Duse included the work in her North American tour of 1902–3 devoted entirely to plays by D'Annunzio. (Photograph by courtesy of the Biblioteca Livia Simoni, Museo Teatrale alla Scala, Milan.)

right Duse in the title role of D'Annunzio's *Francesca da Rimini*, a drama based on the fifth canto of Dante's *Inferno*. Generally regarded as one of his better plays, the poet dedicated *Francesca da Rimini* to the 'divine Eleonora Duse' This lavish production was reported to have cost Duse an estimated 400,000 lire. The première took place at the Teatro Costanzi in Rome on 9 December 1901 with a strong cast headed by Duse and Gustavo Salvini as Paolo. The play's success guaranteed a tour of the major Italian cities before taking the production to Germany, Austria and the United States. (Photograph by courtesy of the Biblioteca Livia Simoni, Museo Teatrale alla Scala, Milan.)

While Italian critics and audiences remained adamant in their refusal to take D'Annunzio seriously as a dramatist, Duse seemed no less determined in her efforts to convert the philistines. At the risk of serious financial losses and sacrificing her own popularity, she insisted upon taking the production of *La Gioconda* on tour from one Italian city to another alongside adapted translations of *Demi-monde* and *La Femme de Claude* by Dumas the Younger. Duse's commitment to D'Annunzio's success as a dramatist knew no bounds. Writing to him on 22 August 1899, she vowed: 'I wish to sacrifice my entire life on your behalf . . . in order to see that virtue triumph which *must never be allowed to perish* – your nobility of soul.'

In the spring of 1901, after engagements in Vienna and Berlin, Duse rejoined forces with Ermete Zacconi in order to tour the Italian cities with a production of *La città morta*. The company visited Genoa, Bologna, Florence, Rome and Venice and, to the management's surprise, audience reactions seemed much more favourable. Duse was beginning to feel that all was not lost.

That same year, she was to create her last great role in a play by D'Annunzio when she appeared in *Francesca da Rimini* (the first part of an uncompleted trilogy). D'Annunzio was by no means the first dramatist to find inspiration in the Paolo and Francesca episode from the Fifth Canto of Dante's *Inferno*, but he brought his own particular colouring to this suggestive tale of adultery, which he himself defined as 'un poème de sang et de luxure'. After months of careful research and detailed preparation, the play opened at the Teatro Costanzi in Rome on 9 December. Duse's interpretation of the ill-fated Francesca was much enhanced by the spiritual quality she gave her part, although the quiet intensity she brought to it showed little rapport with the more flamboyant style of Gustavo Salvini as Paolo.

Visually, the production made a most favourable impression with magnificent sets and costumes based on paintings of the Italian Trecento,[15] and in terms of drama the critics perceived a better grasp of theatrical convention.

Encouraged by the play's success, Duse concentrated almost exclusively upon the works of D'Annunzio from 1901 until 1903. She continued to insist, disregarding the advice of colleagues and impresarios, upon including performances of *La città morta*, *La Gioconda* and *Francesca da Rimini* in the repertoire when planning foreign tours. Drawn by curiosity, foreign audiences reacted with more bewilderment than understanding. The 'mystic sadism' professed by D'Annunzio incensed his detractors, and the resounding failure of plays like *La Gloria* in Naples (1899) and the Nietzschean inspired *Più che l'amore* in Rome (1906) finally succeeded in upsetting his Olympian calm.

Circumstances spared Duse any connection with these fiascos just as a curious irony was to deprive her of the only truly successful tragedy D'Annunzio ever wrote. The same self-interest that had prompted him to give *La città morta* to Bernhardt robbed Duse of the main role in *La figlia di Iorio*, which had absorbed her energies for months. The first performance of this pastoral verse drama in three acts had been scheduled for 2 March 1904 at the Teatro Lirico in Milan. Duse, having just returned to Italy after an exhausting European tour, requested a brief postponement of the opening until she regained her strength. D'Annunzio flatly refused and entrusted the central role of Mila di Codra to the talented young actress Irma Gramatica. In her state of physical exhaustion and grave depression, Duse was even more upset by D'Annunzio's unreasonable behaviour on this occasion, but she suppressed her grievance and handed over her costumes to her substitute, wishing her good luck. As it turned out, Irma Gramatica scored a personal triumph and the play was unanimously acclaimed by the critics.

Fusing provincial realism and strong symbolic elements, D'Annunzio had, at last, managed to produce a play with some semblance of dramatic unity. Written in the space of eighteen days at Nettuno during the previous summer, D'Annunzio had based this tale of violent passions on the folklore and harsh environment of his native Abruzzi. Needless to say, the poetic transfiguration of primitive existence was unmistakably his own. Duse, convalescing at home, telegraphed her friend Emma Garzes, announcing: 'A deserved success to everyone's satisfaction . . . the real consolation is that victory has come without a moment's delay . . . That is how it should be.'

The seven years of intense collaboration between the poet and actress were sadly at an end, and their hopes of creating a theatre on the shores of Lake Albano were buried for ever. D'Annunzio had found a new mistress in the Marchesa Carlotta di Rudinì. Duse emerged from this difficult chapter of emotional turmoil and unsparing activity somewhat scarred and humiliated but infinitely wiser. She buried herself in her work in the firm belief that 'the greatest help in time of need *always comes from oneself'* and, after a brief period of solitude and rest, new projects and engagements were hastily resumed.

In an interview with the drama critic of the *Tribuna* in January 1898, Duse confided her aspirations as an actress and spoke of her search for innovations in the Italian theatre. She spoke of a new form of dramatic art 'essentially noble and pure', and expressed her confidence that Italian dramatists would lead the way.

Pirandello, whose major contribution to modern drama in Italy unfortunately came too late for Duse whom he greatly admired, wryly observed that no Italian dramatist of the period squared up to those ideals. D'Annunzio's writing for the theatre in Pirandello's opinion was essentially based on externals whereas Duse's artistry stemmed from the soul.

Duse and Ibsen

In the end the 'new form of dramatic art' to which Duse aspired did not come from her native Italy as she had hoped, but from Norway's most distinguished poet and playwright of the nineteenth century, Henrik Ibsen.

Ibsen had lived in Italy from 1864 until 1868 and from 1878 until 1885. Recalling his experiences during those eventful years, he expressed his admiration for the realism of Italian acting. Nevertheless, it must have greatly surprised him in later years to find an Italian actress being acclaimed throughout Europe as the most impressive interpreter of his plays.

Halvdan Koht, a Norwegian biographer of Ibsen, has written of the playwright that 'perhaps no one achieved such universal victory for him as the Italian actress Eleonora Duse . . . Her tragic intensity and brilliant intuition made the plays seem forever new: Ibsen had found the perfect interpreter of all his most profound thoughts.'[16]

Duse studied Ibsen's texts with the same attention to detail that she had previously reserved for D'Annunzio's tragedies. She was conscious of inevitable flaws in the French translations upon which she relied and sought advice from informed sources in her anxiety to respect the author's intentions. At the age of thirty-one, the actress felt that she had the necessary experience and preparation in order to play the role of Nora in *A Doll's House* in a translation by the Italian novelist Luigi Capuana, friend and mentor of Pirandello. In an exchange of letters between Capuana and Ibsen as the work progressed, the dramatist insisted that the dialogue should sound natural and unforced. Blatant inaccuracies

in translations of his works from German into French and English
had greatly disturbed Ibsen, and when Capuana suggested giving
the play a happy ending (for reasons never fully explained), the
author understandably refused to allow any such alteration to the
text.

Duse was ready to make her debut as Nora at the Teatro dei
Filodrammatici in Milan on 9 February 1891. Audiences and critics
reacted to this first production of any play by Ibsen in Italy with
puzzlement rather than hostility. Technically, the play was more
convincing than anything ever written by D'Annunzio for the
stage. Yet Ibsen was never to achieve any wide popularity with
Italian audiences who considered his ideals much too cerebral
and indigestible.[17]

For Duse, on the other hand, the Norwegian's drama was a
revelation. His female roles suited her temperament, and she
portrayed these creatures of scruple and inner conflict to perfection. The years 1905 and 1906 marked the high tide of Ibsen in
Europe and, in Lugné-Poe's opinion, the apogee of Duse's powers
as an artist. For some five years during the last decade of the
nineteenth century she immersed herself in assimilating new
Ibsen roles. In studying D'Annunzio's plays, she had been assisted
by the author himself; with Ibsen she had to rely upon the
guidance and experience of others. Duse found herself becoming
totally absorbed in the complex nature of women like Nora,
Rebecca, Hedda, and Ellida. Something in her own nature readily
identified with their conflict between courage and cowardice,
their struggle to reconcile some divine purpose with undermining
temptations and eccentricities. These powerful and destructive
women exercised for the Italian actress a curious fascination that
she had never experienced with the shallow heroines of Sardou.
The problems of interpretation posed by Ibsen's conception of
duty and morality provided the very challenge Duse had been
seeking.

When it came to staging Ibsen's plays, she faced the same
difficulties about suitable casting as those encountered earlier
with the plays of D'Annunzio. Italian actors on the whole were
not responsive to the idea of prolonged rehearsals and close
textual study in order to master Ibsen's world. To quote Duse on
this thorny question: 'They profess to love Ibsen, but they *do not
know how to love him.'*

Italian audiences, like those of Spain and Portugal, found the
Norwegian's plays 'intangible and obscure' and, as one leading

Italian critic was to comment: 'Ibsen very soon went out of fashion in Italy without ever having been in fashion.' Few actor managers shared Duse's scruples about respecting the original script or the author's true intentions. The highly extroverted Oswalds of Zacconi and of Novelli in *Ghosts* (interpretations that infuriated Ibsen) are a salient example of the distortions that resulted from idiosyncratic interpretations.[18]

It is worth remembering that Ibsen's acceptance as a dramatist of any importance was slow to emerge both in his native Scandinavia and in Northern Europe. Bernard Shaw, who shared Duse's passion for Ibsen's drama, recognized the unpalatable aspects of his plays. He rightly attributed much of the coolness on the part of critics and audiences to the intellectual demands Ibsen made on theatre-goers intent upon passive entertainment. Even in Northern Europe audiences disliked the Norwegian's oppressive plots and excessive didacticism and failed to come to terms with his ambiguities and so-called 'religious dimension'. Yet these were exactly the qualities that appealed to his admirers. Shaw extolled Ibsen alongside Wagner as 'the master spirits of the age' while singling out Duse as the first actress to prove herself equal to the new style of acting imposed by Ibsen's drama.

When comparing him with other Northern European dramatists Duse would remark: 'Ibsen promises nothing on the surface . . . but just let him unfurl the sails.' And if Italian audiences were to reject him as they had rejected D'Annunzio, there were compensations on tour as Duse triumphed in Ibsen's plays in one European capital after another – Berlin, Vienna, London, Amsterdam and Copenhagen.

The actress was invited to appear in *A Doll's House* at the Carltheater on 26 February 1892 as part of the cultural programme during the Vienna Exhibition held that year. The drama critic of the *Neue Freie Presse* was struck by the manner in which Duse transformed the personality of Nora as the play progressed. As usual, the theatre was crammed with every theatre personality of note. The well-known critic Paul Schlenther analysed her technique in considerable detail during her season in the Austrian capital. Commenting upon the conviction of every gesture and nuance she brought to the part of Nora, he marvelled at the consistency and power of her interpretation. Nora's trauma suddenly appeared to be shared by everyone in the audience. And the actress's most reliable Italian biographer, Olga Resnevic Signorelli, has contributed her own impressions of Duse's masterly ambivalence in the role: 'As Nora, she acted out a joy which was *not* happiness. Her bright smile failed to conceal the underlying suggestion of solitude; she behaved as if *not wishing to dwell upon her misfortunes* while *having to dwell upon them.*'[19]

German and Scandinavian critics were unanimous in their admiration of her understanding of Ibsen. The occasional note of dissent accused her of indulging in a 'private fantasy on the theme of Ibsen,' but no one questioned her sincerity and impact.

The German critic, Alfred Kerr, felt that the soul of Hedda Gabler held no mysteries for the Italian actress. She lived the part. Few actresses were to express as forcefully as Duse Hedda's inner solitude, or her aversion to the domestic situation in which she felt herself to be trapped.

More than anyone else, Lugné-Poe helped the actress to come to grips with Ibsen's style, and by 1906 *Rosmersholm, The Lady from the Sea* and *John Gabriel Borkman* had become familiar works in her standard repertoire. In her own words, Norway's greatest dramatist had replaced D'Annunzio as 'the beneficent force' and Ibsen's writing for the theatre gave her the necessary inspiration and strength to persevere during a difficult phase of nagging depression and uncertainty.

In January and February 1906, Duse was touring Northern Europe under the management of Lugné-Poe. During the first ten days of February the company appeared in Oslo, where Duse hoped finally to meet her idol. Unfortunately, Ibsen was too ill

The National Theatre in Oslo where Duse appeared in February 1906. (Photograph by courtesy of the Norwegian National Library, Oslo.)

to receive anyone. Accompanied by Lugné-Poe, the actress stood in the snow before Ibsen's house hoping to catch at least a glimpse of the invalid. She was inconsolable and Lugné-Poe believed that this bitter disappointment was the last crushing blow. A warm reception from audiences in the Norwegian capital and words of tribute from the composer Grieg failed to rouse Duse from her despondency. The news of Ibsen's death some months later only increased her sense of personal loss.

Personally, she had learned a great deal from her relentless study of Ibsen's tragic women characters. Their inner torment mirrored something of her own private conflict, and this emerges clearly from a statement by Duse shortly before her decision to retire from the stage in 1909. 'The spirits of the Rosmers may ennoble the soul,' she confided, 'but they destroy every hope of happiness.'[20]

Of all the Ibsen roles Duse attempted, Ellida in *The Lady from the Sea* was the one in which she excelled. Ellida's mysterious and haunting nature brought out the spiritual quality that was to characterize Duse's style of acting in maturity. She frequently expressed her preference for this role and chose *The Lady from the Sea*, not only for her farewell appearance in 1909 but also for her return to the stage some twelve years later.

Published in 1888, the play had been much misunderstood both in Norway and abroad. One Scandinavian critic dismissed the character of Ellida as 'a bizarre psychological case', while another defined the play as 'the creation of a purely negative spirit'. But contemporary assessments would tend to support the view of the Swedish critic, J. A. Runström, who at once defined the play as a 'drama of rare fulfilment'. Runström in his enthusiasm wrote: 'Not only is the characterization masterly and enthralling, but the dazzling assurance with which the plot is conceived and sustained fills one with an admiration that increases the more one studies the work.'

Other actresses watched Duse when she played Ellida with envy and amazement.[21] The German actress, Irene Trisch, claimed that the Italian actress became 'an ageless creature of transcendent beauty' in the role. In Italy the distinguished critic, Silvio D'Amico, made a close study of Duse's development in the part over an extended period of time and he never ceased to wonder at the spiritual aura Duse emanated when she came on stage as Ellida. The senses appeared to play no part in her conception of Ibsen's most elusive heroine. Yet when D'Amico suggested to the actress on one occasion that *The Lady from the Sea* embodied the drama of 'the feminine state of mind', Duse reacted sharply by retorting: 'Nonsense! It is the drama of everyone.'[22]

In Germany and England, Duse found the respect for Ibsen she failed to command in her native Italy. Watching her perform Ibsen's plays, Bernard Shaw judged her performances the best modern acting that he had ever witnessed. And James Agate, who reviewed her last London season at the New Oxford Theatre in June 1923 for the *Sunday Times*, gave the following account of her memorable interpretation of Ellida at the age of sixty-five:

> This play is a godsend to a great actress whose *forte* is not so much doing as suffering that which fate has done to her. With Duse, speech is silver and silence is golden . . . The long second act was a symphony for the voice, but to me the scene of greatest marvel was the third act. In this Duse scaled incredible heights. There was one moment when, drawn by every fibre of her being to the unknown irresistible of the Stranger and the sea, she blotted herself behind her husband and took comfort and courage from his hand. Here terror and ecstasy sweep over her face with that curious effect which this actress alone knows – as though this were not present stress, but havoc remembered of past time. Her features have the placidity of long grief; so many storms have broken over them that nothing can disturb again this sea of calm distress. If there be in acting such a thing as pure passion divorced from the body yet expressed in terms of the body, it is here. Now and again in this strange play Duse would seem to pass beyond our ken, and where she has been there is only fragrance and a sound in our ears like water flowing under the stars.[23]

Her understanding of the role had deepened considerably after a long absence from the stage, and was, if anything, further enhanced by her fragile appearance as serious illness took its toll. Arbitrary alterations to detail were part of the Duse magic as she strived to keep successive performances fresh and convincing. And to those critics who accused her of distorting the original she would reply that the 'spiritual essence' of any character was her main concern.

Loyal admirers discovered something new with every performance and she herself treated every successive appearance in the same role as if it were another opening night. The more ambiguous the character the greater the challenge, and, in the words of Count Giuseppe Primoli, who helped to promote her Paris debut: 'Elle excelle à représenter ces types de femmes à double fond, toutes en nuances merveilleusement compliquées.'[24]

[27]

Duse's incomparable ability to convey human suffering on stage became even more skilful and effective in later years. St John Ervine, when he reviewed her last London appearances for *The Observer*, was to emphasize this particular aspect of her art in a perceptive review that agreed in substance with Agate's more poetic description:

> In some strange and inexplicable way, she is able to communicate sentience to insentient things. Her acting is entirely quiet acting. She does not roar and shout, nor does she throw herself up and down the stage like a demented steam roller. She speaks the most poignant things in a tone that seems no louder than that in which we would make a request for the sugar, and yet she leaves us clearly conscious of the sorrow of those who are lonely in mind . . . There were periods in the play when she enabled us to dispense with language. It was not necessary for us to understand what she was *saying*, because we understand what she was *feeling*. The greatest feat which an actor can perform is to take an audience beyond the barriers of speech.[25]

Unlike other distinguished Italian performers who toured widely and achieved fame throughout the world, Duse never tried to substitute a ceaseless external intensity for inner fire.

The Duse charisma

Just as Sarah Bernhardt was to eclipse the glory of the great Rachel as France's most celebrated tragedienne, so too was Eleonora Duse to surpass the achievements of Italy's most famous actress of the mid-nineteenth century, Adelaide Ristori.

Along with several other distinguished artists, of the 'heroic phase', Ristori had lived long enough to witness radical changes of mood and method in the Italian theatre. Many of those changes were closely associated with the artistry of Duse, who tried to foster new ideas and techniques in her own company. When artists of an earlier generation were invited to comment on Duse's international success, their replies understandably betrayed a note of envy and a lingering nostalgia for the solemn, declamatory style that had brought them fame.

The veteran Tommaso Salvini was critical of Duse's voice and gestures, which he judged to be lacking in harmony. He even went so far as to judge her an 'unstable celebrity' and mistakenly predicted a short-lived success for what he called Duse's 'restricted and anguished' repertoire. Salvini's generation had attached enormous importance to a strong physical presence on the stage. A powerful voice and majestic bearing were the *sine qua non* of fine acting. The 'inner' essence pursued by Duse irked him profoundly although even Salvini was prepared to concede that when it came to expressing the tragedy of unrequited love or spiritual trauma onstage, Duse was unsurpassed. Indeed, wherever Duse appeared onstage for the first time, the same pattern of response repeated itself: 'the puzzled surprise, the totally new experience which could not be immediately absorbed. It took the public, and particularly the critics, a little time to adjust to this new adventure in the art of acting.'[26]

But most of her fellow Italian actors were more approving of Duse's blazing new pathways than Tommaso Salvini, though not all could or would follow. While freely recognizing both the genius and the originality of Duse's performances, Adelaide Ristori admired the subtlety with which the younger actress concealed any deficiencies of temperament and technique. Ermete Zacconi, however, with whom Duse was to form an interesting, if not entirely successful, partnership, expressed the unequivocal view of his own generation of actors when he stated: 'Duse's art was one of genius and meditation – as eloquent in speech and movement as in silence and repose.'[27]

At the turn of the century, conditions in the theatres of France and England were such that actors in those countries were able to measure their success against the reputation of other established artists in the best companies of the day. By contrast, Italian and Spanish artists of any note tended to appraise their achievements in terms of their acceptance abroad. Foreign engagements were avidly sought by Italian artists who could count upon support from Italian emigrants in Paris, London, New York, São Paulo and Buenos Aires. And once they achieved popularity abroad, Italian audiences saw increasingly less of their most prominent actors. There was little reason at the outset to believe that Duse's individual style of acting would ever make her an international star. Offstage, she deliberately cultivated sobriety in her appearance. Her initial appearance onstage could be disconcertingly ineffectual until some all-pervading force was mysteriously released. The following review of her Vienna debut published in the *Neue Freie Presse* on 21 February 1892 sums up the essence of countless first-hand reports of Duse's art. The reviewer on that occasion wrote:

[29]

Her face is anything but beautiful, her voice seems weak; there is nothing about her appearance that draws or attracts one in itself, but suddenly without warning from all these negative features something quite extraordinary emerges, never before witnessed. In that apparent *nothingness* there lives a great artistic soul, by virtue of which the actress becomes rich thanks to her poverty . . . There are silences that last for ten minutes and yet are of the most convincing eloquence; her eyes convey everything . . . In her performance we have experienced moments of silence that mark the supreme expression of human feelings. Duse has brought to us the long-awaited rejection of shouting and gesticulating onstage.[28]

When Duse finally reached Paris in the summer of 1897 to appear at Sarah Bernhardt's own Théâtre de la Renaissance and subsequently at the Théâtre de la Porte Saint-Martin, she had been touring the world for some eight years – in England and Germany, Holland and Scandinavia, Egypt and Russia and North America. To succeed in Paris and win the approval of the formidable French intelligentsia was seen as the final test. A great deal has been written about Duse's first appearance in the French capital on 2 June 1897 in the presence of the great Bernhardt herself. For her debut Duse chose a specially commissioned Italian translation of Dumas the Younger's *La Dame aux camélias*, a role in which the great Sarah excelled. The Italian company could scarcely hope to compete in matters of production or stage presentation with superior French standards. Nerves played havoc with Duse's performance in the opening scenes, but as the play progressed she began to reveal something of her unique stage personality. The notorious *chauvinisme* of Parisian theatre circles had prophesied a cool reception. But when the most influential drama critic of the day, Francisque Sarcey, confided in his review of the performance that 'gradually, her features and whole personality began to radiate something that seizes you and holds you helplessly captive . . .',[29] other influential voices confirmed Duse's triumph – Jules Lemaître, André Antoine, Zola, Paul Deschenel and Marcel Prévost among them. Detailed comparisons of the interpretations essayed by Duse and Bernhardt of Dumas's ill-fated Marguerite Gautier suggest that the two actresses were both memorable in their own way. Bernhardt, sumptuously gowned, offered a much more elegant and pictorial account of the role. Duse, on the other hand, was more subdued and poignant.[30] Until that evening, Bernhardt, who was considerably older than Duse, had never seen the Italian actress perform. Critics and audiences were soon inventing a fierce rivalry between them but, superficially at least, the two actresses were courteous and deferential to each other.[31]

Among the other distinguished French actresses who flocked to see Duse perform were Réjane and Bartet and both expressed their sincere admiration. Also among the countless celebrities who attended Duse's opening night was Bizet's widow who is said to have exclaimed in her enthusiasm: 'Oh, votre Duse! . . . c'est du Bizet en prose!' By general consensus of the critics, Duse's Marguerite was an interesting rather than a definitive interpretation. Subsequent appearances as Sudermann's Magda and Césarine in Dumas the Younger's *Femme de Claude* greatly enhanced her reputation in the eyes of the French critics, who now began to see her as a serious rival to Bernhardt in the same roles. A special charity performance for French artists and critics at the request of Francisque Sarcey, followed by a reception in the Bois de Boulogne, brought this first Paris season to a brilliant conclusion. 'Where Bernhardt was "an army with banners" instantly perceptible and triumphantly sweeping all before it, Duse was the "still small voice" which gradually, but all the more powerfully, undermined all resistance, and at last penetrated to the very heart of her audience.'[32]

A farewell impromptu matinée on 9 July at the Théâtre de la Porte Saint-Martin consisted of a number of scenes from her repertoire, including works by Goldoni and Verga. Expressing the gratitude of everyone connected with the Parisian theatre, Sarcey wrote of that 'belle, inoubliable journée' when 'assurément la Duse nous avait touchés.' Duse acted in Italian, yet language barriers had seemed to disappear. Every detail of nuance and gesture revealed the essence of the women she portrayed; French audiences were astounded by the immediate impact and extraordinary clarity of her performances. Even the exacting Adolphe Brisson (Sarcey's successor as the doyen of Parisian drama critics) was won over by the passion and fluency of Duse's acting, despite his reservations about the purity of her style. Dumas the Younger was delighted to find yet another skilful interpreter of his romantic heroines who could enhance his plays with her individual rendering of certain nuances. Schneider, the drama critic of the *Gaulois* commented: 'La Duse fut, par le public, comme par la critique, consacrée incomparable', and lengthy reviews in *Figaro* and *Débats* expressed the same jubilant note of success.

But Paris and the French were only one of many hurdles in

Duse's career. Whether touring in Italy or abroad, she coura-geously persisted in putting her ideals before any considerations of commercial success, and this attitude frequently brought her into conflict with impresarios, managements, critics, fellow actors and audiences. Desirable engagements and financial rewards were often sacrificed in her determination to tour in a repertoire of her own choice. D'Annunzio's plays, in particular, were something of a nightmare for any management intent upon commercial success. But Duse was increasingly more anxious to enlarge her repertoire. She encouraged Italian dramatists such as Pietro Cossa, Achille Torelli, Galeno Sinimberghi, Edoardo Calandra, Giuseppe Giacosa and Marco Praga to write for a truly national theatre, urging them to pursue some noble ideal in their work, rather than write with the personality of some specific actor or actress in mind. This attitude helps to explain the affinity Duse felt with dramatists like D'Annunzio, Ibsen, Hauptmann and Gorki, whose characters symbolize *ideals*. And when she began to lose all hope of finding an Italian dramatist to equal D'Annunzio's achievement, Duse expressed a keen interest in the Russian repertoire as pro-duced by someone like Stanislavsky.

There was no lack of activity on the Italian stage at the turn of the century, with over a hundred companies devoted to serious drama. Nor was there any lack of female talent as younger actresses began to establish their reputation. Artists like the Gramatica sisters, Tina di Lorenzo, Virginia Reiter, Italia Vitaliani and Clara della Guardia had already scored considerable success in roles created by Duse to which they brought their own distinctive style. Yet few among these able young actresses were capable of match-ing Duse in matters of penetration and refinement.

Ingenuity and a natural talent for improvisation are two qual-ities that have never been lacking in the traditions of the Italian theatre, but Duse was a restless pioneer who sought to temper Latin spontaneity with a deeper understanding of the more arcane aspects of human experience.

In countries like Germany, Austria, Scandinavia, and Russia, Duse followed new trends and methods in the theatre with keen interest. The experimental work of such pioneers as André Antoine and Lugné-Poe, the founders of the Freie Bühne, and the disciples of Stanislavsky made a deep impression on Duse.

As the years passed, the actress surrounded herself with a select circle of friends in Italy and abroad which was dominated by artists and intellectuals with whom she could exchange ideas and work out new projects for the future. She deplored the fact that most Italian actors showed little interest in widening their horizons beyond the theatre. She herself showed interest in writers, musicians, painters and men of science and letters who were capable of enriching her mind and making her aware of other spheres of achievement. And her prolific correspondence with Matilde Serao, Count Primoli, Boito, Dumas the Younger, Lugné-Poe and Marco Praga among many others gives ample evidence of Duse's restless pursuit of something different and better in her career as an actress.

Luigi Rasi could also claim to be an actor and teacher of some vision. Writing in 1903, he saw Duse's contribution to the modern Italian theatre as being one of genuine renewal based on self-discipline and a clear understanding of the transition from past to present as the face of Italian drama changed. Dramatists were astonished and delighted at the way in which she could discover new possibilities or shifts of emphasis in their plays. Her interpretation, for example, of Santuzza at the Théâtre de la Porte Saint-Martin in Paris, touched depths in Verga's powerful regional drama *Cavalleria rusticana* which the author himself felt he was discovering for the first time. Jules Huret, reviewing the play in *Figaro* on 4 July 1897, was struck by Duse's ability to illuminate and transform the smallest detail. He considered her performance as Santuzza an eloquent lesson in how to prepare a role, a lesson from which even the most experienced actors might benefit.

Duse and 'La Dame aux camélias'

Condemned to play certain roles that audiences had come to expect wherever she appeared, Duse tried to make the situation more tolerable by trying to put fresh life into her interpretation of the female roles of Scribe, Sardou, and Dumas the Younger. Struggling to overcome her frustration and annoyance at the thought of yet another performance as Odette, Fedora, Césarine, Fernande, or Marguerite, the rehearsals continued daily in the hope of bringing to light some new meaning or insight. The Italian critic Alfredo Panzini (alias Jarro) named Duse 'the canticle of canticles of all women' as he marvelled at the range of expression she managed to bring out in a long list of heroines who were ostensibly different facets of the same character.

The part of Marguerite Gautier had been turned down by Adelaide Ristori on moral grounds. For Duse, the role was to become her 'cheval de bataille' and she performed *La Dame aux camélias* more than any other play by Dumas the Younger. Duse's development in the part has been carefully analysed by a number of critics but most reliably of all by Luigi Rasi who studied consecutive performances on tour. Reviews of Duse in this play written by critics in Paris, London, Berlin, New York and Buenos Aires consistently refer to a tentative performance in the opening scenes. Yet, as the performance progressed, the most sceptical audience found itself reduced to tears and emotional acclaim. Rasi, for all his experience, could identify no specific school or method at work in Duse's interpretation but he too found her handling of detail as subtle as that of a silversmith at work. Verdi, who described himself as being spellbound by her performance in the final act of the play, was heard to exclaim: 'That little Duse! . . . If only I had seen her Marguerite before composing *La Traviata*. What a splendid finale I might have put together if I had heard that crescendo invoking Armando that Duse has created simply by allowing her soul to overflow.'[33] And the great Stanislavsky in later life was to remember the eloquence of certain extended pauses that would have spelled disaster in any other performer. Here Duse's highly strung temperament served her to full advantage, and Jarro, the one critic who has attempted to describe her vocal technique in any detail, defined her achievement in Dumas's tragedy as 'supreme art'. Jarro's analysis traces out at length the careful modulations and colouring of the voice essayed by Duse in order to register the shifts of conflicting emotion in Marguerite. He speaks of the actress's skilful transitions from head to chest notes that became positively nasal or guttural where necessary; her diction clear and fluent and in perfect accord with her gestures of face and body. In a word, a miracle of transformation and capable of astounding even the other members of the cast as she illuminated some new facet of the role with each successive performance. George de Cuevas, who was to become the founder of Le Grand Ballet du Marquis de Cuevas, saw Duse play Marguerite at the Casino Municipal in Nice as a youth in his teens. He knew nothing about Duse or her reputation as an actress, but he soon found himself caught up in the grief that swept over the entire audience.

Henry James, writing in March 1896 on Dumas the Younger, has provided a more critical and dispassionate account. Expressing his own reservations about Duse's arbitrary interpretation of *La Dame aux camélias*, the critic recognizes in Duse a great actress

with the rare talent of being able to go straight to the essence of
a play:

> We have seen Madame Duse this year or two in her tattered
> translation, with few advantages, with meagre accessories and with
> one side of the character of the heroine scarcely touched at all – so
> little indeed that the Italian version joins hands with the American
> and the relation of Marguerite and Armand seems to present itself
> as a question of the consecrated even if not approved 'union'. For
> this interesting actress, however, the most beautiful thing is always
> the great thing, and her performance – if seen on a fortunate
> evening – lives in the mind as a fine vindication of the play. I am
> not sure indeed that it is the very performance Dumas intended;
> but he lived long enough to have forgotten perhaps what that
> performance was. He might on some sides, I think, have accepted
> Madame Duse's as a reminder.[34]

But *to be once more Marguerite Gautier*, performance after performance, became in Duse's own words an arduous and tormented
process as she struggled night after night to bring the character
to life both 'in form and essence'. The heroines of Sardou and
Dumas the Younger were sapping her mental energies, and Duse
felt trapped by the success of these plays with managements and
audiences.

Duse as pioneer

The conventional and monotonous were wholly alien to Duse's
temperament. Despite the handicap of her own powerful personality onstage, she demanded good ensemble acting from her
company. She insisted that her actors should study their parts in
order to act with greater expression and be less dependent upon
guidance from the prompter. Dramatists like Marco Praga discovered ways of improving their plays as they watched Duse take
the cast through the script. And foreign critics were quick to
recognize the pioneering spirit that singled out her company. The
German critic Paul Schlenther applauded her efforts to enrich
pictorial effects onstage with psychological insights and much the
same sentiments were echoed by the theatre historian Julius Bab
and the dramatist Gerhard Hauptmann. Sad to relate, these qualities were more valued abroad than in Italy. The D'Annunzio
fiasco had taught Duse to mistrust the vagaries of fashion among
Italian critics and audiences. Frustrated time and time again in
her efforts to develop avant-garde theories about dramatic form,
Duse even thought of attempting Luigi Rasi's experiments with

dramatized readings of prose and poetry by authors like Nietzsche, Aristotle, Carlyle, Seneca, Schiller, Goethe, Shakespeare, Petrarch, Carducci and, above all, Dante.

At the height of her fame Duse still had no theatre or circle of her own in Italy, while many younger and much less distinguished artists were securely established with their own permanent company and claque. A brilliant international career had, in effect, alienated Duse from influential theatrical coteries in her own country. Disregarding the fashionable and popular, Duse battled on independently for the ideals in which she firmly believed: 'I have always been my own worst enemy and friend', she would quip, 'and anything else said about me is only idle chatter.' Studious and painstaking, Duse was not only a great actress but an excellent teacher, and she exercised considerable influence over younger actresses who went on to form their own companies. Some of her protégées, like the Argentinian-born Angelina Pagano, who subsequently graced the theatres of Buenos Aires, helped to pass on Duse's impeccable standards of training and discipline to a new generation of actors in countries without any national theatre or established traditions. No actress, whether famous or unknown, ever studied Duse onstage without learning something, and Ellen Terry's first impression of the actress on the London stage speaks for itself: 'Her walk is the walk of the peasant, fine and free. She has the superb carriage of the head which goes with that fearless movement from the hips. And her face! There is *nothing* like it, *nothing*! But it is as the real woman, a particular woman, that Duse triumphs most'.[35]

Duse and the critics

It would be misleading to imply that Duse's particular style of acting was wholly acceptable to every critic or artist who ever saw her perform. The reservations of an earlier generation of Italian actors have already been mentioned. The Italian critic Ferdinando Martini, writing to Giuseppe Giacosa on 2 June 1899, expressed little sympathy for Duse, whose acting he found monotonous, although it should be noted that he was reviewing a performance of D'Annunzio's *La Gioconda*. And an ungallant Giacosa, who owed the success of his play, *Tristi amori*, almost entirely to Duse's interpretation, declared in a letter to their mutual friend Count Primoli that he found Duse a tiresome 'prima donna' whose performances were more often unpredictable and disappointing than brilliant.

In England, Max Beerbohm refused to be submerged by the current Dusemania. After seeing her perform at the Lyceum Theatre in London, he wrote: 'There was never an influence so awe-inspiring as Duse . . . The heaven is rent with superlatives . . . superlatives of a solemn, almost religious order'. The critic went on to concede 'power and nobility in her face', . . . 'charm in her voice', and 'movement full of grace and strength'. But the sensation of some 'great egoistic force' and, worse still, coming from a woman, made Beerbohm feel distinctly uncomfortable and resentful.[36]

On occasion, even James Agate was unimpressed by her moping – 'moping ineffably, if you like, but still moping'.[37] For Bernard Shaw, however, Duse triumphed as an artist of 'exceptional intelligence and sensibility'. Shaw's unstinted admiration for Duse tended to make him cruel in his strictures directed at other well-known actresses. Reviewing Duse's performance of Sudermann's *Magda* in *The Saturday Review* in June 1896, he declared: 'Mrs Campbell has not lived long enough to get as much work crammed into her entire repertory as Duse gets into every ten minutes of her *Magda*.'[38]

Reading Shaw on Duse, one might be tempted to ignore the fact that, like any great artist from whom audiences had come to expect a great deal, the standard of her acting could be variable. First-hand reports confirm that her performances were often seriously affected by nervous tension and poor health. Duse could be sublime in a role one evening and extremely dull in the very same role at the next performance. Some critics made a strength of this weakness. William Archer, the drama critic of *The World*, argued that 'inconstancy was an integral part of her fascination' so that any performance by Duse was never in danger of becoming a mechanical repetition of the same emotions and gestures.[39]

Perhaps Arthur Symons sums up best of all the inherent contradictions in Duse's art when he states, in the opening paragraph of his book:

> Eleonora Duse is a great artist . . . and it is only by accident that she is an actress. Circumstances having made her an actress, she is the greatest of living actresses; she would have been equally great in any other art. She is an actress through being the antithesis of the actress; not, indeed, by mere reliance upon nature, but by controlling nature into the forms of her desire as the sculptor controls the clay under his fingers. She is the artist of her own soul, and it is her force of will, her mastery of herself, not her abandonment to it, which make her what she is.[40]

Duse was adamant that offstage an actress should attract as little attention as possible to herself, and that in her public life she should shun all histrionics. Her quiet life style brought dignity and authority and, as Bernard Shaw observed, whatever Duse lacked in studied elegance and ostentation she wholly compensated for with truth and life. Appearing on stage, as she invariably did, without makeup or elaborate wigs and in the simplest of costumes, Duse emanated a creative power so subtle but so highly charged that it seemed to nearly everyone who saw her to be nothing short of miraculous. She needed only to observe or touch something onstage for that object to take life. Writers as different as James Joyce and Anton Chekhov were so overwhelmed by her artistry that they refused to believe that she was speaking in a foreign language, such was the immediacy of every word and phrase. Actors and critics in France, Russia, Germany and America were to express much the same conviction that they understood every syllable she uttered onstage. And, to quote the exacting Francisque Sarcey: 'When one watches and listens to La Duse, one miraculously *understands* Italian.'

Differences of culture and sensibility were swept away when she began to act, such was the universality of Duse's art. For the first time in the annals of the Russian theatre, the critics of St Petersburg and Moscow spoke with one voice about a foreign artist. The Russian critic Ivanov claimed that he had never seen any other actress make an entrance quite like Duse, who appeared to have been living the part long before the curtain went up. In later years, as Duse's repertoire became more selective, the spiritual overtones became more pronounced in her acting.[41] The German sociologist and philosopher Georg Simmel, observing her in a play by D'Annunzio in 1901 on an evening when she was visibly tired and indisposed, felt that 'A spiritual perception of life embodied the beauty of her stage image' and the words 'religiosity' and 'spirituality' abound in press reviews of her D'Annunzio and Ibsen phases.

Perhaps the last word should go to the actress's lifelong friend and confidante, the novelist Matilde Serao, for whom the Duse magic remained undiminished: 'Without indulging in rhetoric or exaggeration, one could say that Duse acted as naturally as flowers exhale perfume, as stars shine and birds sing . . . she was an actress who performed with all the powers and resources at her disposal – an actress with heart, soul, and wisdom.'[42]

Notes

Full bibliographical references are not provided in the notes for books included in the Select Bibliography.

1 The hierarchy observed in Italian theatre companies in the nineteenth century appears to have been much more rigid and complex than in other European countries. Distinctions were drawn not only between the various categories of leading actors such as *prim'attore* and *prim'attore assoluto* but among the juvenile leads one finds *primo, secondo* and even *terzo amoroso, brillante* or *ingenuo*. In addition, there were the various types of *caratterista* (character actor) and the term *generico* could mean anything from an actor doing walk-on parts to a prompter or a general utility man or stagehand.

2 The Benincasa Company, a minor theatre company of the period.

3 Four of Bernhardt's most successful roles: *La Dame aux camélias* (1852) by Dumas the Younger; *Adrienne Lecouvreur* (1849) by Scribe and Legouvé; *Le Sphinx* (1874) by Octave Feuillet; and *Frou-frou* (1869) by Meilhac and Halévy. With the exception of *Le Sphinx*, Duse, too, soon became associated with these roles.

4 In a letter from Rio de Janeiro dated 28 August 1885 to her friend and confidante Matilde Serao, the actress wrote: 'My heart is full of things both good and bad. But I am perfectly calm and resolute and *all my energies are concentrated on my work*. I feel a little sad for the sufferings of others, but I prefer to bury my own suffering in silence if I am to remain serene.' In addition to the rift with Checchi and the scandal provoked by her affair with Andò, who was a married man, there were other trials to be endured on this ill-fated tour. The enormous theatre in Rio de Janeiro where the company performed had impossible acoustics, and the opening performance of *Fedora* was something of a fiasco. The actors onstage were nervous and ill at ease as they awaited news of a young actor called Diotti, who had been stricken with yellow fever. After several days of atrocious suffering, Diotti died, leaving everyone in the company greatly saddened and depressed.

5 The Freie Bühne was an independent theatre founded by the critic and director Otto Brahm, in 1889 in Berlin for the staging of new, naturalistic plays that were shunned by the German commercial theatre.

The company's first production was Ibsen's *Ghosts* in September 1899. This was followed by performances of plays by Hauptmann, Tolstoy, Zola and Strindberg. The enterprise was successful, but short-lived. Brahm's efforts, nevertheless, inspired the creation of other private theatres and amateur groups in Berlin, Munich, and Vienna.

6 The Independent Theatre was founded in 1891 in London by Jacob Thomas Grein (1862–1935). Born in Holland, Grein influenced British drama at the turn of the century as critic, playwright, and manager. Among other works, the Independent Theatre staged Ibsen's *Ghosts* (1891) and Shaw's *Widower's Houses* (1892). As drama critic, Grein wrote for *Life* (1889–93) and the *Illustrated London News*. As a theatre manager, he did much to promote an exchange of new plays between England and the Continent.

7 Duse's words echo D'Annunzio's own motto: *O rinnovarsi o morire.* (One must renew oneself or perish.).

8 Henry Lyonnet, *Le Théâtre en Italie,* p. 202.

9 *The Letters of D. H. Lawrence,* edited and with an introduction by Aldous Huxley. London: William Heinemann Ltd, 1932, p. 345.

10 Leonardo Vergani, 'Storia di un matrimonio' in *Eleonora Duse,* pp. 32–42.

11 Olga Resnevic Signorelli, *Eleonora Duse,* p. 135.

12 Giovanni Gullace, *Gabriele D'Annunzio in France,* p. 57. See also: Camillo Antona Traversi, *Eleonora Duse: Sua vita, sua gloria, suo martirio,* p. 129.

13 *La città morta* was actually completed before *Il sogno di un mattino di primavera,* but the latter was staged first. Georges Hérelle was responsible for the excellent French translations of D'Annunzio's major plays and novels, which helped to win the poet as much popularity in France as in Italy.

14 Achille Fiocco, *Teatro italiano di ieri e di oggi.* p. 14.

15 This production is reputed to have cost Duse approximately 120,000 lire, a considerable sum of money in 1901. D'Annunzio himself acted as director for the production, and he personally coordinated the costumes by Caramba, the scenery by Rovescalli and the stage furnishings by De Carolis. Luigi Rasi was specially engaged to stage the crowd scenes; indeed, every aspect of the production was handled by some reputable specialist.

16 Halvdan Koht, *Life of Ibsen,* pp. 412–13. (From new revised Norwegian edition 1954.)

17 A similar situation prevailed in Spain where the writer and critic Miguel de Unamuno bitingly observed: 'If any play by Ibsen were to find acceptance with Spanish audiences, I should begin to doubt its excellence.' (See Halfdan Gregerson, *Ibsen and Spain.* Cambridge, Mass.: Harvard University press, 1936.) And even in London, George Bernard Shaw bemoaned the lack of any serious interest in Ibsen as late as the 1920s when he observed: 'The doctrine taught by Ibsen can never be driven home from the stage whilst his plays are presented to us in haphazard order at the commercial theatres.'

18 Ermete Zacconi and Ermete Novelli vigorously defended their approach to the role of Oswald in the face of some severe criticism from authoritative commentators such as Silvio D'Amico. Both actors tended to emphasize the physical aspects of Oswald's madness, although Novelli's histrionics, according to reliable sources, offended most of all.

19 Olga Resnevic Signorelli, *Vita di Eleonora Duse,* p. 101.

20 Olga Resnevic Signorelli, *Eleonora Duse,* p. 341.

21 Sarah Bernhardt apparently studied the text of Ibsen's *The Lady from the Sea* only to decide that the play was not a suitable vehicle for her style of acting.

22 Silvio d'Amico, *Tramonto del Grande Attore,* p. 61.

23 James Agate, *Red Letter Nights*, pp. 71–2.

24 Count Giuseppe Primoli, 'La Duse' in *La Revue de Paris*, June 1897, p. 516.

25 Bertita Harding, *Age Cannot Wither*, p. 218.

26 Eva Le Galliene, *The Mystic in the Theatre*, p. 51.

27 Henry Lyonnet, *Le Théâtre en Italie*, p. 217. Ermete Zacconi was born in 1857, one year before the birth of Duse herself, although he was to outlive her by some twenty-five years. Although they were close contemporaries who achieved success throughout Italy and the world at large, they were poles apart in their acting styles. Yet both artists were true pioneers in their choice of repertoire and efforts to improve standards of production in Italy. Their common admiration for D'Annunzio brought them together in 1898 and 1899, and Zacconi was instrumental in helping Duse to stage her comeback in 1921.

28 Review of Duse's début at the Carltheater in Vienna on 19 February 1892 by an unidentified critic. Quoted by Olga Resnevic Signorelli, *Vita di Eleonora Duse*, pp. 95–6.

29 Victor Mapes, *Duse and the French*, pp. 23–4.

30 To be fair, Italian audiences made much the same comparison between the two actresses. When Bernhardt gave a single performance of *La Dame aux camélias* at the Teatro Paganini in Genoa on 11 December 1898, the French critic Henry Lyonnet who was in the audience heard one Italian say to another: 'Notre Duse est plus pathétique ... mais celle-ci est plus séduisante, plus élégante, plus distinguée et plus fine.' In the opinion of celebrities as varied as André Antoine, D'Annunzio, Ellen Terry and Lily Langtry, Bernhardt gave a much more convincing portrayal of Dumas the Younger's tragic heroine. Duse's firm reply to those critics who accused her of neglecting the glamorous side of roles in the French repertoire was couched in a curious blend of Italian and French: 'Zé né me fardé pas: Zé me maquille moralement.'

Reliable accounts also confirm that with time the artifice of Bernhardt coarsened perceptibly. Henry James detected an unwholesome 'scepticism and cynicism' in the mature Bernhardt. William Archer deplored her 'vulgar virtuosity' in later years while Bernard Shaw fulminated against the French actress's 'circus and waxworks'. By contrast, when Duse returned to the stage in her mid-sixties, her acting appeared to have gained in depth and refinement.

31 It has been suggested that the impresario Joseph Schurmann, who had managed tours for both Bernhardt and Duse, saw some advantage in exploiting any hint of conflict between the two actresses. What is more certain is that the relationship between the two women cooled perceptibly when a disparaging statement about Duse's artistry, attributed to Bernhardt, appeared in print: 'Eleonora Duse is a great actress rather than a great artist; she takes roads that have already been laid down by others. True, she does not ape other actresses; but she plants flowers where they planted trees, and trees where they planted flowers; yet she has never created by means of her art a character that is inseparable from her name; she has never given form to a vision or a figure that makes us think of her alone.' These words rankled in Duse's mind and in later years she commented: 'I refuse to flaunt my ability as an actress; I refuse to put my personal success before that of the play itself; for the interpreter of a work of art must be nothing more than a faithful collaborator intent upon transmitting the author's intentions to the audience without any distortions. It has been alleged by some that in my latest repertoire I have failed to create any new character. No one could have paid me higher praise.'

It helps to put matters into perspective if one remembers that Bernhardt could be just as malicious when discussing some of her French contemporaries. She defined Réjane as 'the most comedian of comedians, and an artist *when she wishes to be*', and she summed up the internationally famous Coquelin as 'an admirable comedian . . . but *not* an artist.'

Clearly, what Bernhardt's acting gained through superb technique and artifice Duse's interpretation equalled by means of intuition and inner depth. Warring factions argued incessantly about their relative merits, but, as Ellen Terry (who knew both actresses well) wisely observed in her memoirs: 'How futile it is to make comparisons! Better far to thank heaven for both these women.'

32 Eva Le Galliene, *Eleonora Duse . . .*, p. 51.
33 E. A. Rheinhardt, *The Life of Eleonora Duse*, p. 140.
34 Henry James, *The Scenic Art*, pp. 263–4.
35 Dame Ellen Terry, *The Story of My Life*, p. 218.
36 Max Beerbohm, *Around Theatres*, pp. 80–2.
37 James Agate, *More First Nights*. New York and London: Benjamin Blom, 1969 (reprint of 1937 edition), pp. 249–50.
38 George Bernard Shaw, *Our Theatres in the Nineties*, vol. II. p. 153.
39 Leonardo Vergani, 'Ritorno a Londra', in *Eleonora Duse*, pp. 173–7.
40 Arthur Symons, *Eleonora Duse*, p. 1.
41 This aura of spirituality has led some of Duse's biographers to enshroud her personality in mystical shadows. To depict the actress as some tragic queen is to minimize Duse's true stature. There were, indeed, moments of great stress and sorrow in her life, but reliable evidence, including Noccioli's sympathetic portrait, confirms that there were also moments of great happiness and satisfaction. Away from the theatre and relaxing among friends, Duse became animated and transformed. And however severe her discouragement and depression, human warmth, compassion and a sense of humour remained integral facets of her temperament.
42 Camillo Antona Traversi, *Eleonora Duse . . .*, p. v.

INTRODUCTION
TO THE DIARIES

Regrettably little is known about the early years and subsequent career of the young actor Guido Noccioli to whom we owe this vivid account of Eleonora Duse at the height of her fame. The diaries, which are preserved in the Biblioteca Teatrale del Burcardo in Rome, consist of two volumes written in a bold hand and tastefully bound in patterned covers. Volume I covers the years 1904 to 1907, when Noccioli completed his first professional engagement with the Fumagalli Company, and then the year with Duse that concerns us here. Volume II covers the period 1907 until 1909 when Noccioli moved on to become a member of the Niccoli Company. Unlike the first, this second volume incorporates numerous press reviews in which Noccioli's own name never appears, suggesting that the actor never progressed beyond minor supporting roles.

Italian publications covering this period of Italian theatre history make no reference to Noccioli apart from recording his brief association with Duse's company. One might safely speculate that he very soon abandoned an acting career for some other aspect of the theatre world or embraced some new profession. The clear image that emerges of the author of the diaries is that of an intelligent and good-natured fellow with a passion for art galleries and museums and a predilection for the masters of the Italian Renaissance. Unusually perceptive for his years, his observations in the diaries about the world of the theatre and its personalities betray all the enthusiasm and generosity of youth.

Guido Giuseppe Antonio Noccioli was born in Florence on 27 May 1883, which means that he was in his early twenties by the time he joined Duse's company. He had received his training as an actor at the Academy of Dramatic Art in Florence under the direction of the much respected Luigi Rasi, and it was here that he met his future wife and made friends with Giuseppe Masi who later recommended him to Duse.

A handful of letters written by Noccioli to his teacher and mentor Rasi suggest that the diaries were kept at the latter's request. During his lifetime Luigi Rasi acquired an impressive collection of documents, souvenirs and personal reminiscences with the assistance of former students and colleagues and these are now preserved in the Burcardo archives. Rasi himself was one of Duse's lifelong admirers and it is quite certain that he urged Noccioli to keep him posted of the company's fortunes during Duse's second tour of South America in 1907.

The young actor has given us a graphic account of his first encounter with the great Eleonora Duse at the Grand Hotel in Florence on 24 November 1906. Stage struck and impressionable, he was completely overcome by Duse's aura of beauty and mystery. His admiration for her artistry comes through on every page, and his loyalty and enormous respect must have endeared him to the actress.

The following entries from Noccioli's diaries are unabridged and extend from 24 November 1906 until 7 November 1907. Duse had engaged a new cast before embarking upon a second tour of South America. The long period of intensive preparation took the company from Florence to Milan and Genoa, followed by short seasons on the French Riviera, Vienna, Hungary and Romania, before sailing from Genoa on the *Umbria* on 30 May 1907 and finally reaching Rio de Janeiro two weeks later on 14 June.

A letter from Noccioli to Rasi written from Genoa on 23 December 1906 and commenting upon a single performance of Ibsen's *Rosmersholm* at the Teatro Paganini betrays the uncertainties and tensions of those long weeks as the company is put through its paces: 'Here one navigates in total darkness. No one knows where we shall be tomorrow or, for that matter, where we shall be tonight. Signora Duse has not appeared so far. The theatre is sold out for this evening's performance with tickets at an exorbitant price. I will send you the reviews from the local press tomorrow.'

INTRODUCTION TO THE DIARIES

Although the diaries are dominated by the personality of Duse herself, other members of the company come to life as Noccioli becomes familiar with their individual character traits and idiosyncrasies: the tyrannical company manager Orlandini, the attractive and flighty Signorina Rossi, the faintly ridiculous Signorina Scalambretti, the much-wronged Almirante and the malicious Beltramo. Noccioli has a sharp eye for the petty intrigues and vain pretensions that characterize any theatre company on tour, and these he records with a knowing wit and frankness.

On a more serious note, the reader is made aware of the strenuous effort and hard work that went into these tours at the turn of the century. Travel conditions could be trying and unpredictable. Actors required sound constitutions and enormous reserves of physical and mental stamina to endure the long journeys, enervating climates, unsuitable theatres, a taxing repertoire of some twenty plays and all the other hazards of alien surroundings. Moments of relaxation, even for a junior actor like Noccioli, appear to have been rare.

Noccioli's correspondence with Rasi from Rio de Janeiro and Buenos Aires voices the general complaint that the company is being worked at a desperate pace. He writes: 'Last Friday we gave *two* performances. Next Sunday *two* performances . . And these endless rehearsals!'

For actor managers there were numerous headaches as they battled with foreign impresarios and managements, coped with the press and adapted to local conditions and customs while struggling to compete with rival companies from Europe offering anything from Grand Opera to cabaret. The financial rewards of Buenos Aires had to be set against the losses incurred in Rosario, and the tributes and gifts of presidents and local aristocrats had to be set against hostile reviews, the threats of student pressure groups and the malice of some anonymous crank. Noccioli's day-to-day account of the company's activities provides an unbiased account of the inevitable stress to which an actor was exposed on tour.

With great reluctance Duse was undertaking this second visit to South America after an absence of some twenty years. Her correspondence reveals that it was only after much persuasion that she finally agreed to sign the contract, and there can be no doubt that the painful events of her first South American tour in 1885 had left her feeling uneasy.

By 1907 Duse was tired and seriously ill. The D'Annunzio

interlude and the death of Ibsen had left their mark. And when Lugné-Poe, who had accompanied her as far as Brazil, found himself obliged to return to Europe, leaving Duse to cope with the Portuguese impresario Faustino da Rosa and his Italian partner whom she completely mistrusted, the actress became increasingly more irritable and depressed. The company's mixed success in Brazil and Argentina, culminating in a commercial fiasco at Rosario, brought further disappointment. All these factors helped to contribute to the general atmosphere of conflict and tension throughout the tour. The news of Duse's bitter disagreement with her company manager Orlandini was first passed on to Rasi in a note written at the Italian Club in Buenos Aires and dated 4 September 1907: 'The latest sensation! Orlandini has incurred the Signora's wrath! A real drama! I shall tell you everything *viva voce.*' The serious consequences of this unfortunate rift and the awkward situations it created for other members of the company as Duse went on to find fault with the entire cast are recorded at length in the diaries with impartiality and understanding. For all his youth and inexperience, Noccioli recognized that all was not well with Duse, and moments of trauma during the tour already pointed to the deep crisis that provoked the actress's decision to abandon the stage in 1909.

To this extent, the Noccioli diaries offer a convincing portrait of Duse at a crucial point in her career. And, notwithstanding the limitations of diary form, the young actor has succeeded in creating a most human and revealing portrait of Italy's best-known stage personality in this century.

Noccioli's association with Duse did not end with this South American tour. After a short period of rest in Italy, Noccioli rejoined Duse's company in November 1907 for an extensive tour of Austria, Germany and Russia.

A letter to Rasi dated 29 January 1908 conveys his impressions of St Petersburg and reports on Duse's personal triumphs throughout the tour notwithstanding the mediocrity of the supporting cast. He comments: 'The critics here, as in Berlin, slate most of the actors in the company while extolling the praises of La Duse – and rightly so.'

In the meantime, Noccioli himself was graduating from walk-on parts to minor character roles and he felt that the moment had come to gain experience with some other company. A contract with the Niccoli Company which was about to fulfil engagements in America gave him his opportunity but Noccioli was somewhat apprehensive about how Rasi would react to the news of his decision. Announcing his imminent departure for America, scheduled for 9 March 1908, Noccioli wryly comments: 'Certainly the change will be enormous', in his awareness that touring with Duse had been a unique experience.

Overleaf: Facsimile of two pages from the original manuscript of the first volume of the Guido Noccioli Diaries. These entries cover the company's successful season in Buenos Aires subsequently offset by severe financial losses and a generally lukewarm reception from audiences in Rosario and Montevideo. (Reproduction by courtesy of Biblioteca Teatrale del Burcardo, Rome.)

THE
NOCCIOLI
DIARIES

1906–07

1906

Florence, 24 November 1906

This evening Giuseppe Masi, whom I asked to recommend me to the director of the Eleonora Duse Company, introduces me to the famous actress. I must confess that this experience provokes emotions beyond expression. I ascend the main staircase of the Grand Hotel as if in a dream. While I wait in the corridor, many actors pass in front of me and I see all of them enter a large salon that is brightly illuminated. There is a rehearsal in progress of *Maria Salvestri*, one of Enrico Corradini's latest plays. At one point Masi detaches himself from me and approaches a group of women standing at the top of the staircase, then he turns towards me accompanied by a lady whose face is concealed under a black veil. He says to her: 'Madam, this is the young man whom I mentioned and who would be happy to join your company.'

The lady unfastens her cloak and lifts the veil covering her face . . . La Duse! She smiles and says: 'Really? How kind. Thank you. Please come and see me again tomorrow with Signor Masi.' She smiles once more with that inimitable pouting of her lips, which reveals the most perfect teeth as she stretches out her hand (one of those famous hands immortalized by D'Annunzio[1]) bidding me: 'Goodbye.' Then she disappears into the salon.

Florence, 25 November 1906

This morning at ten o'clock sharp I am standing at the entrance of the Grand Hotel. Masi too arrives punctually, and together we go up to the Signora's apartments on the second floor. We find her in a towering rage because the handbills advertising her forthcoming season at the Teatro della Pergola are headed: 'Exceptional appearance of Eleonora Duse.'[2]

'Why *exceptional*, for God's sake?', she exclaims pacing up and down the room, 'Such billing may be all right for circus acrobats, but not for me.'

'Signora,' Masi ventures to defend himself, 'The impresario, Signor Rosadi, is to blame. He is responsible for the printing of the handbills.'

'I won't have it!' the Signora retorts. 'I refuse to tolerate ignorant people like Rosadi; therefore suppress those dreadful handbills at once, for I am the one who pays here. And I demand and fully intend to have things done my way.'

She then proceeds to discuss various matters before giving me some instructions and suggestions for the first performance of *La*

The auditorium of the Teatro della Pergola in Florence where Duse began intensive preparations for her South American tour. The company's brief season in Florence extended from 27 November until 19 December 1906. Highlights of the season included a single performance of Ibsen's *Rosmersholm* with controversial sets by the English stage designer Gordon Craig, the stormy première of Enrico Corradini's *Maria Salvestri* and an enthusiastic reception for Maeterlinck's *Monna Vanna*. (Photograph by courtesy of the Ente Teatrale Italiano, Teatro della Pergola, Florence.)

Gioconda, eagerly taking an interest in the smallest detail. This shows with how much dedication to her art the Signora is preparing the production of this play by the poet from Abbruzzi. Dismissing us, she says: 'I shall not rehearse today. It is so bright and sunny outside! I am going into the countryside. I shall see you tomorrow.'

Florence, 26 November 1906
At five o'clock a rehearsal of *Maria Salvestri* in the salon of the Grand Hotel. The author himself attends the rehearsal. The Signora is once more in a black mood. The rehearsal is quite short and almost funereal in atmosphere. Suddenly the Signora dismisses everyone, complaining of a severe headache.

DUSE ON TOUR

Florence, 27 November 1906

A rehearsal of *Maria Salvestri* at eight o'clock this evening at the Grand Hotel. Great excitement. The Signora is in good humour. She smiles a great deal and looks most attractive. Corradini too is thrilled. He appears to be enjoying the foretaste of sweet success. I observe something very odd. The author and cast are still engaged in discussing the play's finale. No one knows as yet how Maria Salvestri will die. The author vacillates and cannot make up his mind. Meanwhile, little by little, as the drama unfolds, La Duse suggests many changes, which are accepted by the author with enthusiasm.

I silently predict a great fiasco. With the exception of the first act, which is very good and executed with considerable originality, the rest of the play in my opinion is worthless.. And what of the performance itself? Who knows! Since the author still does not know what death to give the heroine, so the actors, including La Duse herself, waver between various solutions. Even the great actress fails to convince me in her role, probably because she herself is not entirely happy with the script.

Florence, 28 November 1906

Another rehearsal of *Maria Salvestri* at the Grand Hotel at five o'clock. Further changes are introduced. The author accepts the suggestions of others with a readiness that is positively alarming. At one point, Masi whispers in my ear: 'Don't you get the impression that the Signora is making fun of everyone, especially the author?' I whisper in reply: 'I'm certain you're right!'

The rehearsal continues. In the first act, during the scene with the lover (the actor Robert is most effective in the role), all the stage positions are changed and, one might well add, all the inflections. The Signora says: 'Now we are getting somewhere. I àm hopeful that it will go much better like this.' Then, after a pause, she adds: 'It is common knowledge that beautiful things are rarely improvised and are never easy. Beware of anything that turns out right the first time. Only what is mediocre can be improvised!'

This reasoning is undoubtedly subtle, and it sounds even more subtle when affirmed by Eleonora Duse. I am not altogether certain, however, that the observation is relevant when discussing *Maria Salvestri*.

Florence, 29 November 1906

Still rehearsing *Maria Salvestri* at the Grand Hotel. Eight o'clock in the evening. After numerous suggestions and much argument, both author and cast condemn Maria Salvestri to a frightful death. Her husband will throw her, *with much violence*, from the window. But all this will take place behind the scenes. The husband will then take it upon himself to tell the *distinguished audience* how he has murdered his wife, or better still, of how his wife has had herself murdered for love. We are keeping our fingers crossed!

Florence, 30 November 1906

At three o'clock in the afternoon a rehearsal of *La Gioconda* in the salon of the Grand Hotel. The Signora is taciturn and deathly pale. Grey hairs straggle wildly from her broad plumed hat, which frequently slips to the back of her head causing her to readjust it with a hasty, almost aggressive, gesture. Before her, an enormous wall mirror reflects in frontal view her surprisingly agile figure and thin, emaciated face, with those large eyes that at times assume a strange expression, never witnessed in any other woman.[3] It reminds me of the masterly description of Foscarina given by the author of *Fuoco*.[4] Meantime, while the rehearsal proceeds rapidly with few interruptions, the Signora studies herself in the mirror in silence – one might even say in darkest gloom. Suddenly she speaks: 'You others go on rehearsing. I am leaving. Tomorrow at the same hour there will be a rehearsal of *La Gioconda* for Signorina Rossi and Signorina Zucchini.' And off she goes.

Florence, 1 December 1906

At three o'clock the Signora is already waiting in the salon. She starts rehearsing her scenes with Signorina Luciana Rossi (who plays the role of Francesca Doni) – and the Signora makes a number of interesting suggestions. She is in good form and introduces some quite felicitous nuances. She advises Signorina Rossi to wear something *more seemly and becoming* in the last act.

She then goes on to rehearse her scenes with Sirenetta (played by Signorina Clelia Zucchini, a young pupil of Teresa Boetti Valvassura). The actress slowly begins to read her part, without any vigour or expression. Just as if she were 'rehearsing in her underclothes' to use an Italian stage expression. The Signora watches her with a grim expression on her face and says nothing.

Signorina Zucchini continues with her *cantilena*, self-absorbed and impassive. The Signora intervenes: 'Signorina, are you rehearsing for your own benefit, or for mine?'

The young actress looks dismayed and is silent. Whereupon the

Signora, suddenly roused, exclaims: 'Put some life into it, Signorina! You are like marble! Put some life into it. Put some soul into it, for Heaven's sake!'

This exclamation is beautifully phrased – an exclamation worthy of Eleonora Duse's exquisitely modulated voice.[5] La Zucchini begins to recite her part once more, unfortunately in the same dull fashion. This exasperates the Signora, who jumps to her feet. Shaking with rage, she upbraids the little actress with a torrent of abuse.

Among other bitter accusations, she rails: 'Perhaps you have been deceived into believing that you are a fine actress. Nothing could be further from the truth, Signorina, so get the idea out of your head. Your acting is hopeless! Pitiful! You are nothing better than a pretty child (and even that is questionable) who cannot act any part she is given. Get this sad fact into your head and start studying. If I am obliged to study, then you can study too. The other evening in Vienna, your disastrous performance caused me to break out in a cold sweat, and you completely ignored my pleas for more life. Hopeless! As dense as a piece of stone! You are heartless! Totally insensitive.'

Now La Zucchini mutters: 'That is not true, Signora.' And she bursts into a flood of tears. The Signora replies: 'Go on, cry, cry! It will do you some good. Tears wash away a great many sorrows.'

Then, when the girl continues to sob, she firmly adds: 'That's enough now! A little weep can be interesting, but too much is irritating.' But, since the Signorina remains inconsolable, the rehearsal is postponed until the next day.

In taking her leave, the Signora says to La Rossi pointing to La Zucchini: 'Try to calm her down. Take her for a nice walk. It is such a lovely day!'

Florence, 2 December 1906

A rehearsal in the theatre with sets, furniture and lighting for *La Gioconda*. The Signora finds the furniture for the first two acts quite distasteful. She says over and over again: 'No, no, that simply won't do. It is horrendous. Everything must be changed!' Even the drapes for the third act are altered. Initially, she requests lots of statues; then these are nearly all eliminated. The tapestries too must be changed.

The property man, Luigi Bergonzio, trying to excuse himself, explains: 'But, Signora, this is the same scenery we used last time!' This is enough to enrage her: 'How dare you speak to me about the last time! That is a *cowardly* explanation that I refuse to accept!'

As God decrees, the drapes too are changed. Now everything is in order. Just as well. In the fourth act the lighting for the backcloth strikes her as being inadequate. She exclaims: 'It is far too dark, far too dark!' She could be right! But it looks all right to me.

I try to get her to agree and, little by little, I succeed. The rehearsal is terminated at this point, and we go off to get some sleep.

Florence, 3 December 1906
This morning an urgent summons to the Grand Hotel. The Signora hands me some drapes in old brocade and some magnificently bound books that are to be used for this evening's performance. At the theatre, I find the most exquisite pieces of furniture, chosen by the Signora herself from an antique dealer. Later on, the performance is given before an enthusiastic audience. The theatre is full. The Signora extremely nervous. The furnishings, as usual, are modified at the last minute. The speed with which La Duse makes decisions only to change her mind is quite perplexing.

Throughout the entire evening, the expression on her face is one of great tension. Everything in her behaviour betrays her disquiet, anxiety, fever. She acts extremely well, but not consistently with the same brilliance. It is clear that this evening's performance is marred by her nervous state. In the scene in Act III with Gioconda, she loses control, but in the final act with Sirenetta, she is truly divine! Leo Orlandini (in the part of Lucio Settala) is frankly disappointing. The narration in Act II could hardly be declaimed more poorly, but the audience applauds. And once the audience is satisfied, everyone is satisfied. After all, is the theatre-going public not perhaps one *Great Ignoramus*? Although not entirely suited to the role, Elisa Berti Masi has played the part of Gioconda with a certain charm. This evening La Zucchini in the role of Sirenetta scales some miraculous heights. After the performance, as the Signora is leaving the theatre, she meets the young actress and embraces her, saying: 'Brava, well done!' Perhaps in order to make up for the harsh reproaches of the other day.

Florence, 4 December 1906
A frightful day. The mounting of new sets for Ibsen's drama, *Rosmersholm*. The Signora adores this work. The new sets to which I refer are the creation of a young English painter, Gordon Craig,

the illegitimate son of the great actor Henry Irving. It is a strange affair, all in green and illuminated by ten spotlights. The furniture too is green and covered with the same material as that used for the drapes: at the back of the stage a large glass-paned door looks on to a landscape that is strangely reminiscent of the setting in *Isola dei morti*.[6] Another large door is covered with a blue veil. There are other veils on each side of the stage. Some dream, perhaps? Will the public like it? The Signora is thrilled with Craig's sets.

Florence, 5 December 1906

A performance of *Rosmersholm* before another full house. The Signora is incredibly tense. By seven o'clock she is already dressed and made up. She then sends for the actor, Robert, and goes back over a scene with him from Act IV. Suddenly she pauses and corrects the actor, who invariably replies: 'Yes, Signora! Yes, Signora . . . ' The Signora goes on revising details, and the actor at one point forgets to say 'Yes, Signora' and simply says 'Yes, yes.' The Signora freezes him with those imperious eyes and bitterly reproaches him: 'How dare you show disrespect to me!' And off she flounces to shut herself away in her dressing room. What an unpredictable woman!

The play is an enormous success. The work of Ibsen is certainly not very accessible to the Italian public at large. But the acting of the great Duse in this work reaches dizzy heights. In Act III, after the magnificent narration scene, the audience goes wild with excitement shouting: 'Brava.'

After the performance she is in excellent spirits. Many journalists come on to the stage. The first to offer his congratulations is Corradini. As soon as the Signora sees him, she remarks: 'There he is, waiting to catch me!' alluding undoubtedly to the suspended rehearsals of *Maria Salvestri*. But Corradini reassures her: 'No, Signora! I have come to tell you that your performance has moved me deeply.' She interrupts him: 'So the audience has swallowed it?' and she laughs. 'I cannot say if they were convinced by the play, but like me they found your acting an unforgettable experience', Corradini declares.

Other admirers quickly arrive, all of them expressing their delight and appreciation; the Signora is sitting on a trunk and there, amidst the bustle of technicians and stagehands, she holds an interview.

Suddenly, two women appear. An elderly woman of aristocratic bearing and a rather plain young woman. The younger woman is searching attentively and having spotted La Duse surrounded by journalists, calls out: 'There she is!' Her voice betrays great excitement. She approaches and says something. Duse gets up and moves away from the group. 'I have received all your delightful letters and am most grateful. Just as soon as I finish this series of performances, which is keeping me fully occupied, I shall be very glad to receive your visit.' And she accompanies the young woman towards the exit. She is obviously an admirer, which in the Signora's vocabulary is synonymous with a *bore*!

Florence, 6 December 1906

At three o'clock at the Grand Hotel, a rehearsal of *Maria Salvestri*. Because of one of the Signora's whims, no one is allowed to attend, with the exception, of course, of the actors who have a part in the play. The first to come out is Robert. I ask him what is happening in there. He replies without stopping as he goes off: 'More blessed changes!' After two hours, the Signora and the others come out.

Tomorrow evening a dress rehearsal in the theatre of *Maria Salvestri*.

Florence, 7 December 1906

The Signora is most punctual. At eight-thirty she is already in the theatre. She directs the rehearsal as if it were a performance. The author finds nothing needs to be changed: Things appear to be sailing smoothly. In the third act, a full rehearsal of the grand finale.

As the curtain drops, the Signora has a quiet smile on her lips, a smile of terrifying eloquence, and she remarks to Orlandini: 'It will go down very well!'

A fiasco is assured.

Florence, 8 December 1906

This evening marked the première of *Maria Salvestri*, a drama in three acts by Enrico Corradini, with Eleonora Duse in the leading role. The theatre is filled to capacity. Corradini appears to be nervous; the Signora, on the contrary, seems quite relaxed The moment the curtain goes up, Corradini goes off to take refuge in the dressing room of Signorina Rossi.

The first act is an enormous success. The applause is rapturous, and the cast take numerous curtain calls. The author is delighted, and La Duse takes a deep breath and comments: 'Ah! We are winning!'

The cast gets ready with eagerness for Act II, which is played before an attentive audience. At one point, Signorina Rossi appears and asks: 'How is it going? Corradini wants to know if anything unusual is happening!' At that moment there is an outburst of applause for the story that Orlandini (in the part of Pietro Salvestri) narrates to his brother (played by Masi). But, shortly afterwards, in the scene between Maria Salvestri and her mother (played by Elisa Berti Masi) the audience starts to become restless and bored, making loud comments, laughing and hissing! The moment has come for La Duse to make her exit! Suddenly, there is a crescendo of applause and demands that La Duse should reappear. But La Duse does not appear. She stands alone behind the scenes in silence, with a look of utter disdain on her face. The act ends amidst applause and jeers.

Then the third act opens. Things go from bad to worse! The hissing becomes deafening. In a word: a complete fiasco! Onstage the comments are numerous and varied. La Duse is irritated. She remarks: 'Audiences in Florence are always the same – a boorish lot!' And in the next breath: 'They should at least show some respect for the author and myself. After all, I am *the* Eleonora Duse who has done more than anyone else to enhance the reputation of Italian drama throughout the world.' Quite true! But the public might well retort: 'Even La Duse has no right to drag us into the theatre to listen to such rubbish!'

Upon leaving the theatre, La Duse says to Orvieto[7] who is accompanying her: 'I thought that the times of D'Annunzio were over. Now I realise that things will always be the same . . .!'

Florence, 9 December 1906

We are supposed to be resting, but then suddenly there comes a summons for everyone to appear at the Teatro della Pergola at two o'clock. *Monna Vanna* is rehearsed under the direction of Leo Orlandini. The rehearsal is soon over.

Florence, 10 December 1906

Visita di nozze[8] and *Monna Vanna* are to be rehearsed at the Grand Hotel at three o'clock. The Signora arrives later just as the cast are finishing *Visita di nozze*. She is in a jovial mood. She only rehearses her own scenes in *Monna Vanna* before releasing us for the rest of the day.

Florence, 12 December 1906

A full house and a brilliant triumph during the second act, which

Duse plays as to the manner born. She achieves the most remarkable gestures and modulations. When she utters the phrase: 'That child was named Giannello! . . . Are you perchance Giannello?'[9] the line becomes a poem.

In my opinion, nevertheless, *Monna Vanna* is not a play suited to La Duse's temperament, however beautifully she may act the role.

Florence, 13 December 1906
In the Grand Hotel at five o'clock a rehearsal of *Visita di nozze* and *La locandiera*. A happy occasion and much excitement. Suddenly the Signora's eyes are transfixed in the direction of the prompter's feet (Venafro), feet indeed of a prodigious size, which amuse the Signora and everyone else. So the rehearsal continues with the bizarre sight of the prompter's feet, who remains totally unaware, poor chap, that he is the centre of attraction. During the rehearsal of *La locandiera*, I enjoy myself enormously. The Signora notices how much I relish the play. Suddenly she says to Orlandini: 'Signor Orlandini, I can see that Signor Guido is determined to have a role in *La locandiera*. Give him something to play.'

And so it is agreed that during the Lent season[10] I shall play the role of the Knight's valet, a role currently taken by Giuseppe Masi. I am delighted and overjoyed at my good fortune.

Florence, 14 December 1906
Performances of *Visita di nozze* and *La locandiera*. No sooner does the Signora arrive at the theatre when she asks to see the evening's programme. Upon reading it, she goes into a rage because the programme begins with *Visita di nozze* instead of *La locandiera*. She screams: 'A fine service you render Goldoni!' And she launches accusations at Orlandini, Masi, Bergonzio and myself. The others explain: 'Signora, we followed the pattern of an old play bill, we thought . . .' 'So much the worse!' she retorts. Then, little by little, she calms down and she is persuaded to begin with *Visita di nozze*. The theatre is packed to capacity. The evening is a great success. During *La locandiera* every line is greeted with applause. La Duse is magnificent.

Florence, 18 December 1906
Today it is announced that we shall leave for Vienna on 23 December.

Florence, 19 December 1906
Further orders are given so that the cast of *La locandiera* will leave

tomorrow morning for Milan. The others will leave on 21 December for Genoa, where we shall meet up with them. *La locandiera* will be given at a matinée performance on 21 December at the Teatro Manzoni. The proceeds will go to the Press Association. Needless to say, this sudden change upsets all the actors. We attended the funeral of the actress Udina, the mother of Giannina Udina, who died suddenly last night at the Teatro Alfieri, where the Company of the Marchese Berardi is playing.

Milan, 20 December 1906

We arrived this evening at eight-thirty.

Milan, 21 December 1906

At today's performance there is a good audience. The programme is an attractive one.

La figlia di Jefte[11] is played by Elisa Severi with actors from her own company, the monologue *Lo sciopero dei fabbri*,[12] is recited to perfection by Oreste Calabresi, Alfredo Testoni reads verses from his *Signora Caterina all'Esposizione di Milano* with enormous success, and La Duse acts the whole of *La locandiera*. Such ovations! All the journalists come in a throng to thank and congratulate the illustrious actress. After the performance, the photographer Varischi takes photographs of the cast of *La locandiera*. Exquisite bouquets of flowers are presented to La Duse. The Lord Mayor of Milan, Senator Ponti, goes to the Signora's dressing room to pay his compliments. Tomorrow at one o'clock we depart for Genoa.

Genoa, 22 December 1906

We arrived about six o'clock. Tomorrow at the Teatro Paganini, we give a performance of *Rosmersholm*.

Genoa, 23 December 1906

A black evening at the outset. The Signora is in a state of incredible tension. At least twice, she orders the entire set to be rearranged for, according to her, it has been perversely reduced in scale. Since all the props for this play have already been despatched to Vienna, the property man is obliged to improvise to the best of his ability. This provokes an even greater crisis of nerves. Finally, the curtain goes up. A full house and a tremendous ovation, especially after the third act. The Signora regains her composure. She remarks to Orlandini, as she is about to take a curtain call: 'See how they understand me? People who live near the sea are always deep and contemplative. They love Ibsen, for they are more poetic. The sea, it is the sea that makes them poets.'[13]

Orlandini agrees, but when the Signora is out of hearing, he makes it quite clear that he does not share her optimism. Tomorrow there is no performance.

Genoa, 24 December 1906

The critics are unanimous in their praise for La Duse: the majority of them approve of Ibsen's play. Sabatino Lopez, however, has some reservations and, while praising La Duse, declares that he prefers her in other roles; especially in those plays that have brought her fame. The Signora has left for Rapallo. Tomorrow at the Politeama Margherita we rehearse *Adriana Lecouvreur*[14] and *Diritti dell'anima*.

Genoa, 25 December 1906

It is Christmas Day. The rehearsal is postponed until tomorrow.

Genoa, 26 December 1906

We learn that the Signora has unexpectedly returned from Rapallo because she is feeling unwell and is in a highly nervous state. We rehearse under the direction of Orlandini, who, at one point tells us that the Signora is anxious that those actors who still need costumes for *Adriana Lecouvreur* should get something ready immediately.

The Signora knows perfectly well that according to the terms of her contract, she is obliged to provide the costumes, but since the play only forms part of the repertory in exceptional circumstances, she does not feel inclined to meet this expense. She expresses in anticipation her gratitude to those who agree to her request. And she will certainly bear in mind those who choose to disappoint her.

This last phrase upsets the actors and strikes us as being altogether unworthy of Eleonora Duse. The cast feels that the warning has been added by Orlandini out of some misguided sense of zeal.[15] But nearly everyone agrees to provide something. Only Robert declares that he has no suitable costumes and that he has no intention of buying them, since in his case there are several changes of costume involved (he is playing the role of the Prince of Buillar). Orlandini is sympathetic and promises to discuss the matter with the Signora. Upon leaving the theatre, we are surprised to see posters announcing a performance by Eleonora Duse at the Politeama Margherita in *La locandiera*. We later learn that the Signora had telegraphed from Rapallo to Sabatino Lopez, more or less in these words: 'I shall do as you ask, you old grumbler. I am bringing *La locandiera* and *Visita di nozze!*'

DUSE ON TOUR

Genoa, 27 December 1906

At today's rehearsal we learn that the Signora is once more indisposed.

1907

Genoa, 1 January 1907

New Year's day. The Signora is still unwell. We go on aimlessly rehearsing *Adriana Lecouvreur* and other plays in the repertoire without making much progress. The Signora's daughter Enrichetta[16] has arrived at Genoa.

Genoa, 7 January 1907

Today we leave for San Remo. The Signora has left for Nervi, where she intends to convalesce. Later she will join us at San Remo where we are to go on rehearsing as we await her arrival.

San Remo, 8 January 1907

Climate and surroundings delightful. I have never experienced anything so pleasant. After the cold and wind in Genoa, the spring weather here is most consoling. We rehearse under the direction of Orlandini at the Teatro Principe Amedeo where the Brighi-Coragna Company is appearing.

San Remo, 15 January 1907

The Signora arrives this morning and leaves again this evening for Cap Martin. She gives instructions that we should continue with our rehearsals. We are leaving soon for Nice.

San Remo, 21 January 1907

We are informed that the date of our departure for Nice is scheduled for 25 January. At the theatre of the Casino Municipal, the Company of Amalia Soarez is presenting a season of operetta. The Brighi-Coragna Company left several days ago after playing to empty houses.

Nice, 25 January 1907

We reach Nice to find horrible weather. The Signora arrived two days ago and is staying at the Grand Hotel.

Nice, 26 January 1907

Still raining. Tomorrow at four o'clock a rehearsal of *Casa paterna* at the Grand Hotel.

THE NOCCIOLI DIARIES

Nice, 27 January 1907

The weather is improving. When the sun shines, Nice comes up to one's expectations. A pleasure resort. Preparations are busily under way for the annual Carnival. The Signora comes to the rehearsal, looking in much better health. Tomorrow, we have a rehearsal of *Casa paterna*. This will be given at the theatre of the Casino Municipal, where we are playing.

Nice, 28 January 1907

We have our rehearsal in a room adjoining the stage, but the Signora does not attend. The opening night is billed for 2 February with *Casa paterna*.

Nice, 1 February 1907

This evening I attend a performance of *Heureuse*[17] given by a French company at the Casino. The most appalling mediocrity. Much elegance among the actresses. None whatsoever among the actors. Indeed, one might aptly define the latter as nothing better than 'a bunch of strolling players!'[18]

Nice, 2 February 1907

The theatre is crowded and the performance enthusiastically acclaimed, especially the third act, in which La Duse is interrupted twice by resounding applause. Tomorrow, a rehearsal of *Monna Vanna* at the hotel.

Nice, 3 February 1907

The rehearsal is postponed until tomorrow. I go to the opera to hear Emma Calvé in *Carmen*. A great disappointment. La Calvé is undoubtedly a great singer, but nowadays the voice is past its best. Her experience and artistry permit her to produce certain dissonant notes with considerable aplomb and to cover up many deficiencies of pitch and intonation. Dramatically, however, I find her a splendid Carmen. The tenor Salignac is excellent. He sings with amazing panache and distinction.

Nice, 5 February 1907

The rehearsal does not last very long. The Signora is irritable and nervous.

Nice, 6 February 1907

A wonderful audience and an outstanding success, but the performance is inferior to that of the opening night. The acting in *Monna Vanna* is weak on the part of everyone, including even the Signora. No rehearsal tomorrow.

[63]

The French opera singer Emma Calvé whose interpretation of Bizet's *Carmen* brought her world-wide fame. By the time Noccioli saw Calvé perform at Nice on 3 February 1907, the singer was obviously no longer in her prime. Long before Duse and Calvé became close friends, the French soprano found herself spellbound by Duse's 'sincerity . . . sobriety of gesture and the moving stage presence'. And in her memoirs (*My Life*, translated by Rosamond Gilder, New York/London: D. Appleton & Co., 1922) Calvé confessed that Duse's influence upon her own career was incalculable. (Photograph by courtesy of the Library of Congress, Washington.)

THE NOCCIOLI DIARIES

Nice, 8 February 1907

Tomorrow evening we play *Rosmersholm*. The painter Gordon Craig is in Nice to supervise the mounting of the sets. It goes without saying that he finds his sets badly mounted . . . so angry scenes ensue with the technician, the electrician, the stage manager, the property men and the administration. The most horrendous chaos as insults are exchanged in a bedlam of motley languages and dialects. The English spoken by Gordon Craig bears certain strange analogies to the pure Bolognese dialect of the technician Pompeo Giordani, but it is certainly not in harmony with the Florentine dialect of the stage manager, the Italian of the theatre administrator, the local French dialect of the electrician or the Milanese dialect of the property man. Such sparks are flying! Finally, the painter goes off only to return with the Signora's daughter. A new mise-en-scène! Gordon Craig speaks in English with the young lady who speaks in French to the administrator who speaks in Italian to the technician who curses in Bolognese dialect. At a certain point in these proceedings, the stage manager disappears. A heroic decision! I do not know how the episode has ended.

Nice, 9 February 1907

Since any performance of *Rosmersholm* is calculated to put the Signora's nerves on edge, the evening is stormier than usual, also because of the pandemonium witnessed yesterday. Gordon Craig has written a furious letter to the Signora, accusing the Italians of being incompetent, etc.; the Signora annoyed by the letter, vents her anger on the technician, who vigorously denies the accusations, and on the administrator, who . . . couldn't care less. A good house but a lukewarm reception on the part of the audience. A fashionable cosmopolitan audience does not strike me as being the most likely to appreciate a play by Ibsen. The Signora acts with passion, but her efforts are not rewarded by that noisy ovation that resounds in the farthest corners of the Square in Monte Carlo when she plays *Monna Vanna*.

Nice, 11 February 1907

The performance at Beausoleil is postponed on account of the Signora's illness. The technician Giordani is dismissed and paid the necessary compensation. The reason? Gordon Craig, of course, and his wretched sets![19]

DUSE ON TOUR

Beausoleil, 13 February 1907

We arrive in torrential rain. The theatre is magnificent but unfinished. The passageways leading to the stage are cluttered with mortar and bricks. Just as we arrive, a matinée performance of a variety show is ending. The chaos is indescribable. We find all the dressing rooms crammed with the costumes of music-hall singers, acrobats, comedians, dancers . . . and suddenly, without any warning . . . the lights go out. Pitch darkness! Then after a half-hour of gloom spent listening to the rain, which continues to pour down outside, a candle, a tiny candle flickering timidly, approaches through the darkness. Behind comes another, and yet another, until every dressing room is provided with two candles. The Signora has not arrived yet, and her dressing room is illuminated by two oil lamps that spurt and smoke deliciously – the best that can be done under the circumstances. We are a little apprehensive how this arrangement will be received by the Signora when suddenly our eyes blink with amazement: the electric lighting is restored.

Shortly afterwards, the Signora arrives in an automobile accompanied by Lugné-Poe. And finally, at the appointed hour, the curtain rises.

The auditorium is packed to capacity. But right at the back, beyond a narrow doorway lavishly decorated with stucco and gilt, there are three gaming tables that are also crowded, and while Guido Colonna trembles with anxiety, a deep and monotonous voice can be heard from time to time, saying in French, 'Gentlemen, place your bets.' It is the limit! La Duse says nothing. But the expression on her face is one of terrifying eloquence.

At the beginning of Act II, the scene, as usual, is played virtually in darkness. The electrician has forgotten to provide a lamp for the prompter, who at one point exclaims, 'Good God. I can't see a damn thing', and his gestures are so funny that the actor Robert can scarcely suppress his laughter. The Signora is standing in the wings waiting to make her entrance and nothing of this comedy escapes her.

She summons Orlandini at once and angrily confronts him: 'Signor Robert has no right to be laughing during a performance. Dismiss him immediately!' Orlandini is nonplussed. The Signora makes her entrance on stage. But when the act is over, she turns on Robert: 'You have been laughing all evening!' And Robert retorts: 'That is not true!' And La Duse: 'Be quiet! What is more, you took it upon yourself to change the entire pace of the act; you are always trying to have things your way!' Robert defends himself: 'That is simply not true. It was you who changed position . . .' Whereupon the Signora screams: 'You have no respect for the direction of Eleonora Duse. You are totally lacking in discipline . . . Be quiet and think twice before contradicting Eleonora Duse.' And off she flounces. At the end of the play, Robert is summoned by Orlandini, who informs him that the Signora wishes nothing more to do with him. He is to be dismissed, and she has no intention of paying him any compensation. How will this affair end? Tomorrow evening we play *La Gioconda* at Cannes.

Cannes, 14 February 1907

Upon arrival we meet the Signora's new secretary, Antonio Spinelli; the new stage manager, Mario Almirante, and the new technician, a Roman by birth but domiciled in France for some considerable time. All the other new members of the company contracted by the Signora will join us in San Remo. Former members who have left the company include the prompter Venafro, whose place was taken several days ago by Egidio Faggioli, and the actor Giacinto di Napoli.

The lovely theatre of the Casino Municipal at Cannes is packed to capacity. Before the start of the performance, the Signora has a heated argument with Masi and Bergonzio because the carpets normally used for the set have not been laid on stage. The play is enthusiastically received. The love scene in the first act is played by Duse in a manner that is truly divine.

Robert has written a note of apology to the Signora and all is forgiven. Peace between them has been restored.

After the performance we arrive as a group at the hotel where we reserved accommodation that very afternoon. An unpleasant surprise awaits us. Because we did not forward any luggage, our rooms have been given to other guests! So here we are at one o'clock in the morning, walking the streets of Cannes without any rooms!

We set off on a pilgrimage from hotel to hotel . . . At three o'clock in the morning we finally find somewhere to sleep. Good night! Tomorrow we leave for Nice where we shall give our last performance on the French Riviera with *La Gioconda*.

Nice, 16 February 1907

A magnificent theatre and a superb triumph. After tomorrow we leave for Marseilles where we shall give a single performance of

Monna Vanna. The other actors who are not involved in this performance leave tomorrow for San Remo.

Marseilles, 18 February 1907

We played *Monna Vanna* at the Opera House to a capacity audience. The Signora was given a wonderful ovation. After the second act she was presented a basket of exquisite flowers tied with ribbons in the Italian national colours, a tribute from the Italian colony here. I know that the Signora has donated 500 lire to the local Italian Hospital. We leave tomorrow for San Remo.

San Remo, 20 February 1907

Tomorrow morning at ten o'clock, the entire company will assemble at the Teatro Principe Amedeo. Here is the complete cast list:

Eleonora Duse
Vittorina Verani – Elisa Berti Masi – Luciana Rossi – Laura Tessero Bozzo – Clelia Zucchini – Celeste Bozzo – Margherita Orlandini.
Leo Orlandini
Alfredo Robert – Andrea Beltramo – Giuseppe Masi – Armando Lavaggi – Ubaldo Pittei – Carlo Delfini – Vittoria Capellaro – Guido Noccioli – Mario Almirante – Antonio Spinelli – Egidio Faggioli – Luigi Bergonzio.
Director: Leo Orlandini; Administrator: Giuseppe Masi; Secretary: Antonio Spinelli; Stage Manager: Mario Almirante; Property Man: Luigi Bergonzio.[20]

We still need a technician, because the new one contracted after we left Marseilles has vanished after receiving a considerable percentage of his salary in advance. As from tomorrow, we start rehearsing the entire repertoire at the Teatro Principe Amedeo for our forthcoming tour of South America. The Signora has already arrived in San Remo and is staying at the Hotel Savoia.

San Remo, 22 February 1907

Today at five o'clock, at the Hotel Savoia, the new members of the company are presented to the Signora, and we start rehearsing *L'altro pericolo.*[21] The Signora is favourably impressed by the young actress Vittorina Verani. The part of Fadin is taken away from the actor Lavaggi, not because of any serious deficiencies in his acting but simply because he is physically unsuited to the role.

San Remo, 25 February 1907

This evening a performance of *La Gioconda* before a distinguished audience, but the theatre is by no means full. An enthusiastic reception. Tomorrow a rehearsal of *L'altro pericolo* at the Hotel Savoia.

San Remo, 26 February 1907

The Signora in a foul temper. The minute she enters the room, she announces: 'The rehearsal of *L'altro pericolo* is suspended. The comedy will be withdrawn from the repertoire. I regret this decision because I had hoped to take this fine production to Milan next month. Especially for your sake, Signorina Verani. I am deeply distressed, but I am not to blame!' Then, after exchanging a few words with Orlandini, she mutters, clenching her fists: 'Were I to be reborn, I should ask God to make me a man so that I might give a sound thrashing to certain villains . . .'.

Later, we learn that Count Broglio,[22] who holds the performing rights, has forbidden the Signora to present the play because of some disagreement between them.

There is a rehearsal of *Rosmersholm*. And today Lavaggi suffers another blow: the part of Mortensgard is taken away from him and given to the actor Capellaro. Tomorrow the final performance of *Visita di nozze* and *La locandiera*.

San Remo, 27 February 1907

The theatre is only half full. Both plays, however, are an enormous success. Tomorrow we leave for Milan.

Milan, 7 March 1907

The performance at the Teatro Lirico this evening is magnificent. La Duse is greeted with frenzied applause. A noisy ovation is repeated at the end of each act of *La Gioconda*. The Signora's acting is sublime. Every detail is thrilling in her performance this evening. She surpasses herself. And she is deeply moved by the audience's reactions. At the end of the performance, she locks herself in her dressing room and weeps for thirty minutes. Her dresser tells us afterwards that at one point she exclaimed: 'I have not acted so well for years.'

All the Milanese journalists swarm on to the stage to pay their respects to Italy's most famous and beloved actress, and they beseech her to give an extra performance. She agrees. The Signora would like to present *Casa paterna*[23] but since all the scenery and costumes for the play are already on their way to Vienna, the company will appear in *La locandiera* and *Visita di nozze* instead.

Milan, 8 March 1907

This evening at eight o'clock we rehearse *La locandiera* at the

Palace Hotel with the Signora and when the rehearsal is over she asks Orlandini to send a basket of roses to the actress Emma Gramatica who is appearing at the Teatro Manzoni.

Milan, 9 March 1907

Another great triumph before a full house. The impresarios Suvini and Zerboni present the Signora with an ornamental silver shield bearing her effigy. Tomorrow evening we leave for Vienna.

Vienna, 11 March 1907

(11 p.m. at night) I feel absolutely exhausted. The cold is diabolical. The city covered in snow. It is still snowing heavily.

Vienna, 12 March 1907

The snow is incessant. Tomorrow evening we give our opening performance at the Theater an der Wien with *La Gioconda*.

Vienna, 13 March 1907

The theatre is sold out and the Signora is given the most extraordinary ovation. At the end of the play, there are fourteen curtain calls. Near the stagedoor, despite the heavy snowfall, there are some thirty admirers gathered round the Signora's carriage. The moment La Duse appears, the gentlemen doff their hats and the ladies wave their handkerchiefs. A pleasing spectacle that confirms the devotion shown by these Austrians to our great actress.

Vienna, 15 March 1907

Today at four o'clock, a rehearsal at the Hotel Bristol of *La signora delle camelie*.[24] Tomorrow evening a second performance of *Casa paterna*.

Vienna, 15 March 1907

The theatre is sold out again this evening and the same enthusiastic ovation is repeated. But the Signora's performance is weak and unconvincing. During Act II she seems to be wholly absorbed with her ermine stole, with which she fusses and fidgets throughout the entire act. In the scene with Baron Meller her acting is noticeably careless. Yet the audience applauds her warmly and at the end of the last act, a number of women rush up to the footlights, clapping enthusiastically and throwing flowers on to the stage, waving their handkerchiefs and loudly acclaiming La Duse . . . The Signora acknowledges this wild outburst of enthusiasm and takes eighteen curtain calls. Tomorrow there is a rehearsal of *La signora delle camelie* at the hotel.

[70]

THE NOCCIOLI DIARIES

Vienna, 16 March 1907

An extremely short rehearsal of no real significance. This evening I take myself to the Opera House to hear a performance of Wagner's *Der Fliegende Holländer*. The theatre is full. The opera makes a favourable impression. The production is highly professional. But the voices sound so hard and inflexible. Oh! Italian *bel canto*! How much I have come to appreciate you this evening.

Vienna, 18 March 1907

Tonight, *Rosmersholm* is played to an attentive rather than an enthusiastic audience. The theatre, of course, is packed to capacity. The Signora in excellent form. Gordon Craig's sets have been abandoned and we are now using the old ones. Rovescalli has created much less lugubrious scenery. I am unfamiliar with this

Exterior view of the Theater an der Wien in Vienna at the turn of the century. Vienna was the scene of some of Duse's greatest triumphs and from 1889 until 1909 she appeared in the Austrian capital almost every year. For Viennese critics and audiences Duse incarnated 'the eternally beautiful in dramatic art'. Duse, in return, claimed a special affinity with theatre circles in Austria and Germany where she sensed a deeper appreciation of her particular style of acting. (Photograph by courtesy of the Austrian National Library, Vienna.)

particular set, but the moment I see it I can not restrain my enthusiasm: 'Oh, how beautiful it looks!' I do not realize that the Signora is on stage with Orlandini and she whispers smiling: 'You too are faithful to tradition!' I melt. Tomorrow we have a rehearsal of *La signora delle camelie*.

Vienna, 19 March 1907

Today I complete my cultural tour of Vienna with a visit to the Imperial Museum. I shall take away many pleasant memories of this impressive capital. Two students from the University, Luigi Tapainer and Umberto Arici, prove to be efficient and courteous guides. Thanks to them, I have thoroughly enjoyed my stay in Vienna. Today's rehearsal is a most scrupulous affair. Tomorrow evening we give our last performance in Vienna with *La signora delle camelie*.

Vienna, 20 March 1907

A magnificent theatre and a resounding success. Yet La Duse is not at her celebrated best. For some time now I have not been wholly convinced by her interpretation of this role and she greatly disappoints me this evening. Apart from her invocations to Armando[25] in Act IV, there is nothing sincere, moving, or very powerful in her performance. A great pity! From Act IV onwards the audience goes wild with enthusiasm. The Signora is deeply moved. She remarks to Orlandini, as she goes out to take her eleventh curtain call: 'They are so devoted to me.' And it is true!

After the last act no one in the stalls or boxes shows any signs of leaving the theatre. They rise to their feet, shouting and applauding wildly. When the Signora comes before the footlights on her own, the noise of acclaim is deafening as people cheer from every corner of the theatre and bunches of violets come showering on to the stage from the gallery, boxes and stalls. The stage is soon carpeted by a veritable mass of flowers. As she tries to gather up as many floral tributes as possible, the Signora is crying. The curtain is raised thirty-six times. Here is an unforgettable evening for every true Italian. Tomorrow morning at eight o'clock we leave for Budapest.

Budapest, 21 March 1907

When we arrive the cold weather is dry but still unbearable. There is a wind blowing worthy of a romantic novel. Tomorrow evening we present *La signora delle camelie* at the Vigsinhaz Theatre.

THE NOCCIOLI DIARIES

Budapest, 22 March 1907

The theatre is sold out. A smart audience. The auditorium, which is lavishly decorated, presents a truly magnificent spectacle. The Signora's entrance is greeted by lengthy applause. This evening there are some memorable moments, especially during Act II. But the audience becomes delirious with excitement in Act IV. Those famous invocations to 'Armando' are miraculous. Tomorrow evening our final performance with *Rosmersholm*.

Budapest, 23 March 1907

The theatre packed to capacity. Another resounding success. The Signora acts divinely. Tomorrow we leave for Bucharest.

Bucharest, 25 March 1907

It is midnight. We arrive at last after a desolate journey across a desolate Hungary and over the snow-clad Carpathians. There is snow everywhere. The cold is dreadful.

Bucharest, 27 March 1907

This evening our opening performance at the National Theatre with *Casa paterna*. The theatre is full but not to capacity. An extraordinary ovation. Tomorrow there is to be a rehearsal of *Fernanda*[26] directed by the Signora herself at the Hotel Boulevard.

Bucharest, 28 March 1907

We find the Signora in a state of alarm because of the rumours circulating in the capital about the impending peasant revolution in the countryside. We are convinced, however, that the rumours are exaggerated. Bucharest is to all appearances normal. The rehearsal itself is a short affair.

Bucharest, 29 March 1907

This evening a second performance of *La signora delle camelie*. The theatre is half empty. The latest bulletins from the countryside are causing serious panic. It now appears that the agrarian revolt is a reality. In talking to several citizens of Bucharest today, we hear a pessimistic account of the exploitation to which Rumanian peasants are subjected. Certain details are worthy of a novel. In the capital there is much more activity than normal and groups of demonstrators on every street corner. After Act III we are informed that some government minister has been deposed and substituted by another, who immediately declares a state of siege throughout the entire region where the revolt is brewing.[27]

DUSE ON TOUR

Bucharest, 30 March 1907

This evening we play *La Gioconda* with enormous success. The Signora, however, is greatly perturbed. In fact, the news this evening is much more serious. Last night, a frenzied mob sacked and destroyed one of the royal estates, and this morning the newspapers report the most horrifying incidents. The government is trying to persuade the people that the rising is being fomented by anti-Semitic factions; but the truth is that hunger drives these wretched creatures to the most atrocious excesses. It now seems the revolution is spreading and is fast approaching Bucharest itself, where emergency measures are already being enforced. At the end of the performance, which is given before a sparse audience, the theatre administrator warns us to prepare ourselves for an imminent departure. The Signora is received today by Queen Carmen Silva and advised to leave Bucharest as soon as possible.

Bucharest, 31 March 1907

The news becomes more alarming by the hour. This evening in the theatre we are told that we shall leave tomorrow for Florence. This means that our last two performances have been cancelled, namely: *La moglie di Claudio*[28] and *Fernanda*.

Budapest, 2 April 1907

We are staying in the Hungarian capital until this evening. The Signora has travelled with us as far as Budapest before going on to Vienna. We leave this evening at nine o'clock for Florence.

Florence, 3 April 1907

Midnight. We arrive in a state of near exhaustion.

Florence, 4 April 1907

Today there is a rehearsal at the Teatro della Pergola of *L'altro pericolo* which we shall present on 9 April.

Florence, 8 April 1907

This evening a dress rehearsal at the theatre with sets and lighting. The Signora attends and is still very nervous and tense. She is particularly worried about the mise-en-scène. We learn that the theatre is sold out for tomorrow evening's performance.

Florence, 9 April 1907

A magnificent theatre. The audience gives the first three acts a cool reception. Only one curtain call at the end of each act. La Duse achieves some exquisite touches in these first three acts but

she is far from secure in her role and her acting is all too tentative
... In Act IV, however, she dazzles the audience. Such artistry!
How many beautiful moments she manages to create in this act
and how much feeling, soul and life she expresses! Her face is
something wondrous to behold. Her personal triumph is assured
and the audience's reaction is indescribable. I have lost count of
the curtain calls.

The impresario Rosadi comes backstage to beseech the Signora
to give five more performances, offering to pay her the company's
fees in advance, such is his confidence in a complete sell-out. The
Signora refuses his generous offer. Tomorrow there is a rehearsal
of *Fedora* in the theatre.

Florence, 11 April 1907
Today we have a rehearsal of *Fedora*. Tomorrow a rehearsal of *La
abbadessa di Jouarre*[29] and *Odette*.

Florence, 12 April 1907
Tomorrow we leave for Milan. La Duse will take part in a benefit
matinée for the Milanese actor Sbodio, who has been forced to
retire from the stage because of old age and poor health. The
Signora will perform the last act of *Adriana Lecouvreur*; then on
Monday we shall present *L'altro pericolo*.

Milan, 14 April 1907
The Teatro Lirico is full. The programme long and varied. A
symphony followed by a sketch played by Sbodio, who is greeted
by prolonged outbursts of applause, then *Una partita a scacchi* by
Giacosa[30] played by Elisa Severi, Oreste Calabresi, Amedeo Chiantoni and Egisto Olivieri.[31] This is followed by three musical items
played on the violin by Signorina Frassinetti; then another symphony followed by *L'elogio funebre*,[32] a monologue by Sabatino
Lopez beautifully recited by Calabresi, and then another sketch
played by Sbodio, followed by the last act of *Adriana Lecouvreur*
with La Duse, Leo Orlandini, Andrea Beltramo and Margherita
Orlandini. Finally, there are some *character transformations* by
Fatima Miris.[33] The evening is a great success and the tributes paid
to Sbodio are really very moving. La Duse, naturally enough, is
the major attraction. Her acting on this occasion makes a deep
impression. Endless ovations. Sbodio presents her with his photograph on which he has inscribed: 'To a supreme artist, with my
supreme gratitude.'[34]

DUSE ON TOUR

Milan, 15 April 1907

This evening (although our performance coincides with the opening night of the opera season at the Teatro della Scala and the première of *Gloria*, a new work by Maestro Cilèa) the Teatro Lirico is packed to capacity. The ovation is equal to that witnessed in Florence. The Signora appears to be acting with greater authority and skill. Tomorrow at midday, we depart for Florence.

Florence, 18 April 1907

We are now rehearsing daily at the Teatro della Pergola and preparing the entire repertoire for South America.

Florence, 20 April 1907

Today Orlandini introduces the actress Argenide Scalambretti, the new character actress who is to substitute for Laura Tessero Bozzo, whom La Duse has dismissed with compensation. La Signora never really approved of Tessero Bozzo with her frail physique and sloppy manner of dressing. Her daughter, Celestina Bozzo, has also left the company even though La Duse expressed her willingness to keep the girl on. Our rehearsals continue without anything of interest to report.

Florence, 25 April 1907

Today, during the rehearsal of *Odette*, Signorina Rossi reads her part in Act II without any enthusiasm in a monotonous singsong voice. Orlandini pleads with her to recite the part properly. In reply, she truculently retorts that she is doing her best. Orlandini begins to shout with frustration while Signorina Rossi impudently betrays her amusement . . . He smashes a chair on the floor and bangs his stick on the table until it breaks . . . Bang! . . . crash! . . . thud! . . . the table, too, is soon shattered into bits. At the end of his tether, our director fumes: 'You are all dismissed, the rehearsal is cancelled.' We abandon the rehearsal. The weather is delightful, the air is mild. A grain of remorse prevents us from expressing our gratitude to Signorina Rossi, who goes off in a carriage with a satisfied grin on her face.

Florence, 26 April 1907

A rehearsal of *Seconda moglie*. Orlandini and Signorina Rossi have patched up their quarrel.

Florence, 30 April 1907

We rehearse *La principessa Giorgio*[35] at the Grand Hotel. The Signora is in excellent spirits. She rehearses with passionate dedication.

THE NOCCIOLI DIARIES

Florence, 1 May 1907
In the theatre itself, we rehearse both *Hedda Gabler* and *Rosmersholm* with the Signora.

Florence, 7 May 1907
The final rehearsal of *La principessa Giorgio.* Tomorrow in the theatre, we rehearse *Fernanda* and *La signora delle camelie.*

Florence, 14 May 1907
Yesterday we finished our rehearsals. And so the entire repertoire for South America is ready. Today at two o'clock the full company assembles in the theatre. The Signora comes to bid us farewell. She inquires: 'I trust that you are all happy to be making this long tour overseas?' When we reassure her that our answer is in the affirmative, she adds: 'Excellent! Besides, there are no dangers involved. These are young countries with an important future. I am not sailing with you, but I beg of you not to take this decision amiss. It has nothing to do with any feeling of superiority or personal vanity on my part. I must travel to Paris to bid farewell to some close friends and then go on to London to see my daughter. I shall sail on an English ship from Lisbon. While at sea, I prefer to be alone. These will be fifteen days of complete rest for me.' She exhorts us to keep up our spirits and to be well behaved and respect company discipline. She then kisses all the actresses, who have difficulty in holding back their tears.

Next turning to us actors, she exclaims: 'I won't kiss you, gentlemen . . . for my kisses are the last thing you need or crave . . .' We protest vigorously. She laughs and kisses Orlandini in the name of everyone. All the actors then line up to kiss her hand.

Before departing, having spotted Bergonzio, she kisses him on both cheeks saying: 'Two kisses for my faithful companion', and the old boy is overjoyed while we others looked on enviously.

From today on, the Signora – with her habitual kindness and generosity – is giving us our freedom while continuing to pay our salaries until 29 May when the company is scheduled to sail from Genoa.

Genoa, 30 May 1907
Aboard the steamer *Umbria*. We are due to sail within the next two hours. On deck there is the most incredible activity, a veritable swarm of porters loading trunks and suitcases . . . . There is much gaiety, almost forced and edgy, and no doubt concealing an underlying sense of nostalgia. Many telegrams have arrived from

well-wishers. Among them is one from the Signora wishing us a safe journey. Suddenly Nunes Vais arrives to take a group photograph of the company. I spot the actors Ettore Berti (who has come to bid farewell to his sister Elisa) and Drago in animated conversation with La Scalambretti. The commotion and shouting is quite deafening; the heat is oppressive. In the dining room Pittei is chatting with Lavaggi. Both of them look downhearted. Exquisitely gowned in a silk creation, La Rossi annoys everyone with her excessive joviality. La Masi's eyes are quite red from weeping while La Verani and La Zucchini pace to and fro, looking utterly distressed and broken-hearted.

The ship finally sails at five minutes past five. At the quayside a large crowd waves with handkerchiefs and hats. From a nearby campanile numerous bells salute us with their pealing and sonorous chimes. A great flood of emotion suddenly sweeps over us when we are no longer restrained or in danger of appearing ridiculous. But La Scalambretti with a little patriotic speech restores our good humour. Tall, broad and rotund, she appears just like a cook with her large bovine eyes which invariably look bloodshot. Encased in a satin blouse that shines like armour, and leaning against the ship's bow, solemn as a preacher, she declaims with an affected drawl: 'Ah, I feel moved to tears. . . . How it grieves me to leave my beloved Italy! This precious land where we were born and destined to live . . .'. I flee . . . in horror, yet feeling happy.

At sea, Barcelona, 31 May 1907

This evening the ship calls at Barcelona. So far, the voyage has been most enjoyable. We cross the dreaded Gulf of Lions with perfect calm. So much the better! We disembark when it is already dark. The streets are crowded and there is much activity. Accompanied by two other members of the company, I go to the Teatro Apollo where Italia Vitaliani is appearing with her troupe. It is a benefit performance for Carlo Duse with *Il padrone delle ferriere*.[36] At a quarter past nine, the theatre is still empty. I converse with Tolentino, who tells me the season has been disastrous financially. I am anxious to greet Stefani, a former comrade who studied with me at Florence, where we were pupils of Luigi Rasi – a truly excellent and generous maestro – but Stefani is not to be found in the theatre.

Then, we go on to the Teatro de Novedades, where Tina di Lorenzo is giving her farewell performance in Roberto Bracco's

Members of Duse's company leaving for South America aboard the
Umbria at Genoa on 30 May 1907. Although unidentified, some of
the actors in the group are virtually recognizable from Noccioli's
own comments about their individual foibles and traits of character.
(Photographs from the Nunes Vais Collection by courtesy of the
Istituto Centrale per il Catalogo e la Documentazione, Rome)

Luigi Rasi (1852–1918), actor, playwright and Director of the pres-
tigious Academy of Dramatic Art in Florence from 1882 until his
death. An advocate of 'naturalness and simplicity' in acting, Rasi
trained many talented young artists at the turn of the century. A
life-long admirer of Duse, he encouraged his erstwhile student
Noccioli to keep a diary while on tour abroad in the eminent
actress's company. (Reproduction by courtesy of the Biblioteca
Teatrale del Burcardo, Rome.)

Infedele.[37] I watch the second act – a full house with an enthusiastic
audience.

When I get back to the ship, I find Stefani waiting for me on
the quayside.

At sea, 1 June 1907

We are in view of the Balearic Islands. The sea is agitated . . . just
like my stomach. I feel as if an iron band is clamped around my
temples . . . I am keeping my fingers crossed.

At sea, 2 June 1907

We are now crossing the Straits of Gibraltar, with the sea at its
roughest yet. I have spent a terrible night; and I am still suffering

from the after effects.
Ugh! I feel awful!

At sea, 3 June 1907

The ocean is choppy. Seasick passengers wherever one looks.

At sea, 4 June 1907

Our ship has stopped at Santa Cruz de Tenerife in order to refuel. We disembark. The local scene is typical enough but barren. It induces an overwhelming sense of unhappiness. We get back on board without wasting much time. The ship sails as night is falling. The vision of that sombre island is unforgettable.

At sea, 5 June 1907

We are all beginning to recover. The sea is as smooth as a lake and life on board is back to its normal routine.

In second class there are some charming nuns who befriend us. They are civilized and jovial. They are making their way to some mission territory called Santissimo Sacramento. Our Luciana Rossi is already flirting with the ship's doctor. She is invariably dolled up in clothes more suitable for a girl in her teens. La Scalambretti is always dressed in white, with a short skirt and floppy beret. She looks like a deep-sea diver. Pittei has not stirred from his deckchair for three days. He is fast turning into a savage. He has been reading *The Confessions of Famous Courtesans,* which he then passes on to me. But both of us, having read Paul de Kock, had hoped for something more ... how can one put it? ... more salacious. Good Heavens! These confessions are far too circumspect and tame. I prefer Pascoli any day. But I settle for *Dorian Gray* by Oscar Wilde,[38] which is suggestive after a fashion.

But what a bore life is!

At sea, 6 June 1907

To mark our passage over the Equator, some festivities are being arranged. We try to interest Orlandini, but he refuses to have anything to do with the arrangements. Lavaggi, however, has agreed to plan something, but there are all sorts of problems involved in drawing up a suitable programme, especially if one is trying to pander to everyone's vanity. I fear that we shall abandon the whole idea in the end.

Delfini entertains us by singing some ballads. He has a well-trained and extremely pleasant tenor voice.

DUSE ON TOUR

At sea, 7 June 1907

The most terrible seasickness. Such anguish! Such nausea! ...

At sea, 9 June 1907

I surface again, after being confined to my cabin for forty-eight hours. How pleasant to contemplate the sky once more. I have never felt so ill before! And even now on deck, how many wan-looking passengers I encounter. Pittei is almost submerged in his deckchair: Almirante suffers with as much dignity as he can muster. At lunch, for example, when the pangs and nausea in his stomach become unbearable, he leaves the table on the pretext of going off to see some ailing passenger or to witness some display of breakers or the effects of light playing on the surface of the sea ... He rushes off, pays his tribute to the sea, then returns looking tranquil, dignified and composed, exclaiming as he sits back down: 'I have seen ...!' He euphemistically calls it *seeing*! By contrast, Delfini suffers philosophically. When his moment comes, he disappears to his cabin only to return, declaring: 'I feel better now!' I, on the other hand, suffer in public without shame or remorse. I cannot restrain myself. No laws govern my bouts of sickness. Wherever I happen to find myself ... I throw up!

Tomorrow we pass over the Equator. Lavaggi, after much effort, has succeeded in arranging an attractive programme. It reads as follows:

The Symphony: *Amico Fritz*. At the piano, Signor Delfino (a first-class passenger).
An Aria from Mascagni's *Iris*, sung by Carlo Delfini.
Dante's *Inferno* (the third canto), read by Alfredo Robert.
An Aria from Puccini's *Tosca*, sung by Carlo Delfini.
'La scoperta dell'America,'[39] read by Armando Lavaggi.

At sea, 11 June 1907

Last night I was unable to attend the festivities because the sea was rough and I, as usual, was being violently sick. Lavaggi too was unable to be present because somewhat indisposed. Delfini was not feeling well and sang with some considerable difficulty. The greatest success of the evening proved to be Robert ... Afterwards a dance was held in the first-class saloon. The orchestra consisted of a violin, a guitar and a mandoline loaned by passengers travelling in third class.

Seasickness! And still more seasickness!

[82]

THE NOCCIOLI DIARIES

At sea, 13 June 1907

Today a little boy in the third class fell down a stairway, sustaining head injuries. Poor child!

At sea, 14 June 1907

Since eleven o'clock the ship has been stationary just outside the Bay of Rio de Janeiro. We will not be allowed to enter port until tomorrow morning. At long last!

Rio de Janeiro, 15 June 1907

We disembark at nine o'clock and go straight to the theatre. (Evening) A day of great activity in search of suitable lodgings. All the unmarried members of the cast, including myself, prefer to be near the theatre, and we have decided to stay at a French pension. The service is excellent. The price is six milréis[40] per day without wine. We shall drink water instead!

Rio de Janeiro, 16 June 1907

Rehearsals. I observe that our pension is full of amorous young ladies. All to the good! We are guaranteed some amusement! The landlady is a most amiable woman.

Rio de Janeiro, 17 June 1907

It is raining persistently. At seven o'clock this morning, the Signora arrives accompanied by her impresario Lugné-Poe, a French secretary, a masseuse and the latter's husband and two maids. She is staying at the Hotel dos Estrangeiros. Spinelli, the company secretary, assures us that she is in good spirits. On Wednesday, 19 June, we open with *La signora delle camelie*.

Rio de Janeiro, 18 June 1907

The weather is improving. I have been on a sightseeing trip round the city. Chaos everywhere. Old houses being demolished, new buildings going up. Roads ploughed up and new ones traced out, mountains levelled to the ground, or just about to be razed. Confusion wherever one looks. Many black women dress in gaudy colours that range from white to canary yellow or flame red and so forth and so on. Many negroes around sporting stiff collars twenty centimetres high, white linen trousers, black jackets, and yellow ankle boots. An authentic carnival!

Rio de Janeiro, 19 June 1907

This evening our inaugural performance with *La signora delle camelie*. The Signora is extremely nervous. Everyone in the company, for one reason or another, shares her anxiety. Signorina

Luciana Rossi is much irked by Orlandini, who badgers her with one impertinence after another. La Scalambretti who is playing the part of Duvernois is costumed and made up two hours before the play is due to commence. She paces the stage triumphantly, her prodigious bosom virtually bursting out of the most incredible *décolleté* and those formidable haunches swaying ominously . . . As is his custom, Beltramo is already dressed as Duval Père at four o'clock in the afternoon, even though the performance is not due to begin until eight-thirty.

This evening the theatre is full, but not to capacity. The President of the Republic[41] is present, accompanied by members of his family. As she makes her entrance on stage, La Duse is not recognized by the audience. The first act is played with excessive haste. At the end of the act, only one curtain call.

The second act begins amidst the most distracting uproar as the audience noisily rushes back to its seats. La Duse's nerves are on edge; she makes several awkward pauses. Eventually silence is restored. Both audience and actors calm down. Duse's letter scene is magnificently done! The final scene opposite Armando with its lengthy dialogue is played with extraordinary power and feeling and with an infinite variety of subtle undertones and nuances . . . suddenly the audience vibrates with excitement. Standing in the wings, we actors hold our breath. It is, indeed, a sublime moment! As the act comes to an end there is a frenzied outburst of applause with shouts of 'Duse! Duse!' Six curtain calls.

The third act is hastily performed and received with less enthusiasm. Three curtain calls.

Before the curtain goes up on Act IV, the Signora briefly rehearses her scene with Orlandini in *mezza voce* and then becomes impatient because the set is not yet ready. She turns to Almirante, the stage manager, reminding him to supervise carefully the tiny orchestra that is to play behind the scenes. Almirante replies: 'Yes, yes!' The Signora looks at him coldly and snaps: 'Do not reply to me with "Yes, yes" but with "Yes, signora!" ' Almirante is perturbed by this outburst.

The fourth act is badly acted by the entire cast. No one delivers their lines with sufficient attack. The prompter, placed at some distance from the stage, cannot be heard. The Signora's entrance restores some semblance of order. The famous invocations to Armando electrify the audience which shouts its approval, applauds wildly, and brings the Signora to the footlights some six or seven times.

The final act arouses no great enthusiasm although wonderfully acted. It strikes me that these Brazilians have failed to grasp the true quality of Eleonora Duse's genius! We shall see what the newspapers have to say in the morning. Tomorrow at five-thirty in the theatre there is a rehearsal of *Hedda Gabler* and *Fiamme nell'ombra* with the Signora.

Rio de Janeiro, 20 June 1907

All the reviews in the local press have nothing but the highest praise for Eleonora Duse and her company. But only one critic is prepared to concede that Orlandini was an effective Armando even while noting a certain lack of elegance and distinction in his performance. The reviewer also criticizes with some severity the cut of his costume and complains that his dress collar looked positively grubby! An original piece of criticism, to be sure, and somehow worthy of the nation!

At five o'clock this afternoon the Signora is already in the theatre, despite the fact that our rehearsal is scheduled for five-thirty. But all the artists, being familiar with the Signora's whims, are already waiting on stage.

La Duse is in a playful mood. To Signorina Rossi, she quips: 'Your costume was lovely, my dear, but your acting quite appalling.' Then, turning to the entire cast, she goes on: 'Last night you betrayed me at least eighteen times. All of you!' She smiles sweetly and the rebuke, which is wholly justified, is more gentle than any praise she might offer with a scowl. Then she begins to rehearse *Hedda Gabler*. Those of us who are not involved are dismissed.

After the rehearsal, I discover that *Fiamme nell'ombra* is being dropped from the repertoire. The news comes as no surprise.

Tomorrow evening, there is a performance of *Casa paterna*.

Rio de Janeiro, 21 June 1907

This morning Robert told me that another newspaper, whose title I have forgotten, has criticized Orlandini's acting in the most scathing terms! Among other things, the reviewer wrote: 'One is either an actor of genius or one of imitation: Signor Orlandini is neither the one nor the other, and therefore totally negative.' This strikes me as being excessively cruel! I notice how Robert, who is a nice chap at heart, is clearly delighted as he tells me about this attack on Orlandini.

At midday, the news arrives that Masi is ill with severe stomach pains and a high temperature. This comes as a shock, even though we are reassured that his condition is not serious. Meantime, it is decided that I shall understudy the small role of Professor Beka-man in *Casa paterna.*

This evening, at dinner, after the first course, Spinelli arrives with a message from Orlandini, telling me that I am to substitute for Masi! The performance is given before a sparse audience. La Duse acts with inspiration. During Act III, she is interrupted on at least two occasions by outbursts of applause.

Not a single detail of that masterly interpretation which has made her famous in the role is missing this evening. Yet it is disappointing to note that the ovation given to her performance is not so great as one might expect from a public renowned for its spontaneous warmth and exuberance! All my fellow actors reflect with some irony that here in this same theatre, Clara della Guardia, an actress of mediocre talent, scored her most resounding successes. One must console oneself by bearing in mind that pearls were never considered suitable for casting before swine.[42]

Everyone is asked to be at the theatre tomorrow by two-thirty.

Rio de Janeiro, 22 June 1907

We are rehearsing *Fernanda.* Masi is feeling much better. The rehearsal is a lengthy affair. The Signora very cheerful. Tomorrow at one-thirty, a non subscription matinée with *La signora delle camelie.*

Rio de Janeiro, 23 June 1907

A good audience this evening. A triumph almost equal to that of the opening night. Act II is poorly acted but the fourth and fifth acts are much more lively. One comic note: in Act II Orlandini has to say something like: 'I have loved you for a day, for a year, for ten years . . .'. Instead, he says: 'For a day, for a year, for a thousand years . . .' and La Duse exclaims: 'Oh dear!' in such a delightfully comic manner, that those of us standing in the wings can scarcely control our laughter. Tomorrow evening *L'altro pericolo.*

Rio de Janeiro, 24 June 1907

Very few people in the theatre. The first three acts of *L'altro pericolo* make a poor impression. The Signora muddles line after line! The actors who have to converse with her do not know where to turn. The prompter shouts himself hoarse but to no avail. However, by Act IV, although I cannot swear that her performance is equal to that witnessed in Florence and Milan, it is, nevertheless, in its own way revealing. The audience is at one with her, spellbound and ecstatic as it gives her a standing ovation.

We leave the theatre in a group and our conversation turns to the evening's performance. The cast begins to discuss La Duse's merits as an actress. Almost everyone is in agreement that her acting has been very disappointing at this evening's performance, while conceding that in Act IV she did achieve some beautiful moments, even if somewhat lacking in feeling etc. . . . I have the temerity to say that I found her acting deeply moving in the last act, but the others refuse to agree.

It amuses me to reflect that I was the only member of the cast to have watched her in the fourth act, for all the others were then in their dressing rooms getting out of their costumes. It also amuses me to observe how all these fellow actors – decent people – but *actors* after all, are ever ready to declare that La Duse is the greatest actress in the world when they see the theatre filled to capacity! These idiosyncrasies are only to be expected.

The only exception in our company is Lavaggi, who is a fine actor and a gentleman. Although nervous and irascible by nature, he always is capable of balanced and dispassionate judgments. I believe him to be correct when he claims that La Duse of today is no longer the artist of former years – that La Duse of today is purely intellectual and, therefore, in ever greater need of more cultured audiences such as those to be found in Berlin and Vienna . . . Here in Brazil, he asserts, she'll never be able to arouse any great enthusiasm. And this is, indeed, proving to be true.[43]

Rio de Janeiro, 25 June 1907

Today there is no performance. I go to Leme, a beach with the finest sandy shore imaginable and separated from Rio by a mountain covered with luxuriant vegetation. The sea too is green with a transparency the colour of emeralds.

I meet Robert on the beach and accompany him back to the city centre. Robert is lodging with some Italians who are domiciled here, and he tells me that La Duse has made herself very unpopular with the inhabitants of Rio de Janeiro by refusing to receive some minister or other![44] Her behaviour has provoked a great deal of controversy in the press and is thought to have sparked off much of the criticism aimed at the company! Really! A situation all too characteristic of the New World!

Tomorrow evening there is a performance of *La Gioconda*. A full house is expected. We are assured that the box office receipts already amount to a considerable sum. We are keeping our fingers crossed.

DUSE ON TOUR

Rio de Janeiro, 26 June 1907

Ah! At last, I can speak of a truly magnificent evening. The theatre is packed to capacity as on the opening night and the performance a brilliant triumph. This evening La Duse acts with supreme confidence.

Before the curtain rises, she comes on stage and addresses the cast so graciously that we can scarcely believe our ears. All sweetness and affability. Her speech touches on the poor audiences at recent performances. She declares that she herself is not greatly disturbed by this factor and that one must make allowances for the Brazilian public. At one point she says: 'I am almost tempted to say to the impresario: "My dear fellow, if you have brought me all this way only to make money, then you needn't bother", but the next day I reconsider the matter and say to him: "No, my dear fellow, since I am here, here I will remain. And I expect to be paid for my labours." ' Then she goes on: 'Besides, a tour of this nature imposes a certain discipline that is very good for one. For, once a contract is fulfilled, we can derive some moral satisfaction! But if we shirk our duty, there is always a lingering sense of regret and uncertainty that ends in guilt and despondency . . . If only I had done such and such a thing, if only I had said this or that at the time, and so on and so forth. While I debated as to whether we should accept this contract or not, everyone accused me of wasting time, and any such accusation, believe me, distresses me greatly. After all, in order to live with some decorum, it is necessary to earn one's money.'

And she continues by speaking of fortunes to be made, of new paths to be forged – of the mountains levelled or waiting to be razed – of intelligent people who send her books and letters daily, of her elderly maid Nina who has mistakenly packed the costumes for her role in *La moglie di Claudio* in the trunks labelled *La Gioconda*. She discusses lighting, financial details, administrative arrangements, frustrations, diseases and infections, different races and cultures, etc., etc.

Then the performance begins. Six curtain calls after Act I; five after Act II; seven after Act III; and four after the final act.

Tomorrow at two-thirty there is a rehearsal of *Odette* and *Seconda moglie*.[45] Friday: *Fernanda*.

Rio de Janeiro, 27 June 1907

The Signora arrives exactly on the hour. The minute she appears she informs the cast: 'There will be no rehearsal of *Odette* today,

[88]

for we shall not be performing the play until we reach São Paulo. Instead, we are going to rehearse *Seconda moglie* and the closing scenes of *Fernanda*.' Then, while we are awaiting the arrival of Orlandini who has gone to consult a doctor about some minor ailment, she adds: 'Today, for the first time, I enjoy being in Rio de Janeiro.' She smiles, then quickly touching a piece of wood she says . . . 'We might as well respect the old superstition.' Then the Signora begins rehearsing *Seconda moglie* – a quite thorough and scrupulous rehearsal in which La Duse gives ample evidence of her remarkable talents as a company director. But she tires quickly, and from Act III onwards the rehearsal proceeds rapidly without further interruptions.

The Signora, who arrived in a cheerful mood, suddenly becomes melancholy and self-absorbed. Then we go on to rehearse *Fernanda* before being allowed to go home.

Rio de Janeiro, 28 June 1907

Fernanda did not attract a large audience. Yet the whole city should have rushed to the theatre to hear our great actress. She is *truly* great! This evening, the entire cast, including those actors who only the other day were questioning the reputation of Eleonora Duse, praise her performance and declare her unsurpassed. Consigli, one of the impresarios, comes on stage after the performance in a state of utter amazement. As for the public, they become wild with excitement. Noisy and seemingly interminable curtain calls, especially after the third act. And shouts of 'Duse! Duse!' Tomorrow afternoon at a quarter past three there will be a rehearsal of *Hedda Gabler* and *Seconda moglie* at the Signora's hotel.

Rio de Janeiro, 29 June 1907

Today, as we were making our way to the hotel, we meet Spinelli who tells us that the rehearsal is cancelled. The Signora does not wish to see anyone. Returning to my pension, I learn that the local press continues to attack La Duse. Reviewing her interpretation of Silvia Settala, the critics write more or less in these words: 'In the first three acts La Duse was decidedly inferior to Suzanne Desprès: in Act IV, Clara della Guardia has turned in a much better performance! As for *Fernanda*, some twenty-two years ago we heard Duse in the role of Clotilde, which she played reasonably well. All one can say of her performance today is that twenty-two years have taken their toll!'

And the reviews go from bad to worse. These so-called critics are not only cretins but also malicious and insulting! May God forgive them!

Rio de Janeiro, 30 June 1907

For today's matinée performance of *La Gioconda*, there is a magnificent house. A triumph equal to that witnessed at earlier performances. The prompter, Faggioli, is confined to bed with a temperature! The stage manager, Almirante, has taken his place, and I have substituted for Almirante.

Before the curtain rises, the Signora approaches me and shows me a delightful photograph. A nude portrait of a young girl turned away from the camera with her head in profile. She leaves the photograph with me, asking me to show it to Robert. She says: 'Tell him this is the little girl to whom Lucio refers in the play. Tell him to study it carefully. D'Annunzio, in describing her, was inspired by this very photograph.[46] Ah! It is quite exquisite, like a portrait by Ingrès. The original is magnificent!' I carry out her request. Upon seeing the photograph and receiving the Signora's message, Robert is only capable of making some vulgar remark accompanied by obscene gestures . . . Upon returning the portrait to the Signora, I find her chatting with Orlandini. She also shows him the picture, then she beckons to Signorina Rossi and says to her: 'Look, look here! She is even more beautiful than you . . .! Do you see? . . . Such a lovely creature? Oh! She is quite perfect . . . A lovely, lovely child . . .!'

Before and after Act IV, the Signora, who is dissatisfied with the stage lighting, flies into a violent rage. She starts shouting and screaming like someone obsessed: 'God help me! . . . Can one no longer have the simplest instructions obeyed? Damn the lot of you! I am sick and tired of your indifference . . . It is disgraceful . . . an outrage!'

Tomorrow evening at seven-thirty there will be a rehearsal of *Hedda Gabler* at the hotel.

Rio de Janeiro, 1 July 1907

The rehearsal takes place as scheduled. I am unable to attend.

Rio de Janeiro, 2 July 1907

This evening *Hedda Gabler* played to a half-empty theatre. Before the play begins, the Signora demands that the set be modified again and again, by adding or removing certain props and rearranging everything – items of furniture, rugs, knick-knacks, flowers ... I am warned that when she plays *Hedda Gabler* the Signora is always nervous to the point of hysteria. On the contrary, this evening she is radiant and serene and looks quite beautiful. I watch the performance from the front stalls. She scores a personal triumph beyond all our expectations. I am happy to be able to confirm that the Signora gives a masterly account of this difficult role. A whole book would be necessary to analyse her memorable interpretation. It is quite extraordinary how she imposes some new value or meaning on every phrase and gesture; the slightest movement of her body reveals something, and her facial expression is at once so mobile and varied. Her entrance in Act I could scarcely be more suggestive or reveal more clearly the character of Hedda Gabler! And later, in the scene with Thea, she introduces such marvellous details of technique, subtle intonations in every smile or pause ... her miraculous acting in Act II in the scene between Thea and Lœvborg ...[47] and the impressive finale of Act III when she *strangles* the manuscript, symbolizing *their child*, and throws it on the flames. At this point, the audience rises to its feet, and our great actress is led to the footlights some seven or eight times.

Among the other members of the cast only Lavaggi acts with any distinction. La Rossi in the part of Thea looks charming and in the first two acts plays moderately well. But as the play progresses what a disaster! Orlandini, playing Lœvborg, gives a fullblooded romantic interpretation of the role, which completely misfires. Robert makes an exhibition of himself with inappropriate posturings in bad taste, and he plays the great actor with ham gestures and an affected voice distorted by the most curious intonation ... Watching him at close range, it soon becomes evident that he has no understanding whatsoever of the role's requirements.

When the performance is over, I head backstage. La Duse is reproaching La Rossi: 'You were hopeless this evening, Signorina, quite, quite hopeless!' Then, embracing her, she says with a smile: 'Tomorrow at two-thirty we shall rehearse *La moglie di Claudio* and *Seconda moglie* at the hotel.'

Rio de Janeiro, 3 July 1907
The rehearsal is held in the theatre instead of at the hotel. The Signora looks despondent, she moves with some difficulty and seems worn out. The rehearsal is monotonous and not particularly helpful. Suddenly the Signora begins to complain bitterly about

her hotel accommodation. She wails: 'I have never experienced a more unpleasant room! I am plagued by a neighbour who snores and another who coughs incessantly. Such bliss! I cannot wait to leave this wretched place.'

Tomorrow at the hotel there is a rehearsal of *Odette*.

Rio de Janeiro, 4 July 1907

A lively rehearsal with everyone in high spirits. The Signora is in an agreeable frame of mind.

We begin with a display of patriotism. Today marks the centenary of the birth of Giuseppe Garibaldi and our property man, Bergonzio, an ex-Garibaldi soldier, turns up for the rehearsal wearing his red shirt and four medals awarded for valour. The Signora is taken aback but greets him with enthusiasm: 'Bravo, bravo, Bergonzio! I didn't know that you had fought with Garibaldi's insurgents. Bravo! Let me shake your hand!' And she encourages the rest of us to follow her example.

Then the rehearsal finally begins. A rehearsal in a manner of speaking. The Signora, as everyone knows, is tired of the same old plays, so that when the moment arrives for her to say her lines she shouts to the prompter: 'Go on! Go on! You can skip the next bit!'[48]

During the second act she sits apart from the other actors, writing while Orlandini recites his entire part as Clermont Latour. At one point she exclaims, with a broad smile, and in that vibrant tone that is quite inimitable: 'Orlandini! Orlandini! . . .' He looks round: 'Signora, please let me go on with my reading. After all, I have never tackled this role before.' Further exclamations from the Signora: 'Ah, how fortunate you are! That is what it means to be a young actor! I, on the contrary, have even been reduced to playing *Odette*! And when one approaches one's centenary!' (She is clearly referring to the proposal that Ettore della Porta made to her some time ago that we should commemorate Eleonora Duse's fiftieth birthday – a proposal that she has still not been able to persuade him to abandon and that she treats as a joke.) And she goes on: 'Ah! But when that day comes . . . when that great day finally comes, I shall make my escape to Japan! . . . Yes, dear friends, to Japan. And you can all send me a telegram!'

The whole cast is in good spirits and the Signora's words only add to the general mirth. At one point, the uproar becomes so great that she turns round and, still smiling, cries out: 'Children! . . . Children! . . . Quiet now, please!' That is enough to restore order. And so we finally come to the end of *Odette*. I am not sure with how much profit either for us or for the play. But, as far as the Signora is concerned, her opinion is unequivocal: 'These old plays are no longer fit to be heard! It is shameful that we should be expected to go on acting in them. And how are our efforts rewarded? Have you seen the reviews? . . . Have you seen how they acclaim *Hedda Gabler* and our production of the play? Therefore, it simply is not true to say that audiences continue to enjoy watching *Fernanda* and *Fedora* and, God help me! – *La signora delle camelie*! It simply is not true! We are the victims of ignorant and stubborn impresarios . . .'

One might question this reasoning, but to question anything with Eleonora Duse is quite impossible. For she possesses the most extraordinary powers of persuasion. And while she may not always be capable of expressing something profound or even logical, no one finds it easy to contradict her. The allure emanating from that voice and those eyes is enough to disarm anyone. One feels a sudden longing to cry out to her: 'But, of course, you are right, you sweet and delightful creature!' She is continually saying the most paradoxical things, even to the point of talking rubbish. But her voice is so heavenly! Her teeth so perfect, her smile so winning! That is how La Duse strikes one: for, despite everything, despite the fact that she is about to celebrate her fiftieth birthday, despite the lines on her face and her grey hairs, La Duse is *beautiful*.

This evening at the Teatro San Pedro there is a ceremony to commemorate Garibaldi's achievement.[49] The Signora sends the local committee a delightful letter with 800 lire. To Bergonzio she hands an envelope containing some money, urging him to celebrate this *solemn anniversary*.

Tomorrow, at the same hour, there is a rehearsal of *Fedora*.

Rio de Janeiro, 5 July 1907
The rehearsal is suspended. Tomorrow evening, we perform *Monna Vanna*.

Rio de Janeiro, 6 July 1907
Because of the Signora's indisposition, the performance has been cancelled. Tomorrow we give a matinée performance of *Odette*.

Rio de Janeiro, 7 July 1907
There is scarcely anyone in the theatre at today's matinée! Acts III and IV provoke an outburst of applause.

Tomorrow, at two-thirty, there will be rehearsals for *Fedora* at the Signora's hotel.

Rio de Janeiro, 8 July 1907

This morning at the theatre I meet Consigli and, together with Lavaggi, we talk about La Duse and her latest fiasco. Consigli is dismayed. It pleases me to note, however, that in spite of everything his admiration for Eleonora Duse is greater than ever. He keeps on saying: 'What an artist! Such genius! Every Italian actress from Tina di Lorenzo to the Gramatica sisters has been influenced by La Duse!' Then the discussion turns to Brazilian audiences and theatre critics. It is reported that only yesterday one of the city's most prominent critics attended the show at the Palace Theatre where the Vitale Operetta Company is appearing in preference to the matinée starring Eleonora Duse!

We also discuss press reactions to the company in general and the plays in our repertoire. One critic has had the impudence to suggest that Eleonora Duse is even inferior to the supporting actors in her own company! Another critic, launching an attack on Orlandini, says he looks like a sacristan onstage, and the same critic rebukes Robert for posturing like a ballet master! 'And to think,' Consigli angrily exclaims, 'that they have welcomed third-rate French companies with open arms! What *do* they want?'

At two-thirty the cast is assembled at the hotel. Upon entering the salon, the Signora immediately inquires: 'What rubbish are we rehearsing today?' The rehearsal itself begins amidst the greatest uproar. The entire hotel is turned upside down; there are builders wherever one turns. Hammers and picks are causing a terrific noise. During Act I, when Bergonzio has to make his entrance as the porter, the Signora exclaims, clapping her hands: 'Ah, so this is why we are playing this comedy; it's being played for the sake of Bergonzio! Bravo, Bergonzio!' And suddenly she smiles, and the frown that clouded her expression a few minutes earlier disappears, and she looks radiant and transformed. Another Duse now confronts us, younger and more beautiful! And so the rehearsal proceeds rapidly, without any further hitches. Tomorrow evening, we give a performance of *Monna Vanna*.

Rio de Janeiro, 9 July 1907

A reasonable house. No lack of applause. Two curtain calls after the first act, five curtain calls after the second, and three at the end of the play. The Signora is in excellent form. Her acting this evening is most impressive. On the whole, the performance is a huge success, also to the credit of other members of the cast. As usual, the Signora, had some criticism to offer about the lighting effects. The theatre has the most primitive lighting equipment imaginable, consisting of white lamps and gas burners. Thus, despite the strenuous efforts made by Almirante, the lighting effects desired – and these tend to vary – are totally lacking. The Signora can be heard murmuring: 'Ah, that is lovely! ... lovely!' ... only to conclude by saying: 'Really, it is quite pointless bringing any scenery on tour ...'

Tomorrow we have a rehearsal in the theatre at two-thirty of *Seconda moglie* and *La moglie di Claudio*.

On Thursday, the day after tomorrow, there is a gala evening in honour of Eleonora Duse. The programme will consist of *La moglie di Claudio* and *Visita di nozze*.

Rio de Janeiro, 10 July 1907
In conversation with Orlandini this afternoon, I learn that the Signora is constantly receiving anonymous letters written in perfect Italian, and all of them more or less abusive. One of these letters is couched in the following terms: *'You are not La Duse; the real Duse has remained in Italy!'*

Orlandini attributes all this hostility to the Signora's being too much of a recluse. She has obstinately refused to receive the local aristocracy, who appear to be all-powerful in this country. She simply refuses to waste her time socializing in fashionable Rio circles. Here in Brazil, the students, for example, exert considerable pressure. In the theatre, they can swing the balance between success or failure. To make enemies of the student community is to expose oneself to severe reprisals ... I understand that La Duse has decided not to receive some student delegation or other. A grave mistake! Such, at any rate, is the opinion of those who know about local pressure groups. I modestly prefer to back the Signora in these matters.

At today's rehearsal, the Signora is in a black mood. She rehearses *La moglie di Claudio*, then scrupulously takes us through the script of *Seconda moglie*, a play for which she has a special liking. Nothing worthy of note emerges.

Some inevitable gossip among the actors about any colleague who is missing from rehearsals. And other minor intrigues that are commonplace in theatrical circles. Today, the subject of conversation is La Scalambretti, who, having been assigned a walk-on part in yesterday's performance of *Monna Vanna*, goes around saying to everyone: 'Never in my whole career have I been asked to do a walk-on part! This is the first time! The very first time!' Whereupon Orlandini's wife retorts: 'I, on the contrary, have spent my entire career doing walk-on parts . . . But, cheer up! For this evening's understudy might easily become tomorrow's leading lady! That's life!' It is not the first time that La Scalambretti has provided some amusement for her fellow actors. Nor is it likely to be the last!

Pittei comes out with a delightful slip of the tongue in *Seconda moglie*. In Act III, instead of saying: 'I shall pen a line to uncle Frink', he says: 'I shall line a Frink to my uncle.'[50] The Signora can barely suppress her laughter. On the subject of slips of the tongue, the prompter Faggioli tells me a gem concerning the actor Carlo Rosaspina one evening in Budapest during the first act of *L'altro pericolo*. The line went: 'I recall that it was on a summer's day', and Rosaspina said instead: 'I recall that it was a summer's dog',[51] whereupon La Duse retorted between clenched teeth: 'You are the only dog here.'

Rio de Janeiro, 11 July 1907

All of us expect the theatre to be filled to capacity on an evening like this – but quite the contrary! The audience can only be described as adequate, . . . even though the Brazilian President and his family are present. The programme opens with *Visita di nozze*. La Duse, her nerves on edge, is greeted with an outburst of applause and a shower of roses. She is interrupted by applause half way through the play, and at the end she takes three curtain calls. In *La moglie di Claudio* she scores a tremendous success and is interrupted, especially during the second act by continual shouts of acclaim, which become thunderous towards the end. Two doves are released into the auditorium and two baskets of flowers are presented to La Duse onstage. One is particularly beautiful, a tribute from the Brazilian President, with flowers depicting the Brazilian colours. The other bearing ribbons in the Italian colours is from a well-known family here called Jannuzzi. There are also tributes from the impresario Consigli and from a group of students.

Next, the Signora is given a fan made from large feathers and decorated with the exotic plumes of a humming bird. Then, she is presented with a bronze plaque, still unfinished, which will be handed over to her before she finally leaves the city. After the third act, a group of students come backstage and begin chanting wildly outside the Signora's dressing room. The Signora comes to the door, speaks to them quietly, and expresses her gratitude. But as she leaves the theatre they are still there, crowding round her automobile. More cheering and clapping. She gets into the back seat in great haste and, once the door is firmly closed, she smiles through the window, waving her hand with a gesture that seems to say: 'Now you may shout to your heart's content. I am safely out of your reach!' She is mistaken. For no sooner has the automobile started to move away than all the students climb aboard a second automobile to follow that of the Signora, shouting their heads off all the while . . . A decent enough bunch of lads, despite the uproar!

Tomorrow, at the hotel, we shall rehearse *Rosmersholm* and *Fiamme nell'ombra*.

Rio de Janeiro, 12 July 1907

The rehearsal is held in the theatre instead of at the hotel as previously arranged. The Signora arrives late, looking very agitated. She begins to rehearse *Rosmersholm*. In the stalls some cleaners are sweeping the carpets and sending up clouds of dust. La Duse turns on them and snaps furiously: 'Will you stop that at once! May God damn you a thousand times in Italian, Portuguese, Spanish, English, Turkish and Arabic. Is one never to know a moment's peace in this place! The hotel is unbearable; so one comes here, and, if anything, this place is even worse! What do you think I am? A horse? A donkey? A machine? For God's sake! Everybody here does just as he pleases! I seem to be the only one who is expected to behave with some restraint and discipline.'

In the scene with Mortensgard (played by Capellaro), the Signora loses her patience because the actor seems uncertain of his lines and fails to comply with her directions from a previous rehearsal. She screams at him: 'No, no, no! You must try to appear more vicious and malevolent . . . but then perhaps you are always an angel in real life? Lucky you! But you do not know your part! And that won't do. I can tolerate bad acting, but when an actor doesn't know his part . . . that thoroughly upsets me! Tomorrow, Signor Orlandini, you will rehearse this scene once more with Signor Capellaro.'

Indeed, tomorrow there is yet another rehearsal of *Rosmersholm* and *Seconda moglie*. The play scheduled for tomorrow evening is *Seconda moglie*. It will be our penultimate performance because the Signora has ordered two evening performances that are restricted to season-ticket holders to be cancelled and the money refunded.

Rio de Janeiro, 13 July 1907

Few people in the theatre but the play itself is an enormous success. This evening at the Teatro Carlos Gomes the Drama Company of Gustavo Salvini makes its debut with *La morte civile*. Tomorrow at one-thirty a rehearsal in the theatre of *Rosmersholm* and *Fiamme nell'ombra*.

Rio de Janeiro, 14 July 1907

The Signora turns up unexpectedly during today's rehearsal. She has some observations to make to Signorina Verani, who played the role of Elena last night in *Seconda moglie*. She says to her: 'You, Signorina, have one real merit: your approach is straightforward, and you don't go in for ham acting. But you go too far in the opposite direction. You must put more life into the part . . . Last night, instead of leading me, I had to lead you . . . and I was not very successful. You are much too timid! . . . You come face to face with your fellow actors . . . then, without any warning, you turn your back on them and scuttle off . . . Put some life into it, girl, some life, do you hear! Come along now!'

Today's rehearsal of *Rosmersholm* meets with her approval. She even appears to have softened in her attitude to *Fiamme nell'ombra*, which always seems to leave her lukewarm. Tomorrow, at the same hour, we have another rehearsal.

I take myself to the Teatro Carlos Gomes to see Gustavo Salvini play *Otello*. The theatre is quite full and the performance a well-deserved triumph. Gustavo Salvini belongs to a generation of actors that is now much maligned, and he lives in the shadow of his father's glory.

Judging from this evening's performance, Gustavo Salvini is a most scrupulous and polished actor. His interpretation satisfies me on several counts. And if from time to time his effects misfire, his acting on the whole is varied, accurate in detail, finely balanced, and wholly individual. His interpretation of this difficult Shakespearian role is clearly the fruit of long experience and a careful study of the text, and it provides a most illuminating account of this magnificent tragedy. I applaud the performance with warmth and sincerity.[52] It is sad, nevertheless, to observe the mediocrity of the supporting cast, the shabby costumes and sets, all of which are clearly third rate! What a pity!

Tomorrow there is no performance. But on Tuesday they are

[98]

playing *La bisbetica domata.*[53]

Rio de Janeiro, 15 July 1907

The Signora also attends today's rehearsals, and the rehearsal of *Rosmersholm* alone lasts for almost three hours. La Duse's passion for Ibsen is unbelievable. Hers is a true apostolate. Her diction in this play reveals such genius, such a wealth of ideas and depth of vision!

The other actors, naturally enough, end up by loathing Ibsen. They are not accustomed to having to analyse their roles to this extent. Their Latin temperament rebels. And as for the public, it is certainly not sophisticated enough to appreciate this type of play. Yet I believe that the day is not far off when these dramas will finally gain popularity. Much of the glory and credit will be

The distinguished Norwegian playwright Henrik Ibsen whose plays became the focal point of Duse's repertoire in later years. The Italian actress quickly established herself as one of Europe's most subtle and individual interpreters of Ibsen's heroines. Ibsen replaced D'Annunzio as the 'inner light and force' sustaining her career, and she avowed an instinctive rapport with Ibsen's 'poetic realism' and the dramatist's psychological penetration of the feminine soul. (Photograph by courtesy of the Norwegian National Library, Oslo.)

due to Eleonora Duse and a handful of others who have made strenuous efforts to bring about this worthwhile change in public taste.

Most actors refuse to understand this, including leading members of Duse's own company and foremost among them is Beltramo, a character actor, a former director of companies both good and indifferent, an actor who believes that he is acting *in the modern style* without realizing, alas, that he isn't even capable of acting in *the traditional style*. Otherwise, he is a decent fellow and an excellent companion. In my opinion, his one serious fault is his unfortunate habit of speaking disrespectfully about the artistry of Eleonora Duse. He is constantly finding something to ridicule in everything the Signora does or says. Really! Why don't they leave the poor woman in peace!

Rio de Janeiro, 16 July 1907

Today there is a rehearsal of *Fiamme nell'ombra* at the Hotel Corcovado, where Orlandini and his wife are staying, as well as Masi and all the ladies in the Company. I have no part in this play by Butti, but decide to accompany my fellow actors on an excursion to the summit of the Corcovado Mountain, one of the great sights of Rio.

The ascent up this extremely high mountain is in itself an experience, with magnificent scenery all the way. The funicular railway climbs the most incredible slope between enormous crags and rocks, scorched and reddish in colour and inhabited by lizards of every species. Or it penetrates luxuriant vegetation of dense shrubs and tall, slender trees entangled with enormous creepers and every manner of parasitic plant hanging in clusters, like festoons or arboreal stalactites swaying with the slightest breeze.

The sun hovers over the crest of this imposing vegetation, like an immense umbrella of dazzling light, beneath which the atmosphere is fresh and moist, criss-crossed by inumerable currents of air and speckled by multicoloured butterflies that flutter restlessly in mid-air close to the sun. And meanwhile our little train continues its dizzy ascent, gingerly winding its way across an iron bridge, at once narrow and tortuous, which is slung over a bottomless chasm, its depths concealed by a vast plantation of huge banana trees, whose large protective leaves cover the ground below.

The human eye is blinded by the glare of distant light . . . To the right there stretches a strip of the bay surrounded by black mountains and several tiny islands. And nearby is a section of Rio neatly dissected by a green elevation dotted with shanty towns.

Overwhelmed by so much beauty and seized momentarily by dizziness, we go up and up . . . And the scenery is transformed and enriched by further discoveries. The panorama widens, the atmosphere becomes as subtle and pure as the thoughts in our heads at this prodigious height. There is nothing quite like an expanse of wild, uninhabited territory for purifying the soul . . .

And so we eventually reach the hotel at the summit, a large white building of monastic austerity, hemmed in on the left by the mountain, which becomes increasingly more rugged, and on the right by a forest of dark green vegetation looking almost black, and broken by broad, flat avenues bordered by the aqueduct that provides Rio with fresh, crystal-clear water. The silence that reigns here is sacred, broken intermittently by the roaring of the mighty ocean that stretches out beneath us, blue and immense, by the rustling of the wind, or by the gurgling of the streams that run into the reservoirs through vast filters before making their descent towards the great city.

The custodian of this unique spot, along with the mountain streams and forest, is a magnificent black mastiff, tall and highly-strung with a long, noble snout and white markings. Agile and friendly, the mastiff receives visitors with much tail-wagging, and extends hospitality with obvious pleasure and courtesy.

Continuing our ascent towards the highest peak, the path becomes ever more inclined, indeed almost vertical, flanked on the left by the rock and forest and on the right, overlooking the green chasm below, gaping and terrifying.

With dread one thinks of a possible derailment. And, if courageous enough to look out, one is forced to shut one's eyes, feeling suddenly small and insignificant, assailed by a sudden attack of vertigo and a sensation of falling into space. One's whole body suddenly becomes limp and for a second experiences the curious sensation of being lifeless.

Upon recovering, we open our eyes to find that the little train has come to a halt just below the topmost summit of Corcovado, which we soon scale by quickly climbing, four abreast, the steps of the broad twisting elevation that leads to a circular pavilion. It is a spacious and graceful construction made of iron and wood, the ultimate destination on this delightful excursion. Two more steps and we find ourselves on a rectangular terrace with an open parapet on three sides at the level of the mountain's peak. Spreading out before us is a vision of extraordinary beauty and variety. The whole bay can be seen with its sixty tiny islands enclosed by the Serra dos Orgãos,[54] the waters furrowed in every direction by tiny boats and steamers, and several naval vessels. The sea, more calm than the clear sky above, is encircled by an ocean belt that spreads into infinite space on one's right. Further along, is the beach at Leme, the houses along the coastline of Ipanema, and the tall palm trees of the Botanical Garden; then beyond lies the cemetery that appears all white and green. The beach at Botafogo forms a magnificent crescent directly facing the Sugar Loaf Mountain and the red buildings of Rio's Military Academy. Finally, there's a view of all Rio, broken here and there by green hills and enchanting gardens, and way down in the valley below, the great dark shadow of Corcovado itself. We descend as evening falls; the air is cool and the darkness intense: the first evening lights go on in Rio. Overhead, the sky disappears and the thick expanse of darkness is dotted with twinkling stars. We are safely back in the city.

Our farewell appearance with *Rosmersholm*. The theatre is crowded. The scenic arch is decorated with a festoon of laurels and roses and a wide scarlet banner with gold lettering that reads: '*Salve Duse*'. The top of the prompter's box is hidden by an

The celebrated view of the Bay of Guanabara, Rio de Janeiro, as seen from the summits of Corcovado enthusiastically described in some detail by Noccioli. The extended entry for 16 July 1907 betrays a keen eye for visual detail and a genuine flair for colourful descriptive prose. (Photograph by courtesy of The Library of Congress, Washington.)

enormous garland of roses. The balustrade of the gallery is decorated with lots of tiny white flags bearing the same inscription:
'*Salve Duse*'. Long before the performance begins, there is much
coming and going of students – the organizers of this evening's
festivities – as they busy themselves preparing little bunches of
flowers.

Outside the stage door there is a sudden uproar. The door bursts
open under the weight of a group of students all shouting together
in a mixture of Italian and Portuguese. They wish to speak to La
Duse. It is pointed out to them that this is impossible. So they
demand to see Orlandini. He comes to find out what they want.
A Neapolitan acts as spokesman for the others: 'On behalf of all
my fellow students I wish to ask a special favour. We cannot
afford to pay for any tickets for this evening's performance . . .
and we greatly desire to pay our homage to the magnificent and
divine Eleonora Duse as well as to the genius of Ibsen.[55] Therefore
we beg of you to allow us to attend the performance with complimentary tickets.'

In reply, Orlandini tries to raise some objection to this proposal,
but he is silenced by a torrent of eulogies praising the great Duse
and a persuasive little speech along the following lines: 'We
would not insist upon making this plea were we not anxious to
study *Rosmersholm*, and since there are likely to be few opportunities of seeing this play being performed again in Brazil in the
near future, it would be unfair to deprive us of this rare privilege.
We only ask to be allowed to study and admire the play. We are
motivated by a sincere desire to learn rather than to seek mere
pleasure, so we beseech you to let us in gratis.'

These subtle arguments were convincingly expressed, and
Orlandini capitulated. Orlandini had a brief word with Consigli,
and the Impresario agreed that they should be allowed to attend
the performance without paying. And so the theatre very quickly
filled up. The President was present on this occasion too, accompanied by his family. After each act there was vociferous acclaim
for La Duse and showers of bouquets. After Act III, she is presented
with a most beautiful basket of roses and three garlands tied with
red, white and green ribbons. And as soon as the fourth act is
over, a delegation goes onstage to escort La Duse to the theatre
foyer where a huge crowd has gathered. La Duse is still in costume
– the grey outfit that she wears as Rebecca – which features a
large silk veil covering her head and draped around her throat.
Still playing her role, she watches the unveiling of a black marble

plinth inscribed in gold:[56]

ELEONORA DUSE
ROSMERSHOLM
HOMAGE TO GENIUS

Next the Signora is presented with an enormous spray of laurel, together with a large garland of exquisite artificial flowers decorated with a white ribbon bearing the inscription:

TO THE GENIUS OF ELEONORA DUSE.
FROM THE STUDENTS OF RIO DE JANEIRO

Much applause, many eulogies, much raising of hats and, above the din, a loud fanfare of indefatigable trumpets.

Then La Duse is invited to mount an automobile flanked by several students. And off they depart in the direction of her hotel, amidst the most incredible uproar and applause. The procession is headed by a platoon of the Brazilian cavalry and a military fanfare. Then comes the automobile with the Signora – and finally, a long cortège of automobiles crammed with students bearing lanterns. Enormous crowds line the pavements. From a tall balcony flares in white, red and green are lighted; from another balcony flowers are scattered on the crowd. Applause breaks out wherever one turns. Every so often La Duse looks out of the car window and smiles. She is deathly pale. Windows everywhere open at the sound of the trumpets, and faces peer out with every manner of expression – dazed, bewildered, astonished, glowering, smiling, stupefied.

It is one o'clock in the morning when we finally arrive at the hotel, which is brightly illuminated. The square below the Signora's windows is packed with people, and a military band provides music. No sooner does La Duse enter her hotel than the

---

Facing   Duse in the role of Rebecca in Ibsen's *Rosmersholm*. The Italian critic G. A. Borgese wrote of this performance: 'Anyone who has seen Duse interpret Rebecca in *Rosmersholm* will recognize that no one on the Italian stage today is so resolutely avant-garde in matters of stage technique . . . her statuesque poses and moments of silence are almost more significant than the spoken lines . . .' (Photograph from the Nunes Vais Collection by courtesy of the Istituto Centrale per il Catalogo e la Documentazione, Rome.)

[105]

porters lock the main entrance to prevent admirers from pursuing her inside, but, undaunted, some of them clamber through a large window that has been inadvertently left open, and they come rushing into the hotel foyer, causing a terrific uproar. Little by little, order is eventually restored.

At two o'clock in the morning, these pleasant but exhausting revelries finally come to an end. Better late than never! With this reckless display of enthusiasm, some Brazilians have tried to make amends for some of the wrongs done to our great artist by the press. And so we end our season, which has run for almost four weeks. During this period we gave no fewer than ten out of the twelve subscription performances scheduled, including three new plays: *Hedda Gabler, Monna Vanna* and *Rosmersholm*. Plus three matinées for the general public.

The financial rewards have been meagre. The backers are reported to have put up nearly seventy thousand francs, a thing unheard of when Eleonora Duse tours. As for the artistic success of the tour, the local press has waged an intransigent and wholly unjustified campaign against our great Duse, comparing her with second rate actresses who are in every sense inferior. Some critics have even shown themselves to be totally lacking in chivalry towards La Duse as a woman, accusing her of being arrogant and *stupid*. And the public? Indifferent to begin with, and madly enthusiastic as the season progressed.

Tomorrow we leave for São Paulo on board a special train.

São Paulo, 18 July 1907

We have an excellent journey. We travel with the Signora in a luxurious carriage placed at her disposal by the President of the Republic. This morning we stop for almost two hours at some station or other in order to change trains. The Signora is in a most jovial mood and breakfasts in our company after having spent quite some time in our carriage chatting about all manner of things. In the station itself, she does some physical exercises with her masseuse and Luciana Rossi. A large crowd gathers in the station and applauds excitedly.

We open at the Teatro Sant'Ana on Saturday 20 July with *Hedda Gabler*.

São Paulo, 19 July 1907

Today everyone is asked to be at the Hotel Sportsman where the Signora is staying by five o'clock. The rehearsal is to be held in an enormous salon on the ground floor. The Signora arrives fifteen minutes early. From the expression on her face, it is quite obvious that she is suffering from nervous strain. She mutters in a low voice: 'We shall rehearse several scenes from *Hedda Gabler*; the others who are not involved may leave.' So those who have no part in the play gratefully withdraw. The women embrace each other effusively. 'Bye, bye, darling . . . goodbye, dearie . . . until this evening . . . until tomorrow . . . enjoy your outing.' La Duse, seated near the prompter, expresses her annoyance and disapproval. 'Really, what an affected lot they are . . . I suppose they might as well get it out of their system . . . But really, what a bunch of hypocrites . . . quite insincere . . . nothing but hypocrites.'

The rehearsal begins – a rehearsal conducted in whispers, as if in a dream – and almost otherworldly. The Signora continues to be irritable. Lavaggi complains of feeling unwell, La Scalambretti is indisposed, and Orlandini and Spinelli, who have been quarrelling, glare at each other. Robert limps across the stage, moaning about his leg, which is apparently giving him a great deal of pain. La Rossi is wearing a most attractive new outfit and cannot resist admiring herself in the mirror every five minutes. Orlandini's wife is as gloomy and silent as a tomb, and as for me . . . I make myself scarce.

São Paulo, 20 July 1907

A most unfortunate opening night even though there is a good house. Only one curtain call after each act and not much enthusiasm on the part of the audience. The Signora seems quite listless, and *Hedda Gabler* is obviously not a suitable play for South American audiences.

Tomorrow, at the hotel, there is a rehearsal of *Fiamme nell'ombra*.

São Paulo, 22 July 1907

This morning the Signora gives full vent to her resentment against Brazil and the Brazilians. This outburst is apparently provoked by some comments made by the impresario Consigli, which were subsequently repeated to La Duse. She rants: 'The Management has the effrontery to go around saying that I am being paid too much! I have sent word back to them that if they wish to cancel the performances in São Paulo nothing would please me more. I am sick and tired of their nonsense, and I flatly refuse to tolerate any more interviews, receptions, or any other futile activities calculated to waste my precious time. It is outrageous! To listen to these wretches, one would think they actually expected me to

[107]

The old Teatro Sant'Ana in the Rua Boa Vista in São Paulo where Duse's company appeared from 18 July until 4 August 1907. Built by the Brazilian industrialist Antonio Alvares Penteado, the theatre was inaugurated on 18 May 1900. The building was used as a theatre until 1911 and subsequently demolished in 1912. (By courtesy of the Estado de São Paulo.)

sit down and eat spaghetti at the same table. Me! Eleonora Duse! Who do they think they are dealing with? Do they forget that I have been touring the world for twenty years? I am a serious artist and not some charlatan! Fools that they are! Why did they bring me here in the first place? Elsewhere I can count on loyal audiences who appreciate true art and are willing to pay for the privilege. Where is the great fortune they claim I am making here? It is a well-known fact that in Europe I can command six or seven thousand lire for each performance. Here they have guaranteed me ten thousand, but my personal expenses are higher, so where is the profit at the end of the day? No! no! No longer do I believe there's any future for Brazil. These people are fools! What pleasure do I derive from wasting time in this god-forsaken country!'

Then she begins to rehearse the last act of *Fiamme nell'ombra* but as she finishes she remarks: 'It is hopeless trying to rehearse! Anyhow, I cannot feel this part. The more I study it, the less I seem to get out of it. No! no! It is quite impossible. Let's stop now and speak of it no more. Take up the script of *Tutto per nulla*, which is also by Butti.'

Tomorrow at one o'clock the cast for the Butti play will be chosen. Tomorrow evening our second performance with *La Gioconda*.

São Paulo, 23 July 1907

By one o'clock sharp everyone is waiting at the hotel. The Signora, however, does not appear. Parts are distributed for *Tutto per nulla*. Then there is an initial reading of the text. The general feeling among members of the Company is that this second play by Butti will meet the same fate as *Fiamme nell'ombra*.

Delfini, however, is delighted because he is given an attractive part as the juvenile lead. This good fortune also has the virtue, as Lavaggi maliciously points out to me, of suddenly restoring Delfini's confidence in La Duse's genius! Just think what a good part can achieve! For, recently, Delfini has always been the first to assert that Duse's fame is greater than her acting ability nowadays justifies. But, for the moment, he holds a quite different opinion. Today, for example, upon coming away from the rehearsal, the cast discusses the play and the leading lady's role, and we are all in agreement that it is not a particularly well-conceived part and totally unsuitable for the Signora. But Delfini, with a devotion hitherto unheard of, argues vehemently that La Duse, with her talents, intelligence, etc., etc., will know precisely how to transform the role into a masterpiece of characterization. We shall see!

One cannot resist quoting a line from *Monna Vanna* when the heroine exclaims in Act III: 'Ah! Men are such fools . . .'[57] It is a great pity because Delfini has some excellent qualities and he is, on the whole, an agreeable companion. But then, no one is perfect.

At this evening's performance there is a magnificent house, and the play scores a veritable triumph. La Duse is at the height of her powers.

Tomorrow at three-thirty there will be a rehearsal at the hotel of *Tutto per nulla*.

São Paulo, 24 July 1907

We rehearse *Tutto per nulla* amidst continuous asides and tittering provoked by certain absurdities in the text and by some of the dialogue that is frankly banal. The Signora's moods alternate between melancholy and cheerfulness. We are still asking ourselves why she persists in rehearsing the play . . .

Tomorrow at one o'clock another rehearsal and in the evening our third subscription performance with *Magda*.

São Paulo, 25 July 1907

The rehearsal is held in the theatre instead of at the hotel. The Signora does not attend. At this evening's performance of *Magda* a packed house, but not quite equal to those of the two previous evenings. A wonderful success. Innumerable curtain calls, especially after Acts III and IV.

Tomorrow at three o'clock a rehearsal of *Tutto per nulla* at the hotel.

São Paulo, 26 July 1907

Today, once again, the rehearsal is held in the theatre instead of at the hotel. The Signora is nowhere to be seen. Some interesting news . . . La Scalambretti is about to become engaged to a wealthy Italian businessman who has settled here in São Paulo. I say *about to become engaged* because she has not yet made up her mind. He is head over heels in love with her and prepared to marry La Scalambretti tomorrow if she will only consent. But she wants time to consider the matter. Meantime, the rest of us are looking forward to throwing confetti!

Tomorrow at one o'clock another rehearsal of *Tutto per nulla* in the theatre and in the evening the fourth subscription performance with *Seconda moglie*, which is new to São Paulo.

São Paulo, 27 July 1907

The rehearsal has been cancelled. No reasons are given. This evening the theatre is not exactly full. The first two acts are well received; then a tremendous ovation after Acts III and IV. La Duse is jumpy and tense to the point of appearing to be paralysed. Yet her acting is superb, especially from Act II onwards. I watch the performance from the front stalls, in order to have a better view of the stage. And so I am able to study every single detail of her extraordinary facial expressions and the thousand-and-one subtleties and nuances that make the Signora's acting unique. Her interpretation of the role certainly ranks among the most beautiful and complete performances in my experience.

Tomorrow at one-thirty there is a matinée for the general public at reduced prices with a performance of *La signora delle camelie*.

São Paulo, 28 July 1907

A full theatre today and an enthusiastic audience. The Signora is as nervous as ever. After the last act, as she comes to the footlights with Orlandini to thank the audience as they give her a frenzied ovation, she is muttering: 'Cretins . . . Imbeciles!'

This strikes me as going too far! But it is true that by and large audiences here are intellectually somewhat inferior to European audiences. Even the Italian section of the community consists mainly of butchers, grocers and the like. One only needs to overhear some snatch of their conversation during the interval or after the performance in order to form some impression of their intellectual level.

I myself have heard some amusing comments well worth the telling. The Italians who are engaged in the following conversation are dressed in the height of fashion and have just been watching *Hedda Gabler* from their private box or the most expensive seats in the stalls. After the final act of *Hedda Gabler*, one young man sums up the plot for another who has missed the performance as follows: '*Hedda Gabler*? A very weird lady indeed, who plays the piano and then commits suicide!' But at this point a fair-haired young man is passing who claims to have been backstage and he chimes in: 'It wasn't Hedda Gabler who was playing the piano: there was a pianist hidden in the wings!' And there, in a nutshell, is a complete account of Henrik Ibsen and Eleonora Duse!

Another amusing comment overheard after a performance of *Casa paterna*: 'What's so special about *that* acting? They speak just like us. If that's all it takes, then even I can consider myself a great actor!'

And, to conclude, one final gem criticizing Eleonora Duse after a performance of *Seconda moglie*: 'My dear chap, she's a good actress, that much I'll grant you, but she's far too old, and her face is not nearly so expressive as that of Della Guardia! As for the play itself! Well! It's a nice plot! But why does she have to go and kill herself? I just don't understand it! It would have been a better play if she hadn't killed herself!'

Frankly, comments such as these discourage one! Today, outside the stage door, La Duse's carriage is surrounded by such an enormous crowd of admirers that the rest of the cast find it impossible to leave the theatre until the Signora has made her departure. When she sees the entire cast waiting at the stage door, she asks what is happening, and we explain about the crowd blocking the exit. She says: 'Perhaps I should sleep here this evening! Then, after a pause, she draws her large silver-grey veil over her hat and around her throat, exclaiming: 'Don't worry, they will do us no harm when they see this face!' and out she marches to face the crowd courageously. The moment she appears the fans begin clapping their hands and shouting: 'Brava Duse', but her carriage is gone in a flash.

Tomorrow at three o'clock we rehearse Fulda's one-act comedy *A quattr'occhi* and at four o'clock there is yet another rehearsal of *Tutto per nulla*.

São Paulo, 29 July 1907

After the rehearsal of *A quattr'occhi* with La Verani, La Zucchini, Robert, Pittei and Capellaro in the cast, the Signora arrives shivering from the cold[58] and wrapped up in an enormous black cape with a sable collar. Then the rehearsal of *Tutto per nulla* begins. The Signora reads her part. Every so often she shakes her head or quietly smiles and says to the prompter: 'Remove that line . . . cut that . . . and that . . .'

During Act II she is visibly shocked by a scene of some violence in which Roberto has to strike Alberico. She cries out: 'Good Lord, how vulgar . . .! We must try to tone this scene down . . .' and she rehearses this particular scene over and over again, changing the stage positions a number of times and constantly introducing new and surprising details. She then goes on to make further cuts to Act III. Suddenly she exclaims: 'Perhaps we should replace *Tutto per nulla* with a performance of *Poco o nulla*.[59] Hhmm! It is difficult to say which is better. I can see myself still changing the play on the night of the performance . . . I am still uncertain about the details . . . Let's start with *Tutto per nulla*, and then go on to the last act of *L'altro pericolo*.'

Tomorrow there is a rehearsal of *A quattr'occhi* and in the evening our fifth subscription performance with *Monna Vanna*.

São Paulo, 30 July 1907

A good audience and a reasonable ovation. The Signora looks calm and relaxed.

Tomorrow we meet in the theatre to rehearse *A quattr'occhi*, then at the hotel a reading of *La donna del mare* by Ibsen!!! The exclamation marks are meant to convey the feelings of those actors who have been given a part in the play. Everyone is nervous at the prospect.

São Paulo, 31 July 1907

The prompter is in bed with a bad cold. The temperature has suddenly dropped after a day of incessant rain. The cold is unbearable! At the hotel we find the Signora ready to start the rehearsal. We begin reading the script immediately.

Almirante is auditioned for the role normally played by Faggioli (having substituted for the same actor in *La Gioconda* during the Rio season). He sits beside the Signora and begins to rehearse his part. As he reads, he keeps fidgeting absent-mindedly with his legs. The Signora watches him in silence, her whole expression betraying annoyance. Then, without any warning, she snatches the script from his hands and, offering it to Orlandini, she snaps: 'Do me a favour: you read it. This fellow is getting on my nerves!'

Poor Almirante is left speechless while the other actors try unsuccessfully to hide their amusement. He does not stir from his chair, as if rooted to the spot. But the Signora relentlessly lashes at him in the next breath: 'Get up and give your place to Signorina Verani!' That is the last straw! Almirante gets up and, mingling with the other members of the cast, mutters under his breath: 'That is what one gets for doing people favours!'

After the reading is over the Signora speaks sharply to the cast: 'Tomorrow I do not wish to see anyone with the script in their hand. This play must be word perfect as soon as possible so that we can be ready to perform it during the second week of our season in Buenos Aires.' Then she dismisses us.

Tomorrow at the hotel there will be a rehearsal of *La donna del mare* and in the evening a non-subscription performance in honour of Eleonora Duse with the one-act comedy *A quattr'occhi*, followed by *La moglie di Claudio*.

São Paulo, 1 August 1907

Today's rehearsal is called off. This evening, an excellent house, although by no means packed to capacity. Two curtain calls for the cast of *A quattr'occhi*.

During *La moglie di Claudio* two curtain calls after the first act; seven after the second, and four after the third. The Signora is a bundle of nerves. The prompter is still on sick leave, and Almirante is asked to take his place. During the first act, perhaps because he is prompting too loudly, or because the Signora has a genuine grudge against this goodhearted and conscientious fellow, she keeps on muttering between one cue and the next: 'Will you be quiet ... be silent ... lower your voice!' One can imagine the effect this torrent of abuse has on Almirante.

The São Paulo Academy of Music and Drama has presented a gold medal to the Signora with a diamond inset in the shape of the sun and the medal is inscribed with the words:

TO THE GENIUS OF ELEONORA DUSE
FROM THE SÃO PAULO
ACADEMY OF MUSIC AND DRAMA

She is also given a silk screen decorated with flowers by an Italian couple Signor and Signora Camba, and there is a huge basket of flowers from the Management.

Tomorrow we shall rehearse *La donna del mare*.

São Paulo, 2 August 1907

Today's rehearsal is cancelled. Tomorrow evening we give our farewell performance with *La locandiera* and *Visita di nozze*. We leave next Monday for Santos where we embark for Buenos Aires.

São Paulo, 3 August 1907

This evening everyone is in a state of excitement and nervous tension. A magnificent house and a tremendous ovation for both plays. And so this short season in São Paulo comes to an end. There have been six subscription performances, including three works new to São Paulo – *Hedda Gabler, Seconda moglie* and *Monna Vanna* – plus one matinée performance for the general public and a gala evening in honour of Duse, which was also open to the general public.

The financial rewards during this short season have been relatively better than those at Rio, but not sufficient to recoup the losses incurred by the Paradisi–Consigli Management, which has had to put up a net sum of one hundred thousand lire. The artistic success, on the other hand, is now being loudly acclaimed in both the Italian and Brazilian press, but the Brazilian public has failed on the whole to grasp the real significance of Duse's achievements. The more subtle details of her acting have been lost on the majority of theatre-goers in Brazil.

We are all hoping that in Buenos Aires La Duse will fare better and see her reputation restored. Rumour has it that the impresario Faustino da Rosa will make money on the Buenos Aires season because all the subscription performances have been sold out. We shall see. Our departure has still not been confirmed. We are awaiting a telegram from Santos announcing the arrival of our steamer.

Tomorrow morning the Signora will pay a courtesy visit to the Italian Hospital Umberto I and at two-thirty she will leave for Santos.

THE NOCCIOLI DIARIES

São Paulo, 4 August 1907

The Signora departs in a black mood. Today I encounter Orlandini, who in the course of our conversation tells me, among other things, that the moment we return to Italy she will disband the company. She is dissatisfied with all the actors. She claims that we have become slack and insubordinate, that we no longer act with any conviction or enthusiasm, and that we no longer seem to appreciate the great privilege of appearing alongside one of the world's greatest actresses.

To be fair, this is simply not true. If the actors no longer appear to be equal to the standards of acting demanded by the Signora, this is almost entirely due to her own erratic behaviour. Her own nervous condition has led to more than one crisis in recent months and has put everyone else's nerves on edge. The tension she generates onstage paralyses everyone, old and young, veterans and novices, good and mediocre alike . . . Every cue brings a sharp rebuke muttered between clenched teech, a baleful look, or some gesture of despair. And the actor on the receiving end finishes up by losing his nerve. We can only hope things will sort themselves out.

Tomorrow morning at ten o'clock we leave for Santos.

Santos, 5 August 1907

On board the steamer *Il Brasile*. A most delightful and interesting journey from São Paulo to Santos. The descent from the plateau by rail is most enjoyable. The scenery breathtaking. A long chain of gently undulating slopes, densely covered with the most incredible vegetation: the lushest greens, imposing silhouettes, austere and rugged landscapes. Every so often, unexpected bridges miraculously cross some enormous chasm. The sheer dimensions give one vertigo.

Then, after all this splendour, one is suddenly dumped in Santos – dusty, hot and squalid. At the station cafeteria, we thankfully settle down with a beer and a sandwich.

After a long wait, we are finally led on board the ship. The first impression is grim! The ship is spacious enough, but we cannot help comparing our quarters, no matter whether first or second class, with the luxury and comfort we enjoyed aboard the *Umbria*.

La Scalambretti and La Zucchini are so horrified that they decide to pay the difference and travel first class. We junior members of the company, however, resign ourselves to our fate, although some voice their protests because Lavaggi and Pittei have been given a magnificent cabin to accommodate four passengers below deck, while the rest of us are crammed into miserable cabins down in the bowels of the ship, together with the other impecunious passengers. We can only hope that the sea will remain calm.

We are due to leave at five o'clock.

The River Santos looks beautiful with green banks on either side. On the right there are signs of habitation with the odd house, but the left bank appears to be deserted except for the dense flora and fauna at the level of the water.

The gong summons us to lunch.

6 August 1907
A fine day. We are sailing smoothly at a fair speed.

8 August 1907
Yesterday the sea was rough and stormy. Almost all the passengers were confined to their cabins, even the hardiest members of our group. Only Bergonzio and Faggioli could face lunch. I find out this morning that Signorina Verani is suffering from convulsions. Today the weather is fair again. We are already sailing up the River Plate, its surface livid and muddy but otherwise placid. When he comes into breakfast this morning, Beltramo is sporting a green smoking jacket, black trousers and a polka-dotted cravat. We are due to arrive in Buenos Aires around four o'clock and expect to be on land again by five o'clock.

Before breakfast we sight Montevideo: flat territory everywhere with a green mountain lying to the left, which gives the city its name.

The pilot comes on board to navigate the ship as far as Buenos Aires, for on a previous voyage this same ship apparently remained stuck in a mud flat for forty-eight hours. Today lunch is served two hours earlier than usual.

By five o'clock we are entering the port of Buenos Aires. Twilight has already descended. A great crowd has gathered on the quayside.

La Verani's mother and brothers live in Buenos Aires. Amidst the shadows she spots her relatives (mother, brother and a little niece), and she begins shouting: 'Mamma, Mamma, Mario . . .' On the quayside three shadows can be seen springing forward simultaneously, a moving sight, as if guided by one great heart. Three handkerchiefs are waving and then three figures are huddled together until they almost form a single shape. La Verani collapses into the arms of La Masi, laughing and sobbing at the same time, overwhelmed and hysterical with joy. It seems to take an eternity to complete the landing formalities, especially for the four people in this touching little episode who have probably been dreaming of their reunion for ages!

But, when the formalities are finally completed and our baggage is checked (another tiresome business!), La Verani disembarks. Not a single word is exchanged between the actress and her relatives, but they fall on each other with such passion that every onlooker feels the beating of those hearts as they embrace each other. Despite the growing shadows, we can see their tears as they look into each other's eyes, joyful and happy as they prepare to recapture, however briefly, the consolations of a family reunion. This episode stirs us deeply as we watch from the rails. The rest of us disembark tomorrow.

Buenos Aires, 9 August 1907

At seven o'clock we are already ashore. We head straight for the Teatro Odeon, where we are due to open. Our impresario Da Rosa is ill. Today, at the same theatre, Coquelin is performing at a charity matinée on behalf of the local actors' nursing home. Also appearing there are Mimì Aguglia, Giovanni Grasso and Maiorana (members of the Sicilian troupe that is currently appearing at the Teatro San Martín),[60] with Act V from *Morte civile* and Ugo Ojetti's one-act drama *Il garofano*.

Among the singers taking part, the name of Maria Farneti catches my eye. This evening Coquelin is giving his farewell performance with *Les Précieuses ridicules* by Molière and a comedy in three acts by Musset. I have found lodgings in an Italian pension much frequented by actors. The landlord is a certain Marziano, a Neapolitan by birth and the theatre hairdresser. His wife is a true native of Bologna, voluminous, cheerful and an extraordinarily good cook. Her *tagliatelle* are celebrated in theatrical circles. I am delighted at my good fortune!

Buenos Aires, 10 August 1907

This evening I went to the Teatro San Martín. It is a benefit performance for Mimì Aguglia. The theatre is full. They play *Il garofano* by Ojetti and *La lupa*[61] by Verga. These are followed by a farce in which Musco makes the audience split its sides with laughter. Giovanni Grasso is billed to appear in the Verga play, but one of the cast comes onstage to announce that he is indisposed. Maiorana substitutes for him with great success. I learn afterwards that Grasso's indisposition is nothing more serious than a hangover after attending the baptism of a child born to some Sicilians who are resident here! This is confided to me by the theatre administrator, who urges me not to breathe a word to anyone.

Tomorrow evening there is a performance of *Juan José*.[62]

Buenos Aires, 11 August 1907

The Signora arrives in Buenos Aires this morning. She is staying at the Palace Hotel. I am told that her daughter has also arrived from England. Tomorrow evening we open with a performance of *A quattr'occhi* and *La moglie di Claudio*.

Today at the Teatro Odeon I attend a gala matinée in honour of the *Círculo de la Prensa*. Grasso, Mimì Aguglia and Maiorana present a sketch by Brogi called *Teresa*[63] with enormous success. This is followed by a splendid song recital with the participation of Garbin, Grassi, De Luca, Didur, La Farneti, La D'Albert and La Longasi Ponzone.[64] Thunderous outbursts of applause. Afterwards, Angelo Musco recites some verses by Nino Martoglio; then a German choir sings two items after which two Spanish actors, José Tallaví and Laura Socías, perform a dramatic sketch titled *El flechazo*.[65] The theatre is packed to capacity. This evening at the Teatro San Martín, the actor Grasso appears in *Juan José* before a full house, which gives him a standing ovation. Mimì Aguglia also scores a personal triumph. Aguglia is pregnant; indeed, she is soon to give birth. She plans to stay on in Buenos Aires and will only rejoin the company after the birth of her child.

Tomorrow evening's offering is *Il diritto di vivere* by Roberto Bracco.

Buenos Aires, 12 August 1907

The theatre *au complet*: a wonderful audience. A spectacle in itself. La Duse's entrance is greeted by rapturous applause. One curtain call after the first act. Constant interruptions during the scenes with Claudio in Act II and two curtain calls at the end of the act; then two curtain calls after the third act. In a word, a rather cool reception.

The reasons? There are a number of valid reasons. The audience this evening is much too anxious and bewildered. First, because of La Duse's temperament as a woman; second, because of the nature of the play itself; and third, because of La Duse's reputation as an artist. Their attention is clearly divided: people feel it necessary to study La Duse's physical presence, even the lines on her face; then, they try to come to grips with the drama, which

An unsigned caricature published in the *Revista Dramática Argentina* in 1907 to coincide with Duse's appearances in Buenos Aires. The artist's impression of the actress at the height of her fame subscribes to the popular image of an actress of rare intensity who triumphed in tragic roles. (Reproduction by courtesy of the Biblioteca Teatrale del Burcardo, Rome.)

represents a new experience for the theatre-goers here; and finally, they must reconcile themselves to the acting style of La Duse who is completely different from any other actress on the stage today. In the end, I am confident that Eleonora Duse will win them over.

On Wednesday, for our second subscription performance, we will present *La Gioconda*. Thursday will be our first performance for the general public when we present *La signora delle camelie*. Tomorrow at two o'clock in the theatre we shall rehearse *La donna del mare*.

Buenos Aires, 13 August 1907

The rehearsal takes place as arranged, but without the Signora. All the reviews in the Buenos Aires press declare that La Duse has surpassed all expectations. So much the better!

Buenos Aires, 14 August 1907

A full house this evening again, and an even warmer reception than on our opening night. Audiences are beginning to react with greater enthusiasm.

The Signora, however, continues to be testy and unpredictable. She is displeased with everything and everyone. She goes on accusing us of being sluggish and lacking in dedication and swears that she has no intention of appearing with the present company in Paris. From certain confidences made by Orlandini, it seems he is personally out of favour. There is one angry scene after another. What an unhappy state of affairs!

Buenos Aires, 15 August 1907

This evening, the first performance for the general public of *La signora delle camelie*. A magnificent house. The ovation is even greater than on previous evenings. Acts II and IV especially arouse tremendous enthusiasm. The Signora acts with much feeling and gives a wonderful performance. There is, however, one lamentable incident this evening. At the end of Act IV Orlandini slightly modifies the stage positions so that in the showdown with Armando the money is thrown quite by accident straight into the Signora's face. As soon as the curtain comes down, she gets up, livid with temper and as dangerous as any harpy, tearing at the veils around her throat and howling: 'Ah, dear God, have we come to this? How dare you attempt any such villainy with me. It is unspeakable ... you base trickster!' Orlandini mumbles an apology: 'Forgive me, Signora ... It was quite unintentional ...' 'Ah! I thought as much! ... Besides, you deliberately changed positions onstage without my permission. You are full of whims ... You must have everything your own way ... You continually disobey my instructions ... but I will have you know I give the orders here!'

And a stream of recriminations come pouring out from her lips like lava from a volcano. The angry scene that ensues is beyond description. It is impossible to capture in words the bitterness, anger, and spite that consume the Signora at such moments. The rest of the cast looks on *in terror* – that is the only word to express our dismay. Mimì Aguglia and Angelina Pagano, already contracted as juvenile leads with La Duse's Company, are waiting to greet her, but the Signora promptly shuts herself away in her dressing room and refuses to see anyone. We are all asking ourselves what the outcome of this ugly scene is likely to be.

Tomorrow evening we give our third subscription performance with *Magda*.

Buenos Aires, 16 August 1907
The usual splendid house, packed to capacity, and the performance a triumph that surpasses all previous evenings. During the third act La Duse is interrupted several times by frenzied outbursts of applause. The Signora appears to be in good humour and acts with inspiration and enthusiasm ... a superb piece of interpretation.

Tomorrow at one o'clock a rehearsal of *Tutto per nulla* in the theatre and at four o'clock a second rehearsal to be directed by the Signora at the hotel for Signorina Verani and Signorina Rossi in *Bacio* by Banville.[66]

Here is a conversation accidentally overheard between two Italians who watched this evening's performance from the gallery. A young man with excitement in his eyes and voice asks of his companion: 'Well then ... What do you think?' And the other replies as if in a daze: 'I feel mortified!' There is a novel expression to ponder, yet wholly appropriate if one is trying to sum up the feelings that most people must experience when watching and listening to Duse for the first time and finding themselves spellbound by her sheer artistry.

Buenos Aires, 17 August 1907
This evening the theatre is not quite so full. The applause is polite rather than enthusiastic. And the performance of *Seconda moglie* certainly does not achieve the success it deserves considering the play's intrinsic merits, the strong cast, and the Signora's brilliant

interpretation in the title role. This evening she is in excellent
form and performs, as only La Duse can, when she is at her best.
Orlandini looks solemn and unbending. The Signora is still not
speaking to him. We, at least, are all rather pleased (weak creatures
that we are) about his fall from grace. We like to think of it as
providential and as just retribution for the somewhat authoritarian
regime Orlandini has imposed on us since becoming the company's director. The powers vested in him by the Signora were
going to his head! A cold shower every so often for those in
authority is no bad thing!

Tomorrow we give *La Gioconda* at our first matinée performance.

Buenos Aires, 18 August 1907

Today I do not attend the performance. I am told the house was
full and the play a colossal success. Tomorrow at one o'clock there
is a dress rehearsal in the theatre of *Odette* in preparation for the
evening's performance. The company is working at a frantic pace!
No one can deny the fact! But the real question is just how long
we can keep up this effort . . .

Buenos Aires, 19 August 1907

A receptive audience! A tremendous ovation! La Duse acts beautifully this evening as the heroine in *Odette*. Such an improvement
on her performance in the same play during our Rio season! She
continues to be in a happy frame of mind – to everyone's relief.

She has not yet made her peace, however, with Orlandini, and
it looks as if they will never settle their differences. I learn from
Spinelli that before we left Santos, the Signora forwarded a letter
to Orlandini releasing him from his contract for next year's season.
This explains recent comments made by Orlandini that are not
very complimentary to the Signora and his declared intention of
never more working with Duse's company.

For some time now everyone has been aware of the Signora's
resentful behaviour towards Orlandini. I remember one evening
in Florence, during the second act of *La Gioconda*, while Orlandini
was playing the opening scene with Robert, and the Signora,
standing behind the scenes, was making exasperated gestures and
muttering: 'Good God! Good God! . . . What *is* the man saying! . . .
What *is* he trying to do? . . . Ugh!' And during a performance of
La signora delle camelie, at the end of the third act when Armando
reads the notebook and closes it, throwing it to the ground, La
Duse impatiently screamed at him: 'Bang! Come on now . . . Throw
it down . . .' and as he performed in the fourth act: 'Just listen to

him . . . Just listen to that! . . . Dear God, how can I play Margherita opposite this man . . . God help me! . . .'

These are minor episodes that help to explain the strained relations between them today.

Tomorrow we shall rehearse *Tutto per nulla* in the theatre.

Buenos Aires, 20 August 1907

A dispirited rehearsal. Tomorrow evening we give a performance of *Rosmersholm*.

Buenos Aires, 21 August 1907

A respectable audience and a full house. The first act of *Rosmersholm* is played in total silence. There is a single curtain call after each subsequent act, so, all in all, a somewhat cool reception, even if one can speak in terms of success.

Tomorrow there is a rehearsal of *Fedora* in the theatre, and tomorrow evening we have been invited to perform the second act of *La moglie di Claudio* at the Teatro Coliseo.

Buenos Aires, 22 August 1907

The benefit performance at the Teatro Coliseo for the Theatre Managements of Buenos Aires consists of a variety of offerings. The theatre itself, which is enormous, is crowded. Not a single empty seat! The programme opens with *Música de camera*, a one-act play performed by the Podestá Company[67] without much success. Then Emma Carelli sings the romanza from Mascagni's *Cavalleria rusticana*, and the duet that follows with the tenor Armanini. This is more to the audience's taste, with noisy demands for an encore. This is granted. Then La Duse performs the second act of *La moglie di Claudio*. A brilliant performance acclaimed with lengthy applause. The fourth item on the programme consists of the last scene from the fourth act of *Carmen* sung by María Gay and Zenatello. A storm of applause and cries for an encore, which is not granted this time. Finally, a duet from the last act of *Gli Ugonotti*, magnificently sung by La Laragne from the Paris Opera and by the tenor Gautier. Another great triumph. All in all, a most interesting evening, which has brought in thousands of lire for *the poor impresarios!*

Buenos Aires, 23 August 1907

Today at one-thirty a rehearsal in the theatre of *Fernanda*. And this evening the actual performance of the play, which has aroused more interest than any other play in the Signora's repertoire this season.

Tomorrow at seven-thirty there is a rehearsal of *Il cantico dei cantici* for La Verani. Then Lavaggi and Beltramo will rehearse the first act of *L'altro pericolo* at the theatre; following with a rehearsal of *Fedora* to be directed by the Signora herself at the hotel.

Buenos Aires, 24 August 1907

The Signora is in high spirits. She rehearses her own scenes from *Fedora*, jesting all the while and vowing that she will be the last actress to play the role: 'Ah! . . . How bored I am with this role . . . how bored!'

This evening's performance of *L'altro pericolo* is given a warm reception, especially Act IV.

Tomorrow there is a matinée performance of *Fernanda*.

Buenos Aires, 25 August 1907

The theatre is crowded and the performance a deserved success.

Tomorrow at one-thirty a rehearsal of *Adriana Lecouvreur* is scheduled and in the evening a subscription performance of *Fedora*.

Buenos Aires, 26 August 1907

The usual, inevitable sell-out. The first act is received in silence. La Duse muddles on incredibly. After the second act, there is one curtain call. The play's success becomes manifest during the third act when the Signora finally makes up her mind to take herself in hand and by Act IV she is acting beautifully.

Tomorrow at one-thirty we have a rehearsal of *La abbadessa di Jouarre* and *La locandiera*. Tomorrow evening there is no performance!

Buenos Aires, 27 August 1907

The ensemble scenes from *La abbadessa di Jouarre* are worked over by the cast. Before the rehearsal of *La locandiera* begins, Spinelli arrived with a letter from the Signora which Orlandini had been asked to read to us.

It is a most interesting letter. Its contents virtually constitute a lesson in how to achieve the style demanded by Goldoni's plays. The Signora's letter stresses the importance of playing him with panache and consummate elegance. She also analyses the appropriate gestures and details of make-up, etc.

Her words bring back memories of my own happy schooling as a drama student with Luigi Rasi, whose demonstrations of Fulgenzio's tantrums and Lindoro's jealous tirades[68] were perfect cameos of Goldonian characterization. Those were indeed happy days – and I feel gripped by an inexplicable nostalgia and sadness for the rest of the day.

Tomorrow at two o'clock the Signora will conduct a rehearsal of *La abbadessa di Jouarre*. Tomorrow evening, however, there is no performance.

Buenos Aires, 29 August 1907

A good audience and a warm reception. Even *Il bacio* meets with the audience's approval.

Buenos Aires, 30 August 1907

A day of intense activity. In the afternoon our third subscription matinée with *Il bacio* and *La locandiera,* and in the evening our tenth subscription performance with *Magda! La abbadessa di Jouarre* is withdrawn from the repertoire because certain good ladies who have subscribed to the season and see themselves as custodians of public morality have invoked ecclesiastical censorship. Any further performances of this *immoral* work are forbidden by the authorities. The Signora is extremely annoyed. This evening she shows signs of physical exhaustion. Back in her dressing-room, she collapses in a faint, but fortunately this attack is not serious, and she soon recovers.

Buenos Aires, 31 August 1907

This evening we present *La signora delle camelie* for our eleventh subscription performance. An unqualified success, but the Signora has all the symptoms of constant strain and nervous tension.

Buenos Aires, 1 September 1907

Today marks our fourth subscription matinée with *Fedora*. The theatre, needless to say, is crammed and there is no lack of applause. Yet the Signora is not at her best.

Tomorrow at one thirty there will be a rehearsal in the theatre of *Tutto per nulla* which is billed for Friday, 6 September!!!

Buenos Aires, 2 September 1907

The Signora participates actively in today's rehearsal. This evening, before a full house, we give our twelfth subscription performance with *Monna Vanna*. A lukewarm success – not to say frigid.

Tomorrow at two o'clock yet another rehearsal under the Signora's direction of *Tutto per nulla*. In the evening there is no performance!

Buenos Aires, 3 September 1907

We rehearse *Tutto per nulla*. The Signora reads her part! Otherwise, she seems cheerful and every so often urges the prompter: 'Take that out . . . and that . . . cut here . . . and there!' By dint of so many cuts we quickly reach the finale.

The reviews in the morning press voice serious reservations about *Monna Vanna* and accuse La Duse of having been surprisingly dreary and colourless in her acting.

Buenos Aires, 4 September 1907

Today at one-thirty a rehearsal in the theatre of *Tutto per nulla* and *Il cantico dei cantici* for Là Verani, Lavaggi and Beltramo.

This evening we give our thirteenth subscription performance with *A quattr'occhi* instead of *Il bacio* as announced. Also *La locandiera*. Fewer people in the theatre but the usual enthusiastic applause.

Buenos Aires, 5 September 1907

At one-thirty in the theatre we rehearse *Il cantico dei cantici* and at two-thirty we rehearse *Tutto per nulla* with the Signora.

One could almost say that today's rehearsal of *Tutto per nulla* is our most fruitful and promising attempt so far. I wouldn't say that the Signora has mastered her part, but she is now following the prompter with greater ease! These days she seems to prefer leaving everything to Providence!

Buenos Aires, 6 September 1907

At one-thirty there is a performance in the theatre of *Tutto per nulla* and at six o'clock the entire cast reassembles in the theatre for another rehearsal with the Signora. She arrives punctually on the hour. She takes us through the important scenes from Acts II and III over and over again until eight-thirty, then the performance itself begins with *Il cantico dei cantici* followed by *Tutto per nulla*.

The first act is moderately successful. It is a real pleasure to watch the Signora as she skilfully improvises and gives and takes cues. By Act II she appears to be almost in control of her part. Frankly, she turns in a good performance. The second act is given a tremendous ovation and Act III too, although here certain details tend to get out of hand and the standard of performance is noticeably uneven.

Things could have been worse. One amusing slip of the tongue by the actor Robert in the second act is worth mentioning. He is supposed to say: 'Oh, I had forgotten these poor flowers' instead of which he says: 'I had forgotten these ... plowers.' Naturally enough, the audience remains unaware of anything unusual.[69]

Buenos Aires, 7 September 1907

This evening marks our nineteenth subscription performance with *Hedda Gabler*. The Signora is rather nervous. Before the play begins, she comes onstage and as usual changes and rearranges the furniture. She even makes the stagehands alter the scenery so that certain defects can no longer be seen from the auditorium. She then starts ranting because the mantelpiece is not Norwegian but in the style of Louis XVI. But eventually she calms down.

The performance receives a warm ovation.

Buenos Aires, 8 September 1907

We perform *Odette* for our fifth subscription matinée. A special performance of *Adriana Lecouvreur* in the Signora's honour is announced for Tuesday, 10 September. This evening at eight o'clock we go over the script of *La principessa Giorgio* at the Signora's hotel.

We shall do the play tomorrow evening to mark our sixteenth subscription performance.

Buenos Aires, 9 September 1907

A large audience and a warm ovation, especially after Acts II and III. La Duse is magnificent.

Buenos Aires, 10 September 1907

A gala performance in honour of Eleonora Duse. A performance open to the general public. An atmosphere of great excitement in the theatre. Throughout the performance the audience is attentive. Thunderous applause all evening. After Act IV many baskets of flowers are presented to the Signora and a shower of flowers is thrown onto the stage from the boxes and stalls. The impresario Da Rosa presents the Signora with an exquisite brooch: a butterfly set in diamonds. During Act V, the one act in which La Duse can be said to have attained true greatness, the sheer finesse of her acting provokes the most incredible scenes in the theatre. She takes curtain call after curtain call at the end of the play.

Tomorrow at one-thirty we are scheduled to rehearse *Amore senza stima* in the theatre.

Buenos Aires, 11 September 1907

This evening we give our seventeenth subscription performance with a repeat performance of *La Gioconda*.

DUSE ON TOUR

Buenos Aires, 12–13 September 1907

A rehearsal of *Amore senza stima*. Parts are distributed for *La moglie ideale*.

Buenos Aires, 14 September 1907

Today, on the stage of the Teatro Odeon, a delightful party is held to celebrate the baptism of Mimì Aguglia's baby daughter. The little girl is aptly named Argentina, and she is a very pretty child.

Champagne is served with the compliments of Da Rosa. The Signora sends a magnificent basket of flowers, and all the other members of the company present the new baby with a silver sewing case. There is much rejoicing and banter between the journalists, the Sicilian confraternity, and the Italian actors who are invited to the party. La Verani plays some dance tunes on the piano while the rest of us take to the floor. Musco recites two sonnets in Sicilian dialect amidst much applause. Maiorana, who is a most handsome young fellow, finds himself greatly admired by the ladies. The absence of Giovanni Grasso from the festivities does not go unnoticed.

Buenos Aires, 15 September 1907

Today Eleonora Duse achieves a veritable *tour de force*. We give our final matinée performance with *Hedda Gabler* and in the evening another performance for the general public, at reduced prices, of *Adriana Lecouvreur*.

Things go extremely well during the matinée but the evening performance is a quite different affair! By then, the Signora is in a state of utter exhaustion. Adriana dies much before her time at this performance! Yet, despite everything, the audience greets her with a noisy ovation.

Buenos Aires, 16 September 1907

Our final subscription performance and farewell appearance with *Amore senza stima* which, allowing for the somewhat frantic rehearsals, turns out reasonably well. The Signora, although still fatigued and listless, is much applauded. At the end of the performance, the audience rises to its feet. Flowers and tributes in abundance are thrown on to the stage.

Tomorrow we leave for Rosario.

Rosario, 17 September 1907

Buenos Aires is cloudy and overcast when we set out on our journey this morning. *En route* it begins to rain and by the time we finally arrive at Rosario, there is a heavy downpour. The Signora and her daughter travel on the same train. The journey is rather boring. The pampa which is depressingly flat has precious little that is picturesque or interesting enough to attract one's attention apart from the tiny settlements that loom into view every so often. The shacks (incredible though it may seem) are actually inhabited by human beings!

Even Rosario creates a dismal impression at first sight. To reach the theatre from the station, I do believe that a boat would have been more suitable than the carriage that awaits us. I also come to the conclusion that the sewerage system here is something of a myth. And to think that Rosario is a city reputed to have made notable progress by those who knew the place some twenty years or so ago!

The Teatro Colon, where we shall play, is a fine theatre, even if somewhat pretentious and ornate. Tomorrow evening we open with *Fedora*.

Rosario, 18 September 1907

A good house, although by no means packed to capacity. A dismal performance on the whole. The Signora is feeling unwell . . . the theatre is cold and badly heated, and as for the play – suffice it to say that is *is Fedora!* A most unfortunate debut.

Tomorrow evening we play *Hedda Gabler*.

Rosario, 19 September 1907

Fewer people in the theatre this evening. The local critics have written at length about La Duse's disappointing debut. Not merely are they prepared to argue that she is not a great actress, but they dare to suggest that her acting is downright mediocre.

This evening the Signora gives a strong performance. But all her efforts prove to be futile. The audience shows itself to be neither convinced nor moved by Hedda Gabler's predicament. The atmosphere in the theatre is distinctly cool.

A gala evening for the general public has been announced for the day after tomorrow in honour of La Duse. She will appear in *La signora delle camelie*.

For our third and final subscription performance we shall perform *Adriana Lecouvreur*.

Rosario, 20 September 1907

In reviewing *Hedda Gabler*, the critics have not shown themselves to be any more indulgent than in their assessment of *Fedora*, with one or two notable exceptions.

DUSE ON TOUR

Rosario, 21 September 1907

The performance is cancelled because of the Signora's indisposition. La Duse is obviously ill, but there is another factor that has led to the cancellation of this evening's performance: the abysmal box office receipts. Only two seats have been sold in the front stalls! This means that our last subscription performance is announced for tomorrow night with *La signora delle camelie*.

Rosario, 22 September 1907

The Signora is still too ill to appear. So the performance is postponed until the day after tomorrow.

Rosario, 24 September 1907

A good house. The Signora looks tired, weak and remote. For the first act she has a large fur brought onstage. Act by act, her physical weakness becomes increasingly apparent. Those miraculous invocations to Armando in Act IV, even though said in a whisper, nevertheless make a deep impression on the audience. Ironically enough, this evening brings the only warm applause heard throughout this short but altogether unhappy season. By Act V the Signora can scarcely be heard. Margherita's sudden cry when she sees Armando enter the room is almost inaudible – a mere whisper. There is lengthy but restrained applause at the end of the performance. Once offstage the Signora exclaims: 'I don't know how I managed to keep going'. She certainly looks very ill.

Tomorrow evening we return to Buenos Aires.

Buenos Aires, 25 September 1907

We open tomorrow at the Teatro Coliseo, where we shall give four performances at popular prices. Given the extraordinary size of the theatre, it is quite clear that even with reduced prices the box office receipts will be considerable. For the first two evenings the theatre is already sold out.

Our play on the first night will be *Fernanda*.

Buenos Aires, 26 September 1907

A magnificent house and a successful opening. The Signora is in good form and gives a most convincing performance. Her personal

---

Facing: The theatre poster announcing a gala performance of *La signora delle camelie* in Rosario on 21 September 1907 with Duse in the title role. The cast list confirms that Guido Noccioli had a walk-on part in the play as the messenger. (Reproduction by courtesy of the Biblioteca Teatrale del Burcardo, Rome.)

TEATRO COLON

TEMPORADA 1907

Empresa LUIS CARPENTIERO ❋ Dirección: FAUSTINO DA ROSA

Compagnia Drammatica Italiana

DI

Eleonora Duse

El Sábado 21 de Setiembre 1907

GRAN FUNCION EXTRAORDINARIA (FUERA DE ABONO)

A BENEFICIO

DE

ELEONORA DUSE

LA DAMA

DE

LAS CAMELIAS

Drama en 5 actos de A. DUMAS (Hijo)

— PERSONAGGI —

Margherita Gauthier.. .. .. .. ELEONORA DUSE

Armando Duval	Leo Orlandini	Dottore	Vittorio Capellaro
Duval (padre).	Andrea Beltramo	Servo.	Antoni Spinelli
Gastone	Armando Lavaggi	Porta Leitere	Guido Noccioli
Saint Godens	Giuseppe Masi	Erminia	Clelia Zecchini
Gustavo	Carlo Delfini	Duvernois.	Argento Scalambretti
De Gyray	Ubaldo Pittei	Nanetta	Elisa Berti-Masi
Valville	Alfred Robert	Olimpia	Luciana Rosi

A LAS 8·30 P. M.

Precios de las Localidades

Palcos bajos y balcón sin entrada ..	$ 75.—	Tertulias altas 1.ª fila con entrada	$ 4
Palcos altos .. » » ..	» 35.—	Tertulias altas otras filas » »	» .—
Platea con entrada.	» 12.—	Paraiso 1.ª fila » »	» 2.—
Silion de balcón con entrada. ..	» 7.—	Entrada á paraiso	»
Cazuela » » ..	» 7.—	Entrada á palco	»

Mañana Domingo 22 de Setiembre de 1907 — 3ª y última funcion de abono

DESPEDIDA DE LA COMPAÑIA

ADRIANA DE LECOUVREUR

450? — La Capital Rosario

triumph is assured from the outset and her acting in Act III is altogether impressive.

Tomorrow evening we perform *Magda*. Rehearsals of *Scellerata* have also started for Signorina Rossi and the actor Robert.

Buenos Aires, 27 September 1907

The customary full house. This evening the Signora acts like someone 'possessed'. Her acting is truly *divine*, and the entire performance is an unqualified success. Act III is interrupted some three or four times by frenzied outbursts of applause.

The rehearsals for *Scellerata* progress. Tomorrow there is no performance. On Sunday, the day after tomorrow, there is a matinée performance of *Adriana Lecouvreur*.

Buenos Aires, 29 September 1907

The theatre is sold out. An evening of wild ovations. Yet the Signora's performance is somewhat uncertain. In the early acts of the play, she continually misses her cues. But she somehow pulls herself together, as she is wont to do, by the fifth act.

Tomorrow evening we are supposed to be playing *La abbadessa di Jouarre* and *Scellerata* but, once again, the ecclesiastical censors have intervened. So, our farewell performance will be *La signora delle camelie*.

Buenos Aires, 30 September 1907

A triumphant evening, with the theatre once more filled to capacity. Thunderous applause, masses of floral tributes, and, at the end, a deafening ovation. And so our season in Argentina too comes to an end – a season that, apart from the sad interlude experienced in Rosario, has turned out to be a brilliant success, both from an artistic and financial point of view. The management, in particular, has reaped considerable profits.

Tomorrow evening we embark for Montevideo.

In today's bulletin there is a nice letter from Eleonora Duse to all members of the company. Now that we are soon to return to Italy, she would like to express her deep gratitude, etc. A noble gesture on her part!

Montevideo, 2 October 1907

The crossing over the River Plate turns out to be delightful. The weather is fine. Montevideo, the capital, is a most attractive city. We shall play at the Teatro Urquiza. The subscription series consists of six plays.

Tomorrow evening we open with *Magda*.

THE NOCCIOLI DIARIES

Montevideo, 3 October 1907

A good house. The galleries and boxes are sold out. Some empty seats in the stalls. A cool reception on the whole. The Signora is tense, physically exhausted and unable to concentrate. We discover that Orlandini persists in communicating with the Signora by letter, but she too persists in making no reply. To be honest, now that our South American tour is almost over, we should all like to see them patch up their quarrel. Both have made their point. And the time has now come to bury the hatchet.

Tomorrow there is a rehearsal of *Scellerata*.

Montevideo, 4 October 1907

All the newspapers here have expressed their disenchantment with La Duse and her company, with the possible exception of La Verani and Orlandini. And they have nothing but contempt for Sudermann's play.

The drama critic of the Italian newspaper *L'Italia al Plata*, which is published here in Montevideo, writes more or less in these terms: 'We flocked to the theatre in our enthusiasm, fully expecting to experience something memorable, but what a cruel disappointment!' The reviewer then goes on to tear the play to shreds, dismissing it as old hat and conventional, and unsuited to Eleonora Duse's particular style of acting! Well now! This criticism strikes me as being patently unjustified. One can only try to ignore this furore in the press and put trust in the remaining performances. And in the Signora's state of health!

Fedora is billed for tomorrow evening. The same damning newspapers express the hope that the Signora will be more successful with this outdated piece. Dear God! I have no desire to play the prophet of doom but I am apprehensive. My worst fears may prove to be justified.

Montevideo, 5 October 1907

A house similar to that on our opening night, except for the stalls, which are packed to capacity on this occasion. *Fedora* is played with some sound ensemble acting on the part of the supporting cast, but the Signora in the leading role does little to enhance the reputation of her faithful old friend – Sardou! In Act I, during the dialogue between the waiter and the jeweller, the Signora is standing in the wings waiting to make her entrance, leaning against a table. Turning to Masi she whispers, shaking her head: 'Good Lord! What rubbish . . . Just listen . . . listen to that! To think

[133]

that I believed there could be nothing as awful as *Fernanda* . . . but this is even worse . . .!' Needless to say, the play is coldly received.

Tomorrow morning we have the dress rehearsal of *Scellerata* which will form a double bill tomorrow evening with *La moglie di Claudio.*

Montevideo, 6 October 1907

This morning after the dress rehearsal of *Scellerata,* during which our director Orlandini does not once open his mouth, La Rossi decides the time has come to speak out: 'Come now, Signor Orlandini, say something . . . I cannot imagine that I have turned into the perfect actress overnight . . . Tell me, I beseech you, where I am going wrong and how I can improve my interpretation'.

Finally Orlandini speaks and at some length. Naturally, the conversation turns to the quarrel with the Signora, which he feels has put him in an ambiguous position in the eyes of the entire company and seriously undermined his authority as director, etc. . . . Then, turning to La Rossi, he adds: 'You, Signorina, since you enjoy the Signora's confidence, might try to intercede with her on my behalf . . .' 'But I have tried, Signor Orlandini'. Seeing that their conversation is becoming rather intimate, I quietly withdraw.

And then, suddenly this evening, before the curtain rises on the second act of *La moglie di Claudio,* the Signora, in the presence of everyone, throws her arms around Orlandini's neck and kisses him, saying with that magnificent smile on her lips: 'Come now, let's make our peace and forget the whole affair. Everyone in this wretched profession can be mistaken at times . . .' and, since the curtain is already going up, she makes a rapid entrance. Ah! What a relief! Long live universal harmony!

The play is an enormous success this evening. And about time! For the critics are beginning to lose their patience and the public is starting to desert us, protesting that they have been deceived by our advance publicity.

Tomorrow there is no performance.

Montevideo, 7 October 1907

Ecstatic reviews in all the newspapers. Now all the critics are hailing this sudden *revelation.*

Tomorrow evening we play *La Gioconda.*

Montevideo, 8 October 1907

A magnificent theatre and a wonderful triumph.

THE NOCCIOLI DIARIES

Montevideo, 10 October 1907

The critics continue to express their approval but the audiences could be much better. The orchestra stalls remain empty, to the management's despair. This evening's performance of *Hedda Gabler* is enthusiastically received, especially Act III.

Tomorrow evening we give our last subscription performance with *Adriana Lecouvreur*.

Montevideo, 11 October 1907

The audience is much as usual. This evening the Signora acts with inspiration. She performs beautifully in the first four acts of *Adriana Lecouvreur*, and in Act V surpasses all expectations. The enthusiasm of the audience is indescribable. The curtain is raised at least thirty times.

Tomorrow evening there is a gala evening at reduced prices with a repeat performance of *La Gioconda*.

Montevideo, 12 October 1907

Notwithstanding the enthusiasm shown by last night's audience, the reduced prices and the fact that this is a gala evening, the theatre is by no means full except for the boxes and the two galleries, which are crowded. In recompense, there is much applause and many floral tributes.

Tomorrow evening we make our farewell appearance, still at reduced prices, with *La signora delle camelie*.

Montevideo, 13 October 1907

A packed theatre, and an outstanding success. Tremendous ovations after Acts IV and V. The same wild enthusiasm as shown for the Signora's performance the other evening in Act V of *Adriana Lecouvreur*.

Between curtain calls, the Signora bids farewell to the rest of the company. She kisses Orlandini and all the ladies and shakes hands with all the gentlemen, smiling beautifully with a kind word of greeting for everyone. It is a pleasure to see her looking so well and happy.

The curtain goes up, and the Signora bows graciously as the audience gives her a standing ovation. When the curtain is lowered at last, she turns to the cast lined up on stage to say goodbye. A moving and unforgettable evening, marking our last appearance during this South American tour, which began in Rio de Janeiro with *La signora delle camelie* and has ended in Montevideo with the same play.

During our time here critics of every calibre and the most varied audiences imaginable have feasted on the unique personality of Eleonora Duse! But only a few – all too few in my opinion – have come to terms with her true greatness. And now it is too late as we prepare to take our leave and return to Europe and the Old World.

The Signora leaves tomorrow evening on an English vessel *Cap Arcon* which is sailing directly to Lisbon. The rest of us will embark on 17 October on the steamer *Lombardia*, owned by the Italian Navigation Company.

Once in Italy, we shall only be allowed to enjoy a short vacation. The Signora, who, according to the conditions set down in our contracts, has the right to insist that we go on leave for two months without any payment, has generously agreed to pay us half our salary. Deep down, she is really very goodhearted. She has also handed out a number of bonuses: five hundred francs to the prompter, two hundred and fifty francs to the property man, two hundred francs to the stage technician, two hundred francs to the stage manager, two hundred francs to the company secretary, etc. . . . And now it's bon voyage for her and the rest of us.

Montevideo, 14 October 1907
The Signora embarks this evening with the sea at its roughest.

Montevideo, 17 October 1907
Aboard the *Lombardia*. The ship is very comfortable. The weather is fine. Much merriment on board.

At sea, 19 October 1907
Yesterday the sea turned rough. Today, a little less so! After being confined to our bunks for hours on end, we are able to breathe some fresh air again and take some exercise on deck . . . Everyone is showing the ravages of seasickness!

At sea, 20 October 1907
Among the second-class passengers we have discovered a most amusing and delightful fellow. He is on the editorial staff of the Italian newspaper *L'Italia al Plata*, published in Montevideo, Roman by birth and returning to Italy to find himself a wife. His name is Pozzilli. He is mad about the theatre: he knows the name of every singer, actress and actor . . . and has naturally taken to our group. Like me, he suffers the most terrible bouts of seasickness.

THE NOCCIOLI DIARIES

At sea, 21 October 1907

Four o'clock in the afternoon. We have reached Santos. New passengers board ship and among them the business man in love with La Scalambretti. Also travelling on board our ship is Rosita, a famous equestrian star. She is still very striking although no longer so very young.

Rio de Janeiro, 22 October 1907

Once more we are in sight of the marvellous bay of Rio de Janeiro. The weather is extremely hot. Still more passengers join the ship. Our party gains a new attraction with the arrival on board of an Italian singer, Rosina Lucchini.

At sea, 23 October 1907

The sea is quite beautiful. We are all feeling revived and fit, all of us transformed into sea lions. I have met a most engaging young lady travelling in first class, Signorina Lovati, the *prima ballerina assoluta*, whom I so greatly admired at the Teatro Coliseo in Buenos Aires. She is travelling to Italy in order to arrange her release from certain contracts before returning to Buenos Aires to marry her fiancé. So nearly all the arts are represented on board. We have also befriended a Spanish *cantaora* called Juanita,[70] who is already emotionally involved with the ship's purser.

At sea, 24 October 1907

We have now formed our own little circle aboard. Modesty prevents me from adding – a limited but select circle. This comprises the journalist, who has become the life and soul of our group; then there is Lavaggi, as his main ally; Pittei in opposition; and Orlandini in the middle, except when political questions are raised and he becomes a ferocious and intransigent enemy of socialism. Finally there is me, surrounded by all these men of the world.

We amuse ourselves by singing, and here Delfini takes the initiative; we discuss theology because there is a rather oafish priest on board who scarcely knows any Latin, and we quote St Augustine, the gospels of St Matthew, and reflect upon the mystical ecstasies of St Catherine. We reinterpret the Bible and discuss all manner of political issues. What a pantomime! The journalist, Delfini, Faggioli and myself represent the extreme right! And we converse and argue for hours on end. Then the gong sounds for lunch or dinner and someone shouts: 'Come on, lads, let's go', and we eat and eat to our hearts' content.

DUSE ON TOUR

At sea, 25 October 1907

A lovely sea, a lovely voyage, lovely – and hot!

At sea 26 October 1907

Two sensational discoveries amidst the monotonous routine of life on board. Travelling with us is a tiger cub trapped in the Chaco by Doctor Evans, a fellow passenger. He intends to present it to the Zoological Garden at the Villa Borghese in Rome. The other discovery is less ferocious ... but rather more macabre. Also being transported on board, encased and packed like ordinary merchandise, is a corpse that has been disinterred three years after burial.

At sea, 27 October 1907

The heat is becoming oppressive. It is impossible to endure the heat in one's cabin. We stay up late, then try to get some sleep on deck in the open air ... One is tempted to sing the words from *Rigoletto*: 'So we sleep in the open air – that's fine.'[71]

This evening the sea is calm beyond belief. The surface is as smooth as any lake. But it's so unbearably hot!

At sea, 28 October 1907

This evening a gala dinner and dance is being held to celebrate our 'passage over the Equator.' The bridge of the ship is one great blaze of light with innumerable fairy lights in the Italian colours (white, red and green) and decorated with flowers and flags of every nation. The orchestra, consisting of a guitar and two mandolines, has been recruited from the third class. All the ladies appear in full evening dress. Much admired is La Lovati, who dances extremely well. The lemon water ices provide excellent refreshment. Long live such happiness!

But just as the festivities are at their peak, Orlandini corners some four or five of us, complaining bitterly about human ingratitude. He is referring to Masi to whom he has not spoken for several days! Masi, passing nearby, has obviously overheard his tirade. In fact, no sooner has Orlandini gone than Masi arrives to give his version of their quarrel ...

La Scalambretti makes only a brief appearance this evening. Her businessman is confined to his cabin with a swollen foot, allegedly caused by an insect bite. Such a tragedy!

At sea, 29 October 1907

The heat is overpowering. The sea calm. We are now anxiously looking forward to our next stop at Las Palmas.

THE NOCCIOLI DIARIES

At sea, 30 October 1907
The heat is less intense. But the boredom increases daily!

At sea, 31 October 1907
Today we have spotted a great number of dolphins at close range. A heated political argument ensues among our group. The sea has turned a little rough, but everyone is in good spirits!

At sea, 1 November 1907
This morning the priest, who is travelling in first class, celebrated holy mass. From among the passengers on board, only three women attend the service. A great commotion has started up because of the priest's presence on board. It has been leaked that he is travelling at the Italian government's expense because, according to the purser's information, the Italian Navigation Company intends to reestablish the services of a chaplain as normal practice. This rumour has upset a lot of people. Unfortunately, this particular priest is neither bright nor educated; two serious flaws of character that are not exactly in his favour. To make matters worse, during meals he has succeeded – strange to relate – in scandalizing all the ladies at table with certain arguments, which one might term Salesian for want of a better word, when discussing Varazze, etc.[72]

Las Palmas, 2 November 1907
All Souls Day. Magnificent weather. We enter port as dawn is breaking. All sorts of vendors clamber on board selling lace, embroidery, shawls, cigars, etc. Great activity on deck. Much buying and selling.

We go ashore. The city is most attractive. There is a lovely church where one can admire a rich collection of ecclesiastical garments that are made from exquisite materials and richly embroidered; lovely candlesticks, chalices and silver crucifixes, all in Spanish Renaissance style; a seventeenth-century missal tastefully illuminated. There is also a zoological museum nearby, which is well worth a visit.

We set sail once more at four o'clock in the afternoon with a rough sea. This evening the temperature is very much cooler – almost cold.

At sea, 3 November 1907
An ugly sea; the weather so so. We are now counting the days until we reach Barcelona . . . and finally Genoa. The voyage is beginning to seem eternal!

[139]

DUSE ON TOUR

At sea, 4 November 1907

Today a baby girl is baptized in the third class. La Verani and Doctor Evans act as the godparents. Tomorrow we are expected to reach Barcelona.

Barcelona, 5 November 1907

Heavy mist and a turbulent sea. Only two hours in port. The *cantaora*, Juanita, disembarks. She is inconsolable as she bids farewell to her dashing purser. He too looks quite sad and distressed. Poor young things! They were so deeply in love! We depart in the rain. We salute Christopher Columbus, who is looking down on us from his lofty column.

At sea, 6 November 1907

The sea is choppy, and it is very cold and misty. There are many ships crossing each other. Today, La Rossi takes up a collection for the orphans of men at sea.

We have also passed the spot where the *Lino*[73] collided. Our own ship's doctor was serving on board the *Lino* when the disaster occurred. He has told us in detail how it all happened ... A gloomy tale.

Genoa, 7 November 1907

Oh! We have arrived at long last! And what an ugly sea we have crossed. The mists have been treacherous! But now Genoa smiles upon us with her thousand lights, her elevations. Her wonderful port is crowded with military and merchant vessels. No sooner are we on the quayside, after two hours of patient manoeuvering, when we are greeted by the most awful chaos and deafening uproar. It is raining. I recognize Bevacqua[74] exchanging greetings with Orlandini. A telegram arrives from the Signora in Paris inquiring about our voyage and wishing us a pleasant vacation. La Scalambretti, incensed and indignant, confides how her businessman has acted in the most despicable manner and they have parted company for good. Pittei has passed an anxious quarter of an hour after receiving a nasty shock. On the very first day of our voyage, he had entrusted our property man, Bergonzio, with three hundred lire, which the latter was to safeguard for him until we reached Genoa. Upon arrival the money is no longer to be found ... Until, after much searching and rummaging, the lire appear ... *Laus*! The port formalities are complicated. The police come on board to arrest seven passengers for some undisclosed crime. This causes further delay. Then, to our enormous relief, we are finally allowed to land. Much handshaking, kissing and embracing as we make our farewells. It is already night, raining and cold ... But everyone sets off with alacrity ... anxious to return home and be reunited with their families.

NOTES
TO THE DIARIES

1 A reference to D'Annunzio's much-quoted words of dedication on the title page of his tragedy *La Gioconda* (1898): 'Per Eleonora Duse dalle belle mani' ('For Eleonora Duse of the beautiful hands').

2 Duse's season at the Teatro della Pergola in Florence extended from 27 November until 19 December 1906. A single performance of Ibsen's *Rosmersholm* with scenery designed by Gordon Craig was given on 5 December amidst jeers and applause. The next evening Duse gave the first performance of *Maria Salvestri* by Enrico Corradini, which met with a stormy reception by both audience and critics. Six days later, on 12 December, the company presented Maeterlinck's *Monna Vanna* with considerable success.

3 Many of Duse's biographers insist upon describing her as 'plain' and even 'gauche' but this is not borne out by the vast number of photographs that have been preserved covering every phase of Duse's career, right up until a few weeks before her death in 1924. These attest to the reliability of Noccioli's descriptions in the diary, which emphasize the haunting beauty and extraordinary range and subtlety of physical expression in this remarkable woman.

4 D'Annunzio completed his infamous novel *Fuoco* in February 1900. On 1 May of the same year the first instalment of the French translation (titled *Le Feu*) appeared in the *Revue de Paris*, and a press campaign was organized almost immediately against the author. D'Annunzio was sharply rebuked for having basely exploited his affair with Eleonora Duse and for having revealed the most intimate details of their love affair. Duse (alias Foscarina) who was five years older than the poet is seen in the novel as an ageing and insatiable voluptuary. An English translation of the novel under the title *The Flame of Life* was also published in the same year only to be described by one unidentified critic as 'the most swinish novel ever written'.

5   The exclamation in the Italian original is the sonorous *'Per Dio!'*

6   *Isola dei morti (Island of The Dead)*, a landscape painting by the Swiss symbolist painter *Arnold Böcklin* (1827–1901), livid greens and blues dominate, which explains the association in Noccioli's mind.

7   This could refer to one or other of the two Orvieto brothers, Adolfo or Angiolo, both of whom befriended the actress. Adolfo Orvieto (1871–1952), critic and writer, launched *Il Marzocco* (1896), one of the most influential arts magazines to be published in Italy at the turn of the century. Angiolo Orvieto (1869–1967) was a minor poet of some distinction who also wrote for the theatre. He ran his own literary journal *Vita Nuova* (1889) and subsequently collaborated with his brother in editing *Il Marzocco*. Duse's correspondence reveals her esteem and deep affection for the two men, and whenever she visited Florence the actress found a peaceful refuge at Il Poggiolino, the villa where Angiolo and his wife Laura (who was also a writer) lived, in the hills between Montughi and Careggi.

8   A translation of Dumas the Younger's *Une Visite de noces* (1871).

9   The Italian original reads: *'Quel fanciullo aveva nome Giannello! . . . Tu sei Giannello?'* This phrase alone betrays the somewhat arbitrary translation of the French text with the suppression of a significant adjective: 'C'était un enfant blond nommé Giannello . . . – Tu es Giannello? . . .' (*Monna Vanna*, Act II, Scene III).

10   Lent marked the beginning of the new season for theatre companies throughout Italy. Lent also saw the launching or formation of new companies, important cast changes, and the presentation of new productions.

11   *La figlia di Jefte* by Felice Cavallotti was first performed by the company of Giovanni Emanuel on 7 April 1886.

12   *Lo sciopero dei fabbri (La Grève des forgerons)*, a dramatic monologue by the French Parnassian poet, novelist and playwright, François Coppée (1842–1908). It was recited by the great Coquelin himself at the Odéon in 1869 at a gala performance given in honour of Sarah Bernhardt.

13   Once Duse began to immerse herself in Ibsen's plays, she became almost obsessed with his ideals. She revelled in the strange power exerted by his heroines and identified with their sentiments of rebellion and fierce individuality. With the character of Ellida in *The Lady of the Sea*, Duse's identification became almost complete and Ellida's words in Act III, she made her own: 'I think that if only men had chosen from the very beginning to live on the sea – or even *in* the sea – we should have reached a perfection quite different from our present state – both better and happier.'

14   *Adrienne Lecouvreur* (1849), written by Scribe and Legouvé.

15   Noccioli's unkind speculations about Orlandini's behaviour on this occasion seem justified, for however unpredictable or demanding Duse might have been during this tour there is ample evidence elsewhere of

her compassion and generosity. As actor–manager, she took her responsibilities seriously, and her correspondence to intimate friends while on tour reveals her constant concern for the health and well-being of the members of her company.

16 Duse was determined to protect her daughter, Enrichetta Duse Checchi (1882–1961), from the rootless existence to which she herself was condemned as an actress. In 1885, after her marriage to Enrichetta's father, Tebaldo Checchi, broke up, Duse assumed full responsibility for her daughter's upbringing. After being entrusted to caring foster parents in infancy, Enrichetta was educated at boarding schools in Italy and abroad. Subsequently, she married Edward Bullough, a lecturer for some years in Italian and Fellow of Gonville and Caius at Cambridge. Two children were born to the couple, Halley Edward in 1910 and Eleonora (named after her famous grandmother) in 1912.

It is interesting to reflect that the deep religious instinct in Duse's make-up should have found fulfilment in the destiny of her grandchildren, both of whom were to embrace the religious life in the Dominican Order in 1932. For in later life Duse felt an ever greater need for solitude and meditation, turning to edifying works such as the Holy Scriptures, the *Letters* of St Catherine of Siena and, above all, the *Confessions* of St Augustine which gave her enormous consolation.

17 *Heureuse*, written by the Belgian author and playwright Alfred-Néoclès Hennequin (1842–87), whose talent for light comedy made him a pioneer of modern vaudeville in Brussels and Paris in the closing decades of the nineteenth century. Created in collaboration with Millaud, *Heureuse* was first produced in 1903.

18 The Italian original is the disparaging word: *guitti* (poor or inferior strolling players).

19 Duse was unaware of the irreparable damage done by the stage staff to Craig's sets until confronted by Craig himself in a towering rage. Matters were not helped by their inability to communicate with each other in any common language. Without understanding his torrent of abuse, Duse resented Craig's outburst in public and his lack of control in her presence. What might have proved to be a very interesting collaboration clearly became impossible after this unfortunate episode, but, as Duse philosophically stated in a letter to Craig: 'What they have done to your scenery, they have been doing for years to my Art.' Statements in later life from both Craig and Duse make it quite clear that the breach was healed. In his essay of tribute 'On Signora Eleonora Duse', published in *The Dial* in May 1928, Craig wrote: 'She was admirable. She saw at a glance that I was mad. She said to herself, "This is not a scene for an Ibsen play – it's a scene for – something big but it's not Ibsen because I know my Ibsen" and here her mouth grew a trifle hard. But with astonishing good sense she pulled herself together and acted the part of a great actress who is dealing with a madman and who sees it's quite useless to protest. "It is wonderful", she said. Now could anything more sound in its common sense have been uttered?'

20 A brief notice in the *Almanacco del Teatro Italiano* (1907) boldly states: 'With the Lenten season of 1906, another triennium has begun in the theatre. Numerous new drama companies have been formed, and most of the former stage partnerships virtually eliminated. Eleonora Duse has contracted Leo Orlandini as her leading man and reformed her company. *But on the whole her company has turned out to be a collection of mediocrities.'* This broad and damaging statement calls for some qualification. Leo Orlandini, Alfredo Robert and Giuseppe Masi and his wife, Elisa Berti Masi, were considered experienced and competent actors and employed by all the notable theatre companies of the period. Andrea Beltramo, Mario Almirante, Laura Tessero Bozzo (sister of the famous Adelaide Tessero), Margherita Orlandini and Carlo Delfini (Duse's cousin) were all successful character actors with sound training acquired in the companies of some of the most influential actor–managers of the day. True, little or no information exists about some of the younger members of Duse's company, but it is quite clear from Noccioli's testimony that they were carefully chosen on the strength of personal recommendation. Although a prosperous marriage (or early talent unfulfilled) can always terminate an otherwise promising career, it seems highly improbable that Duse would have spent so much of her precious time in 1906 in coaching a bunch of mediocrities in the finer points of interpretation. Without exception, her quest for perfection made her inflexible in these matters. And, as Noccioli observes more than once, the company on occasion was worked into the ground in order to achieve the standards Duse expected of them.

21 *L'Autre danger* (1895) by Maurice-Charles Donnay.

22 *Count Luigi Grabinski Broglio* was for some years director of the Teatro Manzoni in Milan at the turn of the century.

23 Translation of Sudermann's *Heimat* (1893). When referring to performances of this play throughout the tour, Noccioli is inconsistent, sometimes giving the title as *Casa paterna* and elsewhere as *Magda*. Duse could, of course, have used a special translation of the play and preferred to have it billed as *Magda*, a role in which she was universally acclaimed.

24 Dumas the Younger's *La Dame aux camélias* (1848). Duse used a translation in Italian for which she held exclusive rights.

25 A wide consensus of opinion confirms Duse's inimitable skill in handling this particular scene in *La signora delle camelie*.

26 Sardou's *Fernande* (1870).

27 As early as 1888 there was peasant unrest in Wallachia, and in 1907 a general revolt by the peasants erupted in Moldavia and quickly spread to all parts of the Kingdom of Romania.

28 Dumas the Younger's *La Femme de Claude* (1873).

29 Renan's *L'Abbesse de Jouarre* (1886). The controversial nature of the plot caused the play to be censured as immoral in France, and both Antoine and Lugné-Poe failed in their efforts to mount a production of it in defiance of ecclesiastical censorship. Duse encountered a similar difficulty when she tried to present the play in South America where Church influence was still considerable and ecclesiastical censorship strictly enforced. (See Noccioli's entry under Buenos Aires, 30 August 1907.)

30 *Una partita a scacchi* (1873), a play by the versatile Italian dramatist Giuseppe Giacosa (1847–1906) based on the thirteenth-century medieval ballad or *cʌanson de geste: Huon de Bordeaux*. Today Giacosa is best remembered for his *drame à thèse* influenced by Becque and the nascent Théâtre Libre – plays such as *Tristi amori* (1887), *Diritti dell'anima* (1894), *Come le foglie* (1900), and his most polished of all, *Il più forte* (1904), in which one can detect shades of Ibsen.

31 Amedeo Chiantoni and Egisto Olivieri were both experienced members of the excellent company headed by Calabresi and Severi.

32 This was in fact the first performance of Sabatino Lopez's *L'elogio funebre*, presented by the Calabresi–Severi company.

33 Fatima Miris (billed as *Trasformista*). A one-man show comparable with mime. The genre was pioneered by the celebrated Leopoldo Fregoli (1867–1936) who made his name in the traditional *commedia dell'arte* before turning to *trasformismo* (character transformation), which he elevated into an acceptable art form.

Fatima Miris made her own début on 20 October 1903 at the Teatro Storchio in Modena. Within fourteen months she had appeared in all the major cities throughout Italy and soon afterwards embarked upon a tour of the United States. Like Fregoli, Miris wrote most of her own material.

34 The original Italian reads: 'Alla maggiore artista, la maggiore riconoscenza.'

35 Dumas the Younger's *La Princesse Georges* (1871).

36 *Il padrone delle ferriere*, the Italian translation of *Le Maître de forges* by the French dramatist and novelist Georges Ohnet (1848–1918). *Le Maître de forges* was first played at the Théâtre Gymnase in Paris on 15 December 1883 and is generally considered to be the most successful of Ohnet's bourgeois dramas, which are more interesting from the point of view of structure than in details of technique. Many important Italian theatre companies introduced the play into their repertoire, including companies led by Duse, Ermete Zacconi and Ermete Novelli.

37 *Infedele* (1894), a witty and elegant comedy by the Neapolitan dramatist and critic Roberto Bracco (1861–1943). Like Duse herself, Bracco greatly admired the music of Wagner and the dramas of Ibsen, which he tried to promote as an influential journalist. His own efforts in the genre of *drame à thèse* – notably, *Il diritto di vivere* (1900) and *Sperduti nel buio* (1901) – betray the influence of the ideals expressed in the plays of both Ibsen and Hauptmann, but with considerably less power and conviction.

38 As a spokesman for the late nineteenth-century aesthetic movement, which advocated 'art for art's sake', Oscar Wilde (1854–1900) became a fashionable author in Europe at large. His novel *The Picture of Dorian Gray* was seen as a bible of decadent aesthetics and influenced a wide spectrum of European authors from D'Annunzio to Thomas Mann.

39 Literal translation: 'The Discovery of America'. Author unidentified.

40 *Réis* (plural of *real*), the former Brazilian monetary unit, replaced by the *cruzeiro* in 1942. The sum of 6,000 reis in 1907 would have been approximately the equivalent of 50 pence or one US dollar.

41 The sixth President of Brazil who governed from 1906 until 1909 was Affonso Pena (1847–1909), an experienced minister and statesman from Minas Gerais. Under the sound administration of Pena, who dreamed of an industrialized Brazil, Italian immigration increased dramatically in the newly opened region of São Paulo.

42 The Italian original reads: 'l'orzo non è fatto per i ciuchi'. ('barley is not for feeding to donkeys'.)

43 After some bitter experiences in Italy in her determination to gain acceptance for D'Annunzio as a dramatist, Duse became increasingly more impatient with audiences who were unable or unwilling to share her passion for a theatre of 'poetry and ideals'. Yet her impatience with uncomprehending and even hostile audiences in South America seems a little unreasonable when one considers her struggles in Europe itself to promote the plays of symbolists like D'Annunzio and Maeterlinck or idealists like Hauptmann and Ibsen.

44 Duse resented intrusions upon her privacy by an indiscreet press and prying public. She insisted upon the need for peace and solitude when preparing for appearances on tour and refused to receive visitors, however distinguished or important, while engaged in rehearsals or resting between acts during a performance. North American engagements were particularly painful to her because of the brash publicity to which she was exposed. Judging from Noccioli's observations, the social demands upon celebrities touring South America could be equally awkward and irritating.

45 Pinero's *The Second Mrs Tanqueray* (1893). The full title of the play is frequently abbreviated by Noccioli in the original Italian.

46 Duse is referring to the ecstatic description of La Gioconda's beauty narrated at length by Lucio Settala to Cosimo Dalbo in Act II of the play.

47 It is worth noting that Italian translations of foreign plays often adapted not merely the title but even the names of the characters.

48 Duse's correspondence of this period constantly touches upon her total disenchantment with the fashionable heroines of the French repertoire. For example, in a letter to Lugné-Poe, dated 16 May 1905, she wrote '. . . affogavo nel fiume *Sardou et Dumas*'. ('I have been drowning in the river *Sardou and Dumas*.')

49 Celebrations were held throughout South America on 4 July 1907 to commemorate the centenary of the Risorgimento hero's birth, especially in countries like Brazil, Uruguay and Argentina where large numbers of Italian immigrants had settled and where the significance of Garibaldi's twelve eventful years in South America from 1835 until 1848 had not been forgotten.

50 The Italian original reads: 'Al terzo atto, invece di dire: "Scriverò una riga allo zio Frink," (Pittei) ha detto: "Righerò una frinca allo zio . . .".'.

51 The Italian original reads: 'La battuta dice: "Ricordo, era un mattino di estate" e disse: "Ricordo, era un mastino d'estate . . .".'.

52 Gustavo had the difficult task of developing his own interpretation of this difficult Shakespearian role in which his father had excelled. When Tommaso Salvini played the jealous Moor in England and the United States, actors and critics were lavish in their praises. Henry James, who greatly admired Salvini's Othello, analysed his interpretation in some detail, approval outweighing any reservations. The Italian translations of Shakespeare available to Tommaso Salvini and his contemporaries were irritatingly vague and arbitrary; crude pathos often obscured the metaphysical side of Shakespeare's characters in the interpretation offered by most Italian actors of the day. Yet there was enough power in Salvini's performance to excite the envy of Henry Irving and the admiration of Robert Browning.

53 The Italian translation of Shakespeare's *The Taming of the Shrew*.

54 A Serra dos Orgãos (The Organ Mountains), a mountain range in central Rio de Janeiro that forms part of the great coastal escarpment (Serra do Mar) overlooking Guanabara Bay and extends east from Petrópolis to beyond Teresópolis.

55 Two important facts can be inferred from this persuasive little speech. First, by 1907 the name of Eleonora Duse was irrevocably linked with that of Ibsen as the most famous interpreter of the Norwegian dramatist's tragic heroines; second, that the growing importance of Ibsen's influence as a dramatist in Europe was already appreciated by an enlightened minority in South America.

56 A similar plaque was unveiled on the stage of the Teatro della Pergola in Florence as recently as 1977 to coincide with a revival of Ibsen's *Rosmersholm*.

57 The original phrase, which is uttered by Monna Vanna in a lengthy speech, marks the climax of the play. It reads: 'Ah! les hommes sont fous! . . .' (*Monna Vanna*, Act III, Scene II).

58 Late July is the height of the winter season in Brazil when the temperature in São Paulo tends to be perceptibly much lower than that of Rio de Janeiro.

59 There is a note of irony in the word play here: *Tutto per nulla* (*Everything for Nothing*) and *Poco o nulla* (*Little or Nothing*).

60 Mimì Aguglia (1884–1973), Giovanni Grasso (1874–1930), and Toto Maiorana (1862–?), three distinguished Sicilian actors who were to score their greatest successes in regional dialect plays such as those written by Luigi Capuana and Giovanni Verga.

61 *La lupa* (1896), a regional drama adapted from a novella with the same title by the Sicilian writer and playwright Giovanni Verga (1840–1922). Verga made an important contribution to *verismo* in the Italian theatre, notably with an earlier play *Cavalleria rusticana*, adapted from the novel *Vita dei campi* (and best known today as the libretto of Mascagni's opera). As a play, *Cavalleria rusticana* was given its first performance by the Cesare Rossi Company on 14 January 1884 with Flavio Andò (Turiddu), Tebaldo Checchi (Alfio) and Eleonora Duse (Santuzza). Duse's triumph in the role on the opening night at the Teatro Carignano in Turin so greatly overwhelmed Verga that he is reported as saying to the actress as he expressed his gratitude: '*Cavalleria rusticana* belongs more to you than to me.' A French translation of the play was produced at the Théâtre-Libre in Paris in 1888 but made a poor impression. Duse included the play in her repertoire when she made her début in the French capital in 1897 and was much admired as Santuzza in a performance acclaimed by the critics. Unfortunately, Duse was never to interpret *La lupa*, having decided to avoid the limitations of regional drama in her preference for plays of universal interest.

62   *Juan José* (1895). A popular social drama in three acts by the Spanish dramatist Joaquín Dicenta (1863–1917).

63   *Teresa* by Brogi. Presumably a sketch in Sicilian dialect. Painstaking research has failed to reveal any further details about the author or the play.

64   The four singers of any note here are: the Italian lyric tenor Edoardo Garbin (1865–1943); the world famous Italian baritone Giuseppe De Luca (1876–1950); the Polish bass Adam Didur (1874–1946); and the Italian soprano Maria Farneti (1877–1955), internationally acclaimed in the roles of *Iris, Butterfly* and *Isabeau.*

65   *El flechazo* (*Love at First Sight*) (1902), a one-act farce by Serafín (1871–1938) and Joaquín Álvarez Quintero (1873–1944). Together they wrote some 229 comedies, dramas, *sainetes*, and *zarzuelas.* The wit and spontaneity of their writing for the Spanish theatre evokes the sunny atmosphere of their native Andalusia.

66   Banville's *Le Baiser* (1887).

67   The Podestá brothers – Jerónimo, José, Juan, Antonio and Pablo – belonged to a famous acting family of Italian origin which pioneered the concept of a national theatre in the Plate region at the turn of the century. Their remarkable achievements on behalf of better conditions for national authors and artists were admired and praised by people like André Antoine, Lugné-Poe and Duse herself who fully appreciated the sacrifices such enterprises demanded in the face of general indifference and prejudice.

68   Fulgenzio and Lindoro, well-known Goldoni characters. Fulgenzio is the gallant hero of the *Trilogia della villeggiatura* (1761) and Lindoro the protagonist in the *Trilogia di Lindoro* (1764).

69   The Italian original (which cannot be rendered with complete accuracy in English) reads: 'Doveva dire: "Ah, mi dimenticavo di questi poveri fiori" e ha detto invece: "Mi dimenticavo di questi . . . pioveri fuori." '

70   Extensive research has failed to establish any biographical details whatsoever about this fascinating quartet – the equestrian artist, Rosita; the singer, Rosina Lucchini; the ballerina, Signorina Lovati; and the *cantaora* Juanita. Perhaps prosperous marriages terminated their respective careers in the theatre.

71   The original line sung by the Duke in Verdi's *Rigoletto* reads: 'Si dorme all'aria aperta? – bene, bene.' (Act III, Scene V.)

72   The anticlerical sentiments betrayed by Noccioli reflect some of the tensions between Church and State and within the Church itself in Italy at this time. In 1903, the newly elected Pius X set about curbing modernism, and antimodernist measures were ratified in July 1907 with the controversial papal encyclical *Pascendi*. This crusade for religious orthodoxy had far-reaching political and social implications. Noccioli's use of the adjective *Salesian* in all probability alludes to the polemical vein in the writings of Saint John Bosco (1815–1888), the founder of the Salesian order and a native of Piedmont, who deprecated the anticlerical activities of the liberal groups in Northern Italy.

73 The *Lino*: the collision or casualties to which Noccioli refers are mentioned neither in Lloyd's Registers or weekly bulletins of shipping. What the Registers do confirm, on the other hand, is that the *Lino* (built in 1890) remained sea-worthy until the nineteen-twenties.

74 Luigi Bevacqua, a prominent Milanese journalist.

BIOGRAPHICAL
APPENDIX

Vittorio Alfieri (1749–1803)

Italian poet and dramatist. His major tragedies, such as *Oreste, Maria Stuarda, Merope, Saul* and *Mirra* found able interpreters in artists like Tommaso Salvini, Adelaide Ristori, and Ernesto Rossi.

Flavio Andò (1851–1915)

Sicilian actor whose pleasing stage presence and vigorous style of acting led to a succesful career in romantic roles. The highly successful Andò – Duse partnership onstage outlived their brief romance in private life. They were incomparable as Armand and Marguerite in Dumas the Younger's *La Dame aux camélias*. After leaving the Duse Company, Andò went on to form successful partnerships with Virginia Reiter and Tina di Lorenzo.

Andrē Antoine (1858–1943)

French actor–manager and theatre critic. Antoine was considered the leading exponent of naturalism in the French theatre, and in 1887 he founded the Théâtre-Libre in Paris. His company staged dramatized versions of the novels of Zola and the Goncourts, revived the popularity of Henri Becque, and introduced the work of Ibsen, Tolstoy and Strindberg to French audiences. The Théâtre-Libre revolutionized the techniques of stage design, lighting and acting on the principle of strict adherence to objective reality and Antoine's reforms were soon being imitated all over Europe.

Giuseppe Armanini (1874–1915)

Italian tenor who toured extensively. In 1907 he appeared at the Teatro

Coliseo in Buenos Aires in a wide repertoire of operas that included *Zaza*, *Lucia di Lammermoor*, *La Gioconda*, *La Bohème* and *La Sonnambula*.

Emile Augier (1820–89)

French dramatist who wrote controversial thesis plays. *Fourchambault* (1878) deals with the problem of illegitimacy.

Théodore de Banville (1823–91)

French Parnassian poet, critic and dramatist. Like Maeterlinck and Edmond Rostand, Banville contributed to the 'theatre of poetry' as a reaction against the bourgeois drama of Augier and Dumas the Younger. His best known play *Gringoire* (1866) was interpreted in France by Coquelin and in Italy by Zacconi. Banville's verse drama *Le Baiser* was written in 1887 specially for the Théâtre-Libre of André Antoine.

Julia Bartet (1854–1941)

French actress who made her debut in *L'Arlésienne* in 1879. Such was her success that by 1879 Bartet was engaged by the Comédie-Française, where she remained until her retirement in 1919. Her most successful interpretations included Racine's *Bérénice* and *Andromaque* and Marivaux's Silvia in *Le Jeu de l'amour et du hasard*. She withdrew from the stage at the height of her powers.

Luigi Bellotti-Bon (1820–83)

Italian actor–manager. He started acting at an early age and appeared alongside the great tragedian Gustavo Modena. He joined the Reale Compagnia Sarda before forming his own company in 1859. Bellotti-Bon introduced modern criteria by insisting upon good ensemble acting, careful stage production and the promotion of national dramatists. His name is linked with the general revival of Italian theatre in the 1860s and 1870s. He also wrote a number of plays, including the immensely popular *Spensieratezza e buon cuore* (1854).

Sarah Bernhardt (1844–1923)

Celebrated French actress whose splendid voice and powerful acting brought her world fame. She trained at the Comédie-Française from 1860 until 1862 but first came to prominence in 1866 at Paris's second national theatre, the Théâtre de l'Odéon. Her Parisian successes included appearances as Queen Maria in Hugo's *Ruy Blas* and the title role in Racine's *Phèdre*. In the 1880s Bernhardt entered into a fruitful collaboration with Sardou who directed her in roles he had specially created for her flamboyant style of acting. Bernhardt toured extensively and her fame brought her honours and substantial profits wherever she performed. Her numerous tours to the Americas were conducted in a blaze of publicity and, as Henry James wittily observed: 'She has in a supreme degree what the French call the *génie de la réclame* – the advertising genius.' On a more generous note, Lily Langtry wrote: 'This great and overwhelming artist was almost too individual, too exotic, to be completely understood or properly estimated *all at once*. Her superb diction, her lovely silken voice, her natural acting, her passionate temperament, her fire – in a word, transcendent genius – caused amazement ... She filled the imagination as a great poet might do.' After the amputation of her leg, following an injury, further roles were created for Bernhardt to accommodate her disability. She carried on courageously into old age and continued to win the admiration of audiences. In 1907 she published her autobiography, translated as *My Double Life*, and in 1923 a treatise on acting entitled *L'Art du Théâtre*.

Ettore Berti (1870–1940)

Italian actor–manager who began his career on the stage as a child actor. Although he did not accompany Duse on the 1906–07 tour, he had been a member of her company in 1897 when she gave a short season in Paris. On that occasion Berti alternated with Carlo Rosaspina as principal actor. The following year he joined Italia Vitaliani's company and toured with it extensively. One factor that must have endeared Ettore Berti to Duse was his enthusiasm for the plays of D'Annunzio. In 1904, amidst scepticism and indifference, Berti courageously launched his Compagnia D'Annunziana, devoted exclusively to the presentation of D'Annunzio's plays.

Arrigo Boito (1842–1918)

Italian poet, composer and librettist. Today he is best remembered for his opera *Mefistofele* (a fiasco when first performed at La Scala Milan, on 5 March 1868) and his librettos based on Shakespeare's plays for Verdi. His intimate friendship with Duse extended from 1887 until 1898 and was renewed in 1904 when Duse and D'Annunzio parted, right up until Boito's death in 1918. He translated three Shakespearian plays for Duse: *Antony and Cleopatra*, *Macbeth* and *Romeo and Juliet*, although the last of these was never completed, and Cleopatra was the only role she was to interpret on the stage.

Duse had just celebrated her thirtieth birthday when she appeared for the first time in the Boito translation of *Antony and Cleopatra* at a gala performance in her honour at the Teatro Manzoni in Milan on 22 November 1888. The majority of Italian critics were unimpressed by Duse's interpretation of Cleopatra, yet she was urged to perform the role time and time again when she visited Germany and Austria. As a much younger actress, Duse had played Shakespeare's Ophelia and Juliet, and Cleopatra was her third and last Shakespearian role.

In a telegram dated 23 November 1888, announcing the success of Boito's translation, Duse ruefully commented: 'Why did I fail to study Shakespeare sooner?' And, when the great Shakespearian actor, Ernesto Rossi, who was considered to be Italy's finest King Lear, invited Duse to partner him as Lady Macbeth, she declined with some regret, insisting that the preparation of so taxing a role would require at least twelve months of study and some thirty rehearsals.

Edoardo Boutet (1856–1915)

Italian drama critic who wrote under the pseudonym Caramba. From 1905 until 1908 Boutet directed the famous Compagnia Stabile Romana at the Teatro Argentina in Rome. Boutet also acquired a certain reputation as a teacher of acting and dramatic theory.

Enrico Annibale Butti (1868–1912)

Italian lawyer, novelist and playwright. His plays reveal an interest in contemporary ethical and religious problems.

Butti's best known play *Fiamme nell'ombra* was given its first performance at the Teatro Costanzi in Rome by the Talli-Gramatica-Calabresi Company on 18 October 1904. *Tutto per nulla* was written the following year and given its first performance at the Politeama Margherita in Genoa by the Reiter-Carini Company on 10 November 1905.

Martino Cafiero (1841–84)

Prominent journalist who founded and directed the *Corriere del Mattino* in Naples. He was in his early thirties when he first met Duse backstage at the Teatro dei Fiorentini and Duse was overwhelmed by Cafiero's worldly elegance and cultivated tastes. The affair came to a tragic end when the actress found herself pregnant and Cafiero made it quite clear that he was not interested in marriage. Her baby son only lived a few days, but the sad experience proved to be traumatic and haunted Duse for years to come.

Oreste Calabresi (1857–1915)

Influential actor–manager who proved to be equally successful in tragedy and comedy. As a young actor he played minor roles alongside the great Ernesto Rossi and Tommaso Salvini. Calabresi's first real opportunity came when he was invited to take over the roles of the celebrated Angelo Vestri in the Vitaliani Company. Subsequent contracts enabled him to play leading roles opposite some of the best actresses on the Italian stage at the turn of the century, notably Virginia Reiter, with whom he toured extensively, and Irma Gramatica. Considered to be more intuitive than analytical as an actor, Calabresi scored his greatest successes in a contemporary Italian repertoire – the works of Bracco, Verga, Bertolazzi, Giacosa, Rovetta and D'Annunzio. In 1906 he formed his own company together with Elisa Severi.

Emma Calvé (1858–1942)

French soprano who made her début at the Théâtre Monnaie in Brussels on 23 September 1882 as Marguerite in Gounod's *Faust*. In her time, Calvé was considered to be particularly effective in *verista* roles and was much acclaimed throughout Europe and in America in the roles of Santuzza (*Cavalleria Rusticana*) and Carmen. Calvé and Duse were friends and the letters they exchanged have been preserved in private collections. For further details of the friendship between the two women see Calvé's autobiography, *Sous tous les ciels, j'ai chanté* (Paris: Plon, 1940).

Emma Carelli (1877–1928)

Italian soprano who enjoyed considerable success in Italy and abroad and, above all, in South America. Famous for her expressive voice and powers of interpretation, Carelli was especially noted for her appearances as Puccini's *Tosca* and Leoncavallo's *Zaza*. As the wife of an influential left-wing politician Walter Macchi (1870–1955), who subsequently became a theatre impresario, Carelli found herself entrusted with the artistic direction of the Teatro Costanzi in Rome from 1914, when she retired from the stage, until 1926.

Felice Cavallotti (1842–98)

Italian politician and dramatist. His early plays were influenced by neo-romaticism with overtones of Victor Hugo.

Cavallotti's most famous play *Il cantico dei cantici* (1881) was condemned by the ecclesiastical authorities on account of its controversial theme based on quotations from the Bible. His next great success, *La figlia di Jefte*, was given its first production by the company of Giovanni Emanuel on 7 April 1886, and brought into Duse's repertoire in the following year.

Tebaldo Checchi (1844–1918)

Italian actor who belonged to a well-known theatrical family. In 1883 he joined the company of Cesare Rossi and was much admired in a number of leading roles in plays such as *Diane de Lys* by Dumas the Younger and *Ferréol et Rabagas* by Sardou.

He married Eleonora Duse in 1881. After the break up of their marriage en route to South America with the Cesare Rossi company in 1885, Checchi decided to remain behind in Argentina. With the assistance of influential friends in Buenos Aires, he was able to find employment in the service of the Argentine government. After a short period in the Argentine Foreign Office, Checchi was appointed Consul and posted to Newhaven in England where he lived for many years. Eventually he was promoted and appointed to the Argentine Consulate in Lisbon but died shortly after taking up his post in the Portuguese capital. He continued to correspond with Duse who remained legally his wife, and he was reunited with his daughter at Newhaven on at least two occasions. When he died in 1918, he bequeathed a legacy to his wife and daughter. His death coincided with a period when Duse was facing severe financial difficulties. The actress lost most of the money invested in Germany during the First World War on her behalf by Robert Mendelssohn, the Berlin banker, cellist, and patron of the arts.

Francesco Cilèa (1866–1950)

Italian pianist and composer. His early success with operas such as *Gina* (1889) and *La Tilda* (1892), which are now virtually forgotten, caused Cilèa to abandon his piano studies. He then went on to compose the two operas which have survived in the repertoire, namely *L'Arlesiana* (1897), based on a play by Alphonse Daudet, and *Adriana Lecouvreur* (1902), with a libretto by Scribe and Legouvé. *Gloria*, Cilèa's last opera, which was written in 1907, failed to achieve the same success.

Francesco Ciotti (1835–1913)

Italian actor–manager of some importance. He made his debut at the age of eighteen as juvenile lead with the company of Luigi Domeniconi. By the age of twenty-one Ciotti already ranked as *prim'attore assoluto* when engaged to substitute for Alessandro Salvini. He was with Adelaide Ristori's company in 1864, and from 1865 to 1867 with Bellotti-Bon. An actor of some distinction in the traditional mould, Ciotti was noted for his fine stage presence and excellent diction. He played all the standard Italian roles in works by Alfieri, Cossa, Giacosa and Goldoni. Alexandre Dumas the Elder wrote his play *Lorenzino de Medici* specially for Ciotti.

Constant Benoît Coquelin (1841–1909)
French actor and *sociétaire* of the Comédie Française. Coquelin became internationally famous as a *grand comique* who triumphed in a wide repertoire of classical roles and most notably of all in plays by Molière, Beaumarchais and Marivaux. Coquelin toured extensively and made several visits to South America at the turn of the century.

Edward Gordon Craig (1872–1966)
English actor, stage director and designer. Son of the famous English actress Ellen Terry and the architect and stage designer Edward Godwin. (Not Henry Irving, as Noccioli inaccurately states. In fact, Irving's more intimate relationship with Ellen Terry did not begin until 1880). Craig was educated at Bradfield College and then at Heidelberg. He abandoned a promising but short-lived career as an actor in 1897 because he was frustrated by the vogue for realism in the theatre of his day. Craig was striving for revelation through symbolism. He wrote his famous, if somewhat derivative treatise, *The Art of the Theatre* (1905), about the time he began to collaborate with Duse. The actress first invited him to design the sets and costumes for Hofmannsthal's *Elektra*, and when the production had to be abandoned, she invited him the following year to design the sets for Ibsen's *Rosmersholm*. From Noccioli's description of the scenery, one can gauge something of Craig's personal concept of extreme simplicity, where colour, light and movement are all important. After her initial shock, Duse expressed delight with the results, but the critics were almost unanimous in criticizing the sets, which they found oppressive and unnecessarily complicated. Craig himself wrote the programme notes for the production, which was given a single performance at the Teatro della Pergola in Florence on 5 December 1906. His own reaction to this performance was one of unabated enthusiasm. In a letter to Martin Shaw he reported: 'It was a success and is – Duse was magnificent – she threw her details to the wind and went in. She has the courage of 25! She, Ibsen and I played our little trio out and came home happy.' On the strength of this single performance, Craig urged Duse to take the production to Rotterdam and The Hague, but this plan too was subsequently abandoned.

Gabriele D'Annunzio (1863–1938)
Italian poet, novelist, dramatist, short story writer, journalist, military hero and political leader.

D'Annunzio was one of the most prolific and controversial writers in

BIOGRAPHICAL APPENDIX

Italy at the turn of the century and subsequently during the Fascist era. In his novels and dramas, and particularly in his poetry, D'Annunzio indulged in dazzling verbal virtuosity, a passion for life and experience, and an eroticism that made an enormous impact on modern Italian literature. His liaison with Eleonora Duse represented a central and most creative phase in his career as a dramatist. The actress inspired tragedies such as *La Gioconda* (first performed in 1899 and translated into English in 1902) and *Francesca da Rimini* (first performed in 1901 and translated into English in 1902). His most successful play, *La figlia di Iorio* (first performed in 1904 and translated into English in 1907), is a powerful drama about fear and superstition among the peasants of Abruzzi. Unfortunately, Duse, after being replaced by Irma Gramatica at the play's première, was never to assume the role.

The passion, violence, superstition, and amorality of D'Annunzio's life and writings upset many critics in his own day, who deplored his blatant identification with his own Nietzschean–Superman heroes. The most influential Italian critic of the period, Benedetto Croce, called him a dilettante, and Henry James found him vulgar, while other critics objected to his arrogance, egomania, overt sensuality and artiness. The English novelist, Arnold Bennett, however, recognised in D'Annunzio's work, especially in his poetry, the marks of genius. The inherent flaws of structure and salient lack of any action in his plays seriously weakened his extravagant claims as a dramatist. But the sheer verbal beauty and impressive harmony of much of his writing for the theatre makes it worth while reading in the original Italian.

Clara della Guardia (1865–1937)
Italian actress discovered by the famous Adelaide Tessero, who had watched her play in *Celeste* by Leopoldo Marenco in 1885 in Turin. Della Guardia was trained by Giovanni Emanuel and, as a member of his company, she soon graduated from juvenile leads to the ranks of *prim'attrice* alongside Giacinta Pezzana and Alfredo De Sanctis. She became a famous Marguerite, Zaza, Adrienne Lecouvreur and Ellida. She toured extensively and was especially popular with South American audiences. Retiring from the stage in 1919, Della Guardia helped Virgilio Talli for some years to run a drama school. Her husband also spent some time in Brazil as director of São Paulo's Teatro Municipal.

Aimée Desclée (1836–74)
French actress noted for the fire and intensity of her acting, which made her an ideal interpreter of the roles of Dumas the Younger. Desclée was considered an incomparable Gilberte in *Frou-frou* by Meilhac and Halévy and a moving Césarine in *La Femme de Claude* by Dumas the Younger. During her relatively short career, the actress made frequent appearances in Belgium and Italy. Desclée died after a serious illness at the age of thirty-eight.

Suzanne Desprès (1874–1951)
French stage and film actress. The wife of Lugné-Poe, she played numerous leading roles at the Théâtre de L'Oeuvre, where she became the first

French actress to tackle the heroine roles of Ibsen and Hauptmann. She also appeared there in the first French performances of D'Annunzio's *La Gioconda* and *La figlia di Iorio*, and in 1905 she acted opposite Duse in Lugné-Poe's production of *Les Bas-fonds* (1902) by Gorki.

Desprès was unanimously considered to be the leading French interpreter of Ibsen. After seeing her interpretation of Nora in *A Doll's House* at Biarritz on 25 May 1906, Duse sent Desprès her own costume for the role, vowing never again to play Nora. In the early nineteen-twenties she added two more plays by D'Annunzio to her repertoire: *Phèdre* (1909) and *Le Martyre de Saint Sébastien* (1911).

Maurice-Charles Donnay (1859-1945)

French author and dramatist. Donnay began his career in the theatre working in cabaret at the Chat-Noir in Paris. His most significant play *Les Amants* was produced at the Théâtre de la Renaissance on 5 November 1895. *L'Autre danger* received its première at the Comédie-Française on 22 December 1902.

Adolfo Drago (1851-?)

Italian actor who trained as *amoroso* and *generico* in the company run by Cesare Vitaliani in 1870 before graduating to *prim'attore giovane* in other prominent theatre companies. From 1878 until 1879 he was engaged by the much-acclaimed Ciotti and Belli-Blanes Company and in the following year by the celebrated tragedienne Adelaide Ristori. Drago scored some of his greatest successes in Shakespearian roles and played Othello opposite Tommaso Salvini's Iago. Drago retired from the stage in 1897 but made a brief come back as *capocomico* in 1903.

Alexandre Dumas the Younger (1824-95)

French novelist and playwright who specialized in fashionable bourgeois drama and the so-called 'problem play'. Ironically enough, Dumas the Younger's prolific output provided more roles for Duse than any other French or Italian dramatist despite her increasing dissatisfaction with the genre. The heroines of *Demi-monde* (1855), *La Dame aux camélias* (1852), *Une Visite de noces* (1871), *La Princesse Georges* (1871), *La Femme de Claude* (1873) and *Francillon* (1887) all figured in Duse's repertoire at some stage of her career, and in 1885 she created the title role of his play, *Denise*. Her interpretation of Marguerite in *La Dame aux camélias* and Césarine in *La Femme de Claude* were particularly memorable, and Duse was still playing these roles successfully at the age of fifty. The critic Hermann Bahr was so impressed with her Césarine that, in an article published in *Frankfurter Zeitung* on 9 May 1891, he persuaded the impresario Tänczer to arrange a series of performances for Duse in Vienna. Of her Marguerite, Bernard Shaw wrote: 'It is unspeakably touching because . . . exquisitely considerate: that is, exquisitely sympathetic . . . An actress who has understood the author and a greater artist than he.'

Carlo Duse (1866-1937)

Cousin of Eleonora Duse and married to the actress Italia Vitaliani. The younger son of Eugenio Duse and Cecilia Bellotti, Carlo Duse graduated from *generico primario* to *prim'attore*, playing in the company of some of the best actors of the period. As *capocomico*, he proved to be less successful, and in later years was often to be found acting with second-rate theatre companies. His last stage appearance was in D'Annunzio's only truly successful play, *La figlia di Iorio* (1907), acted in the presence of the author himself at his residence, Il Vittoriale, on Lake Garda.

Enrico Duse (c. 1830–?)
Youngest of Luigi Duse's four sons. He played juvenile leads with his father's company before moving on to other theatre companies. Enrico Duse eventually progressed to leading roles with the Pompili company and character parts with the Vitaliani company.

Giovanni Emanuel (1848–1902)
Italian actor who made his debut as *secondo brillante* with the Bellotti-Bon Company. By 1873 he was an established figure in Italian theatrical circles and able to form his own company with a succession of distinguished leading ladies, including Giacinta Pezzana, Virginia Reiter and Adelina Marchi. An adherent of naturalism, he played Coupeau in Zola's *L'Assommoir* (1878) and the title role in Balzac's *Mercadet le faiseur* (1844).

Paolo Ferrari (1822–89)
Italian dramatist who was born in Modena, brought up in Massa, and lived for some thirty years in Milan. He was a versatile author who wrote historical plays, popular comedies in various dialects, and thesis dramas. The play in Duse's repertoire, *Amore senza stima*, was written in 1868 and is based on Goldoni's comedy *La moglie saggia* (1752). From 1883 until 1884 Ferrari directed the reputable Compagnia del Teatro Drammatico Nazionale in Rome.

Ludwig Fulda (1862–1939)
German author and playwright, Fulda wrote some sixty plays, yet today he is best remembered for his translations of plays by Goldoni, Molière, Beaumarchais and Rostand. His verse drama *Der Talisman* (1893) was nominated for the Schiller Prize. An adherent of the school of Naturalism, Fulda was a founder member and director of the *Freie Bühne* in Berlin. A staunch admirer of Ibsen, he helped to promote the Norwegian dramatist's work in Germany. He produced Ibsen's *Ghosts* at Augusta and published an excellent translation of *Peer Gynt* in 1915. The Fulda play in the Duse repertoire was *Unter vier Augen*, written in 1901.

Amalia Fumagalli (1824–89)
Italian actress and contemporary of Adelaide Ristori. Fumagalli began her acting career as a child and by the age of sixteen she was playing juvenile leads. By 1844, she ranked as *prim'attrice assoluta* and proved to be equally effective in tragedy and comedy. In later years she played character roles with the reputable companies of Bellotti-Bon and Sadowsky.

DUSE ON TOUR

Tommaso Gherardi del Testa (1814–81)

Italian dramatist, whose first successful comedy *Una folle ambizione* was performed by Adelaide Ristori in 1844. He was one of the most representative Italian playwrights in the mid-nineteenth century but his fame was short-lived. In retrospect, Gherardi del Testa's plays suggest a pale imitation of Goldoni, Sardou, Dumas and Augier.

Carlo Goldoni (1707–93)

Italian dramatist who virtually overthrew the established *commedia dell'arte* dramatic form by replacing its stock masked characters with more realistic ones, its loosely structured and often repetitive action with tightly constructed plots, and its predictable farce with a new spirit of cheerfulness and spontaneity. Goldoni was remarkably prolific, his entire output amounting to some 250 plays.

Heroines from two Goldoni plays figures in Duse's repertoire: *Pamela nubile* (1750), based on Richardson's novel, and the heroine she played well into maturity, *La locandiera* (1753). *La locandiera* had some famous imterpreters in the history of the Italian theatre, including Marchionni, Ristori, Tessero and Reiter, but Duse, who rarely played comedy roles, was considered an outstanding Mirandolina. Restraint and finesse charaterized her interpretation of Goldoni's spirited and resourceful eighteenth-century heroine. And it was *La locandiera* that Duse chose to perform in the presence of Queen Victoria at Windsor Castle on 10 May 1894.

Emma Gramatica (1875–1965)

Versatile Italian actress noted for the intelligence and subtlety of her acting. She was never to equal the success of her older sister, the distinguished actress Irma Gramatica, despite some memorable performances in plays by Ibsen and Shaw – two dramatists with whom she felt a special affinity.

Irma Gramatica (1873–1962)

Italian actress who played juvenile leads in the company led by Cesare Rossi with Duse as leading lady. Subsequently, she assumed leading roles with the company headed by Ermete Zacconi. Irma Gramatica's style was predominantly lyrical, but the sincerity of her acting and admirable diction assured her worldwide success. As a principal actress with the highly successful Talli-Calabresi company, she created a number of roles, notably that of Nennele in Giacosa's *Come le foglie* (1900), Lisa in Verga's *Dal tuo al mio* (1903), and Mila di Codra in D'Annunzio's *La figlia di Iorio* (1904). She also gave highly individual interpretations of the principal roles in Ibsen's *A Doll's House*, Marco Praga's *La moglie ideale*, and Pinero's *The Second Mrs. Tanqueray*.

Henrik Johan Ibsen (1828–1906)

Norwegian poet and playwright and the creator of modern thesis drama. Ibsen's reputation in Italy is intimately linked with that of Duse, who became recognized throughout the world as an incomparable interpreter of his plays. Duse gave the first performance of Nora in *A Doll's House* in Italy at the Teatro dei Filodrammatici on 9 February 1891. Other memorable interpretations soon followed: as *Hedda Gabler* at the Teatro Manzoni in Milan on 4 June 1898; Rebecca in *Rosmersholm* at the Teatro Lirico in Milan on 11 December 1905; Ella in *John Gabriel Borkman* during a tour of Northern Europe in September and October 1908; and Ellida in *The Lady from the Sea* at the Teatro Duse in Turin on 5 May 1921. Her last Ibsen role assumed after her comeback, was Mrs Alving in *Ghosts* at the Teatro Costanzi in Rome on 4 December 1922 with Memo Benassi as Oswald.

Paul de Kock (1793–1871)

Prolific French writer of discreetly pornographic novels. He scored considerable success with works like *Georgette* (1820), *La Femme, le mari et l'amant* (1829), and *Moeurs parisiennes* (1873). His novels enjoyed enormous popularity in Italy.

Claudio Leigheb (1848–1903)

Italian actor–manager associated with some of Italy's most distinguished theatre companies. Leigheb, who was noted for his excellent diction and polished acting achieved fame as *attore brillante*. He gave memorable performances in comedies by Goldoni and in *pochades* from the French repertoire.

Tina di Lorenzo (1872–1930)

Italian actress of extraordinary beauty and charming stage presence, which made her one of the most popular stage personalities of the period; by the age of seventeen she was already established as *prim'attrice assoluta*. In 1897 she embarked upon a fruitful partnership with Flavio Andò. Their acting styles were in perfect rapport and they toured widely, arousing enormous enthusiasm wherever they appeared. Both artists helped to promote the work of national dramatists, notably the plays of Butti, Giacosa, Bracco and Rovetta.

Aurélien Lugné-Poe (1869–1940)

French actor–manager. As director of the experimental Théâtre de L'Oeuvre (founded in 1893) in Paris, he was responsible for staging the first performances in France of Maeterlinck's *Pelléas et Mélisande* (1892), Ibsen's *Rosmersholm* (1893) and *Peer Gynt* (1896), and Wilde's *Salomé* (1895). Together with Antoine and Gemier, Lugné-Poe was one of the leading pioneers in the French theatre between the epoch of the Théâtre Libre (1887–94) and the period immediately before the First World War. He first came to prominence as an actor in Antoine's theatre company but there were serious differences of opinion between these two remarkable personalities, and Lugné-Poe broke away in order to develop his own theories about theatre reform with his Théâtre de L'Oeuvre. He was instrumental in promoting important new plays by foreign dramatists, and works by Strindberg, Hauptmann and Gorki were brought into the repertoire without ignoring his company's objective to seek out and produce new works by young and hitherto ignored French dramatists.

Lugné-Poe had a real flair for promoting theatrical enterprises. He successfully toured Europe and the Americas with his own company and later proved himself a most able and experienced impresario in arranging foreign tours for Duse. His reminiscences of their collaboration can be found in his published memoirs *Sous les étoiles*, which covers the years 1902–12. Frank to the point of being indiscreet, Lugné-Poe's comments about the great actress on tour, whom he describes as 'surnaturelle pour le bien comme pour le mal', emphasize the inevitable difficulties and strain endured by both management and artists when they embarked upon a long tour of South America at the turn of the century. Duse appeared at the Théâtre de L'Oeuvre in 1905, acting the role of Vassilissa in Italian in Gorki's *Les Bas-fonds* which the rest of the cast played in French.

In 1923 Lugné-Poe produced Shaw's *Pygmalion* in Paris at the Théâtre des Arts. Shaw had met Lugné-Poe when the latter visited London with Maeterlinck as early as March 1895, and in a letter to Richard Mansfield dated 27 March 1895, he wrote: 'Lugné-Poe and the Théâtre de L'Oeuvre are playing here – Ibsen and Maeterlinck: shabby and misunderstood, but artistically first rate. Man of genius, by the Lord.'

Maurice Maeterlinck (1862–1949)

Symbolist poet and playwright and the most famous Belgian writer of his day. He wrote in French and was mainly influenced by French literary trends. As a dramatist, Maeterlinck sealed his reputation with *Pelléas et Mélisande*, written in 1892 and produced at the Théâtre de l'Oeuvre by Lugné-Poe. Debussy set the text of *Pelléas et Mélisande* to music in 1902. That same year, Maeterlinck wrote his historical drama *Monna Vanna*.

Carlo Marenco (1800–46)

Italian dramatist who wrote a number of tragedies on medieval themes and episodes taken from Dante's *Divine Comedy*. *Pia dei Tolomei* was written in 1837.

Virginia Marini (1842–1918)

Italian actress who was in her twenties before taking up a stage career. By 1864 she was engaged as *prima amorosa* at the Teatro dei Fiorentini in Naples alongside Tommaso Salvini and Clementina Cazzola. A natural talent and assiduous study helped her to perfect her interpretations of the heroines of Goldoni, Scribe, and Dumas the Younger.

Nino Martoglio (1870–1921)

Sicilian poet, actor–manager, playwright and film director. Martoglio conceived the idea of forming a troupe of local actors devoted entirely to dialect plays. His company opened at the Teatro Manzoni in Milan on 11 April 1903 with a performance of *Zolfara* by a minor Sicilian dramatist Giusti Sinapoli. Martoglio contracted all the leading Sicilian actors of the day, such as Angelo Musco, Mimì Aguglia and Giovanni Grasso, Jr, and commissioned plays from young dramatists like Pirandello. As a film director, he was responsible for the screen version of Roberto Bracco's thesis play *Sperduti nel buio* (1914) and Zola's *Teresa Raquin* (1915) with the veteran Giacinta Pezzana.

Henri Meilhac (1831–97)
Prolific French writer and dramatist and a representative figure of the *belle époque*. He enjoyed a long and fruitful collaboration with Ludovic Halévy (1833–1908). The combination of Meilhac's wit and Halévy's sensibility resulted in a perfect partnership. Their greatest creation for the stage was *Frou-frou*, which was produced at Le Gymnase on 30 October 1869 with Sarah Bernhardt excelling in the title role.

Angelo Musco (1872–1937)
Another important actor who helped to popularize Sicilian dialect theatre. Musco started his stage career in variety and music hall before being discovered by the Sicilian dramatist Nino Martoglio, who helped Musco to develop into a serious actor. His repertoire consisted of all the major Sicilian authors, notably Capuana and Pirandello; D'Annunzio described him as 'the king of comedy'. Today he is remembered as one of the last great exponents of the *commedia dell'arte* tradition.

Andrea Niccoli (1862–1917)
Influential actor–manager associated with the staging of plays written in his native Florentine dialect. After gaining experience with reputable actor–managers like Cesare Rossi, Belli-Blanes and Giovanni Emanuel, Niccoli eventually formed his own company and became instrumental in promoting the work of the Florentine dramatist Augusto Novelli (1867–1927), notably his popular play, *Acqua cheta* (1909).

Mario Nunes Vais (1856–1932)
Italian photographer. He lived and worked in Florence and became renowned for his portraits of many of the leading artists, actors and men of letters of the day. Nunes Vais was responsible for numerous photographs of Duse at different stages of her career. His magnificent collection was seen to advantage in the Duse Exhibition held in Rome in 1974.

Ugo Ojetti (1871–1946)
Italian journalist, critic and playwright. His one act play *Il garofano* was given its first performance at Turin in 1905 by the Talli-Gramatica-Calabresi company. Today Ojetti is best remembered for his analytical essays on theatre personalities of the day: the dramatists, Maeterlinck and Pirandello; the composers, Puccini, Boito and Verdi, and a whole gallery of actors – including Tommaso Salvini, Ruggero Ruggeri and Duse, whose performances he followed with professional interest throughout Italy and abroad.

Angelina Pagano (1888–1962)
Argentinian actress of Italian parentage. As a girl she studied singing before becoming a drama student at the Reale Scuola di Firenze under

the able direction of Luigi Rasi. Before graduating, Pagano was auditioned by Tommaso Salvini, Duse, and D'Annunzio as part of her final examinations, and this led to a contract with Duse's company. Still in her teens, Pagano was entrusted with the role of Samaritana in D'Annunzio's *Francesca da Rimini* and was singled out by critics as a young actress of considerable promise. Upon returning to Argentina in 1903, she was hailed as 'la piccola Duse' and worked with the leading companies and producers of the day in Buenos Aires. Pagano returned to Italy from 1908 until 1914, where she gained further experience. When war broke out, she decided to return to Argentina once more; there she joined the company of the Podestá Brothers before eventually forming her own company. Following Duse's example, Pagano insisted upon high standards in matters of acting and production. She also became something of a pioneer in her determination to launch works by young national dramatists and to introduce new plays from abroad.

Giovanni Pascoli (1855–1912)

Italian classical scholar and poet from the Romagna region. His lyric poems, with their perfection of form and linguistic innovations have exercised an important influence notably in the work of the so-called *crepuscolari* (or 'twilight') poets such as Corrado Govoni and Guido Gozzano, who were active at the turn of the century.

Silvio Pellico (1789–1854)

Italian writer and patriot. The author of several tragedies in the traditional mould, Pellico's writing for the theatre was characterized by deep patriotic and religious sentiments. His play *Francesca da Rimini* was written in 1814 and performed the following year.

Giacinta Pezzana (1845–1919)

A native of Turin where she came to prominence as a member of the Bellotti-Bon company in the 1860s before moving on to the Teatro dei Fiorentini at Naples. In 1879, Pezzana scored a personal triumph when she created the title role in Pietro Cossa's *Messalina* in Milan. Her next great success came in Zola's *Teresa Raquin* and the author himself wrote to congratulate her: 'Je dois le succès de ma pièce à votre talent supérieur de grande artiste.'

Pezzana's sudden decision to retire from the stage in 1880 when playing with the Compagnia della Città di Torino under the direction of Cesare Rossi was ostensibly due to illness, but other commentators speak of the actress's profound disenchantment with the theatre of the period. From 1895 onwards, she returned sporadically to the stage. D'Annunzio had Pezzana in mind for the part of Candia in *La figlia di Iorio* and Ema in *La nave*, but she assumed neither role because of disagreements over contracts. Pezzana toured extensively, visiting Spain, Russia, Egypt and South America. After several abortive attempts to form a company of her own in Italy, Pezzana settled for some years in Uruguay and directed a Spanish company at Montevideo where she opened a drama school with a government subvention. She returned to Italy in

1914 when war was declared and made several films, including a screen adaptation of *Teresa Raquin*.

Luigi Pezzana (1814–94)

Italian actor. Endowed with good looks and an impressive stage presence, Luigi Pezzana was more flamboyant than subtle as a performer. He played a wide variety of roles, notably in plays by Alfieri, Niccolini, Goldoni and Ferrari. Given his temperament as an actor, Pezzana scored best in the melodramas of Dumas, and was long remembered for his interpretation as the Count of Montecristo.

Sir Arthur Wing Pinero (1855–1934)

Leading English playwright of the late Victorian and Edwardian eras in England. He wrote social dramas calculated to draw a fashionable audience. His later work, in a more serious vein, gained something from the spirit of realism that swept the European theatre towards the end of the nineteenth century when plays began to deal with genuine problems of society and the individual.

Pinero is best remembered today for his brilliantly constructed farces which have survived his serious drama. *The Second Mrs Tanqueray* (1893) established his reputation as a playwright. The role was interpreted by all the great actresses of the day and Pinero became identified with plays demanding sympathy for women saddled with a stricter moral code than men. William Archer, the drama critic of the *London Figaro* and subsequently *The World*, judged Duse's performance as Paula Tanqueray 'one of her most able and extraordinary creations', even if not a part entirely suited to her temperament. The English poet and critic Arthur William Symons has drawn an interesting profile of Duse in the role, comparing her performance with that of Mrs Patrick Campbell. The English actress was obviously the more convincing Paula as conceived by Pinero, and Duse's approach to the role erred in seeking depth where there was none to be found. Symons wrote: 'Paula as played by Duse is sad and sincere, where the Englishwoman is only irritable; she has the Italian simplicity and directness in place of that terrible English capacity for uncertainty in emotion and huffiness in manner. She brings profound tragedy, the tragedy of a soul which has sinned and suffered and tried vainly to free itself from the consequences of its deeds, into a study of circumstances in their ruin of material happiness.

And, frankly, the play cannot stand it . . . Here is Duse, a chalice for the wine of imagination, but the chalice remains empty.'

Luigi Pirandello (1867–1936)

Italian playwright, novelist, and short story writer, awarded the Nobel Prize for Literature in 1934. As an important innovator in the modern theatre, Pirandello scored his greatest successes with *Così è se vi pare* (1917), *Sei personaggi in cerca d'autore* (1921) and *Enrico IV* (1922). He began writing for the theatre in his native Sicilian dialect and collaborated on a number of plays with the Sicilian poet and dramatist Nino Martoglio. A loyal admirer of Duse, Pirandello deeply regretted that their careers never really coincided in the theatre and that Italy's greatest actress was never to perform in any of his plays. He wrote *La vita che ti diedi* in 1923 with Duse in mind and she read the play with genuine interest but the project somehow failed to materialize.

Marco Praga (1862–1929)

Italian playwright influenced by naturalist tendencies in the French theatre of the period. His first play to achieve success was *L'amico* (1886), then *Giuliana* (1887), and an adaptation of Gerolamo Rovetta's novel *Mater dolorosa* (1889).

But Praga's two best known plays are *Le vergini* (1889) and *La moglie ideale* (1890). Duse's sensitive interpretation of the adulterous Giulia in *La moglie ideale* assured the play's success. Other plays by Praga to be included in Duse's repertoire were *L'innamorata* (1891) and *La porta chiusa* (1913). Duse's prestige was such that when she came to interpret his heroines she felt free to influencé or modify significant details in the text. The young Noccioli registers shocked surprise in his diary as he watches Praga concede to Duse's every suggestion. The dramatist himself, recalling the rehearsals of *La moglie ideale* wrote: 'The rehearsals were sheer bliss . . . I stood in a corner thoroughly enjoying myself . . . yes, enjoying myself. Because my poor prose, read thus . . . as Duse read it and made her actors read it – commenting and explaining the text as she went along, demonstrating for the cast's benefit the correct inflections, the appropriate gestures and necessary movements – my poor prose suddenly became tolerable and meaningful, sometimes even amusing . . .'.

Rachel (1821–58)

France's greatest tragedienne during the first half of the nineteenth century. She studied at the Paris Conservatoire in 1836 before taking up an engagement at the Théâtre Gymnase in April 1837. Her acting attracted the attention of the influential French critic Janin, and a contract to appear at the Comédie Française soon followed. Rachel's interpretation of the standard classical repertoire received unanimous acclaim but by the 1840s the actress was also turning her attention to modern roles such as Lebrun's *Marie Stuart* (1840) and *Adrienne Lecouvreur* by Scribe and Legouvé. Rachel was one of the first actresses in the mid-nineteenth century to undertake extensive tours abroad; between 1842 and 1857 she appeared throughout Europe, Russia and the United States.

Luigi Rasi (1852–1918)

Important actor, drama teacher, and theatre historian. Rasi abandoned his university studies in order to become an actor. He soon graduated from secondary roles, and by 1877 he was playing *prim'attore giovane* with the Pietriboni company, with which he remained under contract for five years. Rasi then abandoned acting in order to become director of productions at the Scuola di Recitazione di Firenze, where he was able to engage in theatre research and experiment with new genres and methods.

[166]

BIOGRAPHICAL APPENDIX

One notable experiment introduced by Rasi were verse readings accompanied by music; for example, Byron's *Manfred* with music by Schumann. As a teacher and pioneer, Rasi's influence in Italian theatre circles became renowned. His extensive publications include the standard two volume work on *I Comici Italiani* (1897–1905) and a valuable study of Duse's art.

Virginia Reiter (1868–1937)

Italian actress of singular beauty and expressiveness who began her stage career as a child star. Reiter first came to prominence in 1882 with the company of Giovanni Emanuel. Exuberant by temperament, Reiter acquired discipline under Emanuel's experienced guidance. She scored a personal success in Cavallotti's *La figlia di Jefte*; subsequently, the author dedicated the work to Reiter. By 1887, she ranked as *prim'attrice assoluta* and embarked upon a brilliant career throughout Italy and abroad. At the height of her fame, she absorbed many of the roles associated with Duse, including *La Dame aux camélias, Fedora, Fernande, Odette, Adrienne Lecouvreur* and *Frou-frou*.

Gabrielle Réjane (1856–1920)

French actress who graduated from the Conservatoire in 1874. Her greatest stage successes in the 1870s and 1880s were achieved in productions at the Vaudeville and Variétés. By 1888, Réjane had become one of the most popular actresses on the French stage, with her natural charm and Parisian chic. Her vast repertoire included all the important French dramatists of the late nineteenth century: Meilhac, Sardou, Bernstein, Donnay, Daudet, Bataille and Lemaître. Réjane toured extensively at the turn of the century and was widely acclaimed throughout Europe, Russia and the Americas. The critic James Agate reviewed her London appearances in glowing terms. In 1905 she founded her own theatre company and acquired the Nouveau-Théâtre, which she inaugurated the following year as the Théâtre Réjane.

Ernest Renan (1823–92)

French philosopher, historian and scholar of religion. Renan only began to experiment with writing for the theatre towards the end of his career. Between 1878 and 1888, he wrote four plays, all of which have been rejected by most critics as impossible from the point of view of stage production. Even in Renan's time these five-act dramas appealed only to an intellectual elite.

The one play among them to achieve any success in the theatre was *L'Abbesse de Jouarre* (1886), which was translated into Italian the following year by Enrico Panzacchi and performed by Eleonora Duse and Flavio Andò. Set in a prison during the French Revolution, the imminence of death brings Monseigneur d'Arcy and the Abbess into each other's arms. A child is born of this illicit union, and, saved from the guillotine, the Abbess contracts a marriage of convenience. Antoine and Lugné-Poe both tried to stage the play in Paris, but permission was withheld by the censors on moral grounds. Duse ran into similar difficulties with ecclesiastical censorship in South America, and the play was withdrawn from the repertoire before ever being actually performed during the 1907 tour.

Adelaide Ristori (1822–1906)

Italy's greatest tragedienne in the mid-nineteenth century. From 1837 until 1838 she was juvenile lead with the Reale Compagnia Sarda where she learned much from the distinguished veteran Carlotta Marchionni, whose roles Ristori later assumed. In 1853, she took Parisian audiences by storm and was judged to be superior to Rachel herself by certain French critics. Further successes followed in England and the Americas where Ristori played the regal heroines of Alfieri, Schiller and Victor Hugo. For critics like George Bernard Shaw and Henry James, Ristori offered 'a supreme exhibition of the grand style of acting'.

Carlo Rosaspina (1854–1921)

Italian actor who started his career as a juvenile lead in his father's company. After gaining further stage experience with well known actors like Gaspare Lavaggi and Adelaide Tessero, Rosaspina was engaged as *prim'attore assoluto* by the reputable Bellotti-Bon company. He retained this rank in subsequent engagements with Cesare Rossi, Luigi Rasi and Duse. Rosaspina's unaffected and controlled style made him the perfect leading man for the great actress, and they scored a notable success together in *La signora delle camelie, La moglie di Claudio* and *La seconda Mrs Tanqueray*. In Italy he created the title role in Hauptmann's *Fuhrmann Henschel* (1898) at the Teatro dei Filodrammatici di Milano in 1899 and the difficult role of Gianciotto in D'Annunzio's *Francesca da Rimini* at the Teatro Costanzi in Rome on 2 December 1901.

Cesare Rossi (1829–98)

Italian actor–manager of considerable influence. Rossi was a versatile actor with a vast repertoire who came to prominence in the Bellotti-Bon company between the years 1860 and 1871.

By 1877, Rossi was able to launch his own company, which became semi-permanent when he leased the Teatro Carignano in Turin for six months annually. The years from 1881 to 1884 were particularly brilliant for Rossi's company, thanks to his leading actors, Eleonora Duse and Flavio Andò. The company toured South America from 1885 until 1886. When Duse and Andò left the company upon their return to Italy, Rossi engaged another distinguished trio of principals in Ermete Zacconi, Teresa Mariani and Graziana Glech (protegée and pupil of Adelaide Ristori).

Odoardo Antonio Rovescalli (1864–1936)

Italian stage designer much in demand by all the best theatre companies at the turn of the century. He collaborated with Duse for a number of important new productions, perhaps most notably of all for the first performance of D'Annunzio's *Francesca da Rimini* at the Teatro Costanzi in Rome in 1901, a production singled out by critics for its great visual

beauty. Rovescalli also worked abroad for artists like Coquelin and Sarah
Bernhardt in Paris, and Maria Guerrero in Madrid.

Eustase Thomas Salignac (1867–1945)

French tenor who subsequently became a renowned teacher of singing.
From 1896 until 1903 he made regular·appearances at the Metropolitan
in New York, where he sang all the leading tenor roles in the French
repertoire. From 1897 to 1899 and 1901 to 1904, he appeared during
every season at Covent Garden. In 1913 he became director of the Opera
House at Nice and in 1924 Professor of Elocution at the Paris
Conservatoire.

Gustavo Salvini (1859–1930)

Italian actor and son of the great Tommaso Salvini and Clementina
Cazzola. He was engaged as *attore generico* by the Achille Dondini
company in 1878 against his father's wishes. Gustavo was never to
achieve the success or reputation of his famous father despite some
notable interpretations of Shakespearian roles. He was engaged by Duse
for the first production of D'Annunzio's *Francesca da Rimini*, which
opened at the Teatro Costanzi in Rome on 9 December 1901, but contemporary reviews of this interesting collaboration suggest that Salvini
and Duse were temperamentally unsuited as stage partners.

In *La morte civile* (1861) by Paolo Giacometti (1816–82) Gustavo had to
compete with his father's masterly interpretation of Corrado, which
Tommaso Salvini had played throughout Europe and the Americas.
Victor Hugo found him 'inimitable' in the role when he took the play
to Paris, and even Henry James, who found Giacometti's social drama
about the indissoluble nature of marriage 'meagre and monotonous',
defined Salvini's performance as Corrado 'a most moving creation'.

Tommaso Salvini (1829–1915)

The most famous Italian tragedian of the nineteenth century alongside
Ernesto Rossi (1827–96) and Adelaide Ristori (1822–1906). Tommaso
Salvini began his career as an extra in the company of the famous Gustavo
Modena, who predicted a brilliant career for the young Tommaso Salvini
when he tested him in Egisto's monologue from *Merope*.

In 1845, at the age of sixteen, he moved on to become *secondo amoroso*
in the Compagnia Reale di Napoli. In search of wider acting experience,
Salvini next joined the company of Domeniconi where he partnered
Adelaide Ristori. The young actor now went from strength to strength
and excelled in heroic roles such as Oreste, Saul, Othello and Hamlet.

An actor of noble presence and exceptional physique, Salvini prepared
his roles with the utmost care. Poets like Victor Hugo and Robert
Browning extolled his praises while contemporary actors like Irving,
Booth and Sonnenthal expressed their wholehearted admiration.

Victorien Sardou (1831–1908)

French dramatist who exploited the formula of the *comédie-vaudeville*
successfully launched by Scribe around 1825. His major plays formed an

integral part of the standard repertoire of every French and Italian actress of note in the late nineteenth century. At the height of her fame, Duse assimilated four Sardou plays into her repertoire: *Théodora* (1884), *Odette* (1881), *Fernande* (1870) and *Divorçons* (1880).

Gaetano Sbodio (1844–1920)

Italian actor and dramatist who became a major interpreter of the *commedia verista* in Lombardy. Between the years 1883 and 1897, Sbodio wrote some twelve plays in Milanese dialect. At his best in character roles, he enjoyed enormous popularity as 'an actor of human warmth and sincerity'. His farewell appearance at the Teatro Lirico in Milan in 1907 was long remembered as one of the most emotional evenings in the annals of the city's theatre history. The sketch to which Noccioli refers in the diary was a one-act play by Carlo Bertolazzi (1870–1916) in which Sbodio played one of his favourite roles for the last time as the 'veggion del Pio Luogo Trivulzio' in *Ona scènna de la vita*. Sbodio had played the same role when the sketch received its first performance in 1890.

Augustin-Eugène Scribe (1791–1861)

French dramatist and master of the well constructed play. Scribe was a prolific writer who specialized in plays of popular appeal. His comedies and dramas expressed the values and predilections of bourgeois society and extolled the virtues of commercial prosperity and family life. Scribe's melodrama *Adrienne Lecouvreur* (1849) about an actress who falls in love with a nobleman, unaware of his high rank, was interpreted by all the great actresses in the late nineteenth century, and most successfully of all by Sarah Bernhardt, Helena Modjeska and Eleonora Duse.

Matilde Serao (1856–1927)

Greek-born novelist and journalist who lived and worked in Naples and Rome. Together with her husband Edoardo Scarfoglio, Matilde Serao founded the *Corriere di Roma* before joining the staff of the *Corriere di Napoli* where she achieved enormous popularity with a column entitled 'Api, moscari e vespe' ('Bees, blue-bottles and wasps'). Subsequently, she wrote for *Il Mattino* and *Giorno*. The best of her romantic novels is *Il paese di Cuccagna*, published in 1891.

Elisa Severi (?–1930)

Well-known actress admired for her beauty and expressive voice. Her natural talent for the stage compensated for any lack of formal training. In 1894 she was contracted by the Paladini-Talli company and by 1905 she was an established leading actress. In 1912 she became a member of the famous Compagnia Stabile Romana directed by Ettore Berti.

Carmen Silva (1843–1916)

The name by which Queen Elizabeth of Romania was more commonly known. The German born wife of Prince Carl I, Elizabeth was a woman of wide cultural interests. She wrote books inspired by tales from Romanian folklore and studied music and painting. She had a special regard for Italian literature, especially for Dante's *Divine Comedy*, which was read and discussed at court in her own intimate circle.

Constantin Stanislavsky (1863–1938)

Russian theatre and opera director, actor, teacher and theoretician. One crucial problem studied by Stanislavsky was how actors might avoid giving mechanical performances when obliged to go on playing the same part night after night. In order to combat this danger, he advocated constant study and psychological penetration of the role. As Olga Signorelli points out in her authoritative study of Duse, it was only in later life that Stanislavsky, who was an intransigent opponent of the star system, came fully to appreciate the Italian actress's extraordinary identification with the roles she interpreted. Analysing Duse's performances, Stanislavsky found to his satisfaction that here was an actress who shared his own firm belief that the true artist 'reads between the lines' in order to discover the true essence of the role.

Hermann Sudermann (1857–1928)

German writer and dramatist associated with the naturalist movement in Germany. His play *Heimat*, performed for the first time in 1893, brought him fame throughout the world. The main protagonist Magda is a celebrated opera singer who returns to confront her past in the narrow, provincial home town that she had left in disgrace. The role was interpreted by all the leading actresses of the period, and these included Sarah Bernhardt, Eleonora Duse, Mrs Patrick Campbell and Minnie Madden Fiske, among others. *Heimat* was not a play much admired by the French, although the doyen of Parisian critics, Francisque Sarcey, found Duse's interpretation of Magda much more acceptable than that of Bernhardt. In a letter to his ailing wife written in late November 1892, Sudermann described Duse as the perfect Magda. He wrote: 'Try to imagine our ideal Magda and then add thousands and thousands of surprises and revelations.' High praise, indeed, when one considers that Sudermann was upset by certain arbitrary changes in the text perpetrated by the Italian translator without his permission.

José Tallaví (1878–1916)

Spanish actor of striking originality who was noted for the seriousness with which he prepared his roles. By 1904 he was appearing at the Teatro de la Comedia in Madrid with considerable success; and soon afterwards he began touring South America where he enjoyed enormous popularity. In 1911 Tallaví formed his own company. Equally effective in comedy and tragedy, Tallaví was long remembered for his masterly interpretation of Oswald in Ibsen's *Ghosts* and in Benavente's incisive satire *Los malhechores del bien* (1905). Laura Socías, his leading lady on this occasion, appears to have been an actress of secondary importance.

Adelaide Tessero (1842–92)

Italian actress named after her famous aunt, the tragedienne Adelaide Ristori who fostered her early career. By 1859, Tessero had become *prim'attrice* in her own right with the Torelli company in Piedmont where she acted both in dialect plays and classical dramas. Adelaide Tessero was a famous interpreter of Leopoldo Marenco's *Marcellina*, and her wide repertoire ranged from Schiller to Sardou and Dumas – and from the historical dramas of Paolo Giacometti and Pietro Cossa to the thesis plays of Paolo Ferrari.

Alfredo Testoni (1856–1931)

Bolognese journalist, poet, author and dramatist who subsequently developed an interest in directing for both stage and screen. An experimentalist of some note in Bolognese theatre circles, he wrote plays both in Italian and in his native dialect. Today Testoni is mainly remembered for his dialect poems about *Sgnera Cattareina* (1900) from which the extracts in Italian, *Signora Caterina all'Esposizione di Milano* (*Signora Caterina at the Milan Fair*) mentioned by Noccioli were taken; and for a major play *Il Cardinale Lambertini* in which Ermete Zacconi scored a personal success when he appeared in the title role at Rome on 30 October 1905.

Achille Torelli (1841–1922)

Neapolitan dramatist who wrote his first plays before the age of twenty. Torelli's first real success was *I mariti* which the Bellotti-Bon company produced for the first time in Florence in 1867. His next play to achieve lasting popularity was *Scrollina* (1880), of which the vivid dialogue and harmonious structure were acclaimed by critics. As a young actress, Duse scored a personal success in the title role.

Teresa Boetti Valvassura (1851–1930)

Italian actress who, after a sound training in the influential Bellotti-Bon Company, played leading roles in a number of important theatre companies, notably alongside actors like Giovanni Emanuel and Giacinta Pezzana. Her dramatic temperament was best suited to plays by authors such as Dumas the Younger and Sardou, and she was highly considered for her interpretation as Francillon, Tosca and Fedora. After leaving the stage for a brief period she directed the Accademia dei Filodrammatici di Milano.

Giovanni Verga (1840–1922)

Sicilian novelist and playwright of the *verismo* school, the Italian equivalent of the naturalism that Zola had made popular in France. His major plays reflect these realistic tendencies. *Cavalleria rusticana* (1884) and *La lupa* (1886) survive in the modern Italian repertoire as outstanding examples of the genre with their themes of love and jealousy, their terse dialogue, Sicilian intensity and primitive peasant environment.

Italia Vitaliani (1866–1938)

Italian actress and the cousin of Eleonora Duse. By the mid 1880s Vitaliani was established as a juvenile lead and engaged by the Cesare Rossi Company where she played alongside Duse, then the company's leading lady. By 1892, Vitaliani was directing her own company in the face of serious financial difficulties. In compensation, she was free to choose her own repertoire. Contemporary reviews suggest that Vitaliani was a notable interpreter of *Hedda Gabler, Maria Stuarda, Magda* and *Zaza*. When Luigi Rasi died in 1919, she took his place for some years as director of the Reale Scuola di Recitazione in Florence.

Ermete Zacconi (1857–1948)

Italian actor–manager and, together with Ermete Novelli (1851–1919), one of the most prominent figures in theatrical circles at the turn of the century. After starting his career in his father's theatre company, Zacconi gained further experience alongside all the great actors of the day – Lambertini and Majeroni, Vestri, Dominici, and Battistoni. From 1885 until 1887 he was engaged by Giovanni Emanuel before moving on to become leading actor with the companies of Cesare Rossi and Virginia Marini.

From 1897 onwards Zacconi headed his own company. On two occasions, he briefly joined forces with Eleonora Duse: first in 1899 for the first Italian productions of D'Annunzio's *La Gloria* and *La città morta*, and then in 1922 when Duse made her comeback. He toured indefatigably throughout Europe, South America and Egypt and was still acting in his eighties. His repertoire was vast and ranged from nineteenth-century classical drama to thesis plays by Rovetta and Giacosa. He gave memorable performances of *Othello* and *King Lear* and other major roles in his repertoire were Cossa's *Nerone*, Musset's *Lorenzaccio*, and Oswald in Ibsen's *Ghosts*.

Giovanni Zenatello (1876–1942)

Famous Italian baritone and teacher of singing. He married the Spanish mezzo-soprano María Gay (1879–1943), and both artists enjoyed an international reputation before finally settling in New York, where they opened their own academy of vocal studies.

Emile Zola (1840–1902)

French novelist whose stage adaptation of *Thérèse Raquin* (1873) was never published, and the work proved to be a complete fiasco when performed in Paris. The Italian production, starring Giacinta Pezzana, came six years later, and its success in Naples ensured the play's popularity throughout Italy for some considerable time. As an exponent of naturalism, Zola formulated his own theories about the theatre and dramatic presentation, and he exercised an enormous influence over André Antoine and the adherents of the *Théâtre-Libre*.

SELECT
BIBLIOGRAPHY

Select Bibliography

Agate, James, *Red Letter Nights: a survey of the post-Elizabethan drama in actual performance on the London stage, 1921–1943*. New York: Benjamin Blom, 1969 (reprint of 1944 edition).

Antoine, André. *Memories of the Théâtre-libre*. Translated by Martin A. Carlson. Edited by H. D. Albright. Coral Gables, Florida: University of Miami Press, 1964.

Antona Traversi, Camillo, *Eleonora Duse: sua vita, sua gloria, suo martirio*. Pisa: Nistri-Lischi, 1926.

Beerbohm, Max, *Around Theatres*. New York: Alfred A. Knopf, 1930.

Bellonci, Goffredo *et al, Cinquenta anni di teatro in Italia*. Rome: Centro di Ricerche Teatrali. Carlo Bestetti, Edizioni d'Arte, 1954.

Berenguer Carisomo, Arturo, *Las ideas estéticas en el teatro argentino*. Buenos Aires: Instituto Nacional de Estudios de Teatro, 1947.

Boettcher, Friederike, *La Femme dans le Théâtre d'Ibsen*. Paris: Librairie Felix Alcan, 1912.

Boglione, Giuseppe, *L'Arte della Duse*. Rome: Tipografia Istituto Roosevelt, 1960.

Boito, Arrigo, *Lettere di Arrigo Boito*. Raccolte e annotate da Raffaelo de Rensis. Rome: Novissima, 1932.

SELECT BIBLIOGRAPHY

Bordeux, Jeanne, *Eleonora Duse: the story of her life*. London: Hutchinson & Co., n.d. [1924].

Bracco, Roberto, *Nell'arte e nella vita*. Lanciano: Gino Carabba Editore, 1941.

Camilleri, Andrea, *I teatri stabili in Italia 1898–1918*. Bologna: Cappelli Editore, 1959.

Corsi, Mario, *Le prime rappresentazioni dannunziane*. Milan: Treves, 1928.

Craig, Edward Gordon, 'On Signora Eleonora Duse' in *Life and Letters*, September, 1928.

D'Amico, Silvio, *Tramonto del grande attore*. Milan: Mondadori, 1929.

Duse, Eleonora, *Undici lettere di Eleonora Duse e Gabriele D'Annunzio*. Gardone Riviera: Quaderni dannunziani X–XI, 1958.

Ferrugia, Gemma, *La nostra vera Duse*. Milan: Sanzogno, 1924.

Fiocco, Achille, 'Lettere della Duse' in *Scenario*. Numbers 3 and 4, 1951.

——*Teatro italiano di ieri e di oggi*. Bologna: Cappelli Editore, 1958.

Fromm, Harold, *Bernard Shaw and the Theatre in the Nineties*. Lawrence: University of Kansas Press, 1967.

Fusero, Clemente, *Eleonora Duse*. Milan: dall'Oglio Editore, 1971.

Gatti, G, *Le donne nella vita e nell'arte di Gabriele D'Annunzio*. Modena: Guanda, 1951.

Guerrieri, Gerardo, 'Sasper, Sachespar, Shakespeare ovvero l'interpretazione di Shakespeare in Italia dal '700 al '900' in *500 Anni di Teatro in Italia*. Rome: Centro di Ricerche Teatrali. Carlo Bestetti, Edizioni d'Arte, 1954.

—— *Eleonora Duse e il suo tempo 1858–1924*. Rome: Canova, 1974.

Gullace, Giovanni, *Gabriele D'Annunzio in France. A study in cultural relations*. Syracuse, New York: Syracuse University Press, 1966.

Harding, Bertita, *Age Cannot Wither. The story of Duse and D'Annunzio*. London: George G. Harrap & Co. Ltd, 1949.

Jacobbi, Ruggero, *Teatro in Brasile*. Bologna: Cappelli Editore, 1961.

James, Henry, *The Scenic Art*. Edited with an Introduction and Notes by Allan Wade. New Brunswick: Rutgers University Press, 1948.

Knepler, Henry, *The Gilded Stage: The lives of four great actresses (Rachel; Ristori; Bernhardt; Duse)*. London: Constable & Co. Ltd, 1968.

Koht, Halvdan, *Life of Ibsen*. Translated and edited by E. Haugen and A. E. Santaniello. New York: Benjamin Blom, 1971. (From the new revised Norwegian edition 1954).

Lawrence, Dan H. (ed.), *Bernard Shaw. Collected letters 1874–1897*. London: Max Reinhardt, 1965.

Le Galliene, Eva, *Eleonora Duse: The mystic in the theatre*. London: The Bodley Head Ltd, 1966.

Liberati, Franco. *Eleonora Duse. Biografia aneddotica* . . . Palermo: S. Biondo, n.d.

Lugné-Poe, Aurélien Marie, *Sous les Étoiles: Souvenirs de Théâtre 1902–1912*. Arthème Fayard et Cie., 1932.

——*Ibsen*. Paris: Les Editions Rieder, 1936.

Lyonnet, Henry, *Le Théâtre en Italie*. Paris: Librairie Paul Ollendorff, 1900.

Mantegari, Pompeo (ed.), *Eleonora Duse: reliquie e memorie*. Milan: Editrice Tespi, n.d.

Mapes, Victor, *Duse and the French*. New York: Publications of the Dunlap Society, 1898.

Martínez Sierra, Gregorio, *Un teatro de arte en España 1917–1925*. Madrid: Ediciones de la Esfinge, 1926.

Mazzali, Ettore, *D'Annunzio*. Milan: Nuova Accademia, 1963.

Mazzoni, Ofelia, *Con la Duse, Ricordi e anedotti*. Milan: Alpes, 1927.

Meyer, Michael, *Henrik Ibsen 1883–1906*. 3 vols. London: Rupert Hart-Davis, 1971.

Morales, Ernesto, *Historia del teatro argentino*. Buenos Aires: Lautaro, 1944.

Nardi, Piero, *Vita di Arrigo Boito*. Milan: Mondadori, 1942.

Nicastro, Luciano, *Confessioni di Eleonora Duse*. 3 vols. Milan: Gentile, 1945–46.

Noble, Iris, *Great Lady of the Theatre, Sarah Bernhardt*. New York: Julian Messner Inc., 1960.

Ordaz, Luis, *El teatro en el Río de la Plata*. Buenos Aires: Ediciones Leviatan, 1957.

Pandolfi, Vito, *Antologia del grande attore*. Bari: Laterza, 1954.

Pardieri, Giuseppe, *Ermete Zacconi*. Bologna: Cappelli Editore, 1960.

—— *Il teatro italiano e la sua tradizione*. Matera: Basilicata Editrice, 1967.

Pierazzi, Rina Maria and Duse, Carlo Vittorio, *Eleonora Duse e la guerra*. Turin: Istituto Editoriale, n.d.

Pullini, Giorgio, *Teatro italiano del novecento*. Bologna: Cappelli Editore, 1971.

SELECT BIBLIOGRAPHY

Radice, Raul (ed.), *Eleonora Duse – Arrigo Boito. Lettere d'Amore*. Milan: Il Saggiatore, 1979.

Rasi, Luigi, *La Duse*. Florence: R. Bemporad e Figlio, 1901.

Rensis, Raffaello de *Arrigo Boito. Capitali biografici. Florence: G. C. Sansoni Editore, 1942.

Rheinhardt, E. A., *The Life of Eleonora Duse*. London: Martin Secker, 1930.

Rhodes, Anthony, *The Poet as Superman. A life of Gabriele D'Annunzio*. London: Weidenfeld & Nicolson, 1959.

Ridenti, Lucio, *La Duse minore*. Rome: Gherardo Casini Editore, 1966.

Robichez, Jacques, *Le Symbolisme au théâtre. Lugné-Poe et les débuts de l'oeuvre*. Paris: L'Arche, 1957.

Sarcey, Francisque, *Quarante ans de théâtre*. Paris: Bibliothèque des Annales, 1900–1902. 8 vols.

Schlenther, Paul, 'Eleonora Duse' in *Deutsche Rundschau*. XIX. Berlin: 1893.

Setti, Dora, *Eleonora Duse and Antonietta Pisa. Carteggio inedito*. Milan: Ceschina, 1972.

Shaw, George Bernard, *The Quintessence of Ibsenism*. London: Constable & Co. Ltd, 1932.

—— *Our Theatres in the Nineties*. 3 vols. London: Constable & Co. Ltd, 1932.

Signorelli, Olga Resnevic, *Eleonora Duse*. Rome: Gherardo Casini Editore, 1955.

—— *Vita di Eleonora Duse*, Bologna: Cappelli Editore, 1962.

Silveira, Miroel, *A contribuição italiana ao teatro brasileiro*. São Paulo: Edições Quíron/MEC, 1976.

Simoni, Renato, *Teatro di ieri. Ritratti e ricordi*. Milan: Treves, 1938.

Sozzi, Giuseppe, *Gabriele D'Annunzio nella vita e nell'arte*. Florence: La Nuova Italia, 1964.

Symons, Arthur, *Eleonora Duse*. New York and London: Benjamin Blom, 1969 (reprint of 1927 edition).

Talli, Virgilio, *La mia vita di teatro*. Milan. Treves, 1927.

Tennant, P. F. D., *Ibsen's Dramatic Technique*. Atlantic Highlands, N. J.: Humanities Press, 1965.

Terry, Dame Ellen, *The Story of My Life*. London: Hutchinson, 1908.

Vannucci, Pasquale, *Eleonora Duse*. Rome: Società Editoriale Idea, 1959.

Vergani, Leonardo, *Eleonora Duse*. Milan: Aldo Martello Editore, 1958.

Waxman, Samuel Montefiore, *Antoine and the Théâtre-Libre*. Cambridge, Mass: Harvard University Press, 1926.

Young, Stark, *Essay on the art of the theatre*. New York: Charles Scribner's Sons, 1925.